THE NORTH AMERICAN

➻

WHISKEY
GUIDE

— FROM —

BEHIND THE BAR

TO AVA AND GAVIN LEBLANC.
TO BOONE HARTLEY BERKEY ... WELCOME TO THE WORLD, SON.

PAGE STREET
PUBLISHING CO.

Copyright © 2018 Chad Berkey and Jeremy LeBlanc

First published in 2014 by
Page Street Publishing Co.
27 Congress Street, Suite 103
Salem, MA 01970
www.pagestreetpublishing.com

Distributed by Macmillan; sales in Canada by The Canadian Manda Group; distribution in Canada by The Jaguar Book Group.

22 21 20 19 18   1 2 3 4 5

ISBN-13: 978-1-62414-687-9
ISBN-10: 1-62414-687-2

Library of Congress Control Number: 2018948135

Cover and book design by Page Street Publishing Co.
Photography by Tamara Lee-Sang

Printed and bound in China

THE NORTH AMERICAN

WHISKEY GUIDE

—FROM—

BEHIND THE BAR

REAL BARTENDERS' REVIEWS OF MORE THAN 250 WHISKEYS—INCLUDES 30 STANDOUT COCKTAIL RECIPES

CHAD BERKEY
GENERAL MANAGER OF THE AERO CLUB BAR
and **JEREMY LEBLANC**
HEAD MIXOLOGIST AT THE ALTITUDE SKY LOUNGE AND AUTHOR OF
THE BEST CRAFT COCKTAILS & BARTENDING WITH FLAIR

PAGE STREET
PUBLISHING CO.

CONTENTS

INTRODUCTION

North American whiskeys are more popular than ever. The whiskeys we cover in this book are produced in either the United States or Canada. They are made from a variety of different grains produced from a mash bill that usually mixes together rye, wheat, corn, malted barley and oats. The legal requirements for production vary by the type of grains, the percent or proof of alcohol and the length and manner of their aging. Regulations vary above and below the Canadian border, but here's our take on it.

For bourbons, ryes, wheats, malts and Tennessee whiskeys to be labeled "Straight," they must have a mash bill consisting of at least 51% of their particular grain, be distilled no more than 80% ABV (160 proof) and be aged for at least two years in new charred oak barrels. Tennessee's number one difference is that most of them perform a process that filters their whiskey through sugar maple charcoal, unique to their state.

Blended American Whiskey is required to contain at least 20% straight whiskey. Blended whiskey that contains the minimum of 51% straight whiskey of a particular grain can legally use that grain in its label description—for example, blended bourbon or blended rye. Note that these are the ones your bartender is probably going to offer you if you order a whiskey and Coke.

Corn whiskeys must contain 80% or more corn and be distilled at no more than 80% ABV (160 proof). Their hillbilly cousins, white whiskeys and moonshine, are distilled from a variety mix of corn and sugars and are bottled right off the still.

Our neighbors from the north have some different rules and regulations when it comes to making whiskey. Their versions are mostly blended with a minimum age of three years, but most brands spend a little more time in the barrels.

In this book we have chosen 250 North American whiskeys from the back bar of the Aero Club Bar in San Diego. These brands were selected from a wall of over 900 whiskeys because they are among the most frequently ordered by our patrons. Our goal is to taste, review and report our findings from a combined 40 years of experience from behind the bar. We have spent countless nights interacting, observing and questioning our patrons and peers trying to answer questions such as "What's a good whiskey?" or "What whiskey do you recommend?" We as service providers do our best to please our customers who simply say, "Give me something good." Answering these questions can be quite difficult as each individual has different tastes and styles. Our strategy and solution was to combine our wealth of knowledge along with blind tastings from four professional bartenders. Our team was not influenced by brands or labels and wrote their reviews on what they honestly thought after smelling and tasting the whiskey. As bartenders, it's important for us to satisfy our guests, and nothing pleases us more than to help them find that "perfect" whiskey that suits their taste and pleases their palates.

In addition, we added a variety of unique whiskey craft cocktails, along with some classics with a twist. These rare libations were all handcrafted by mixologists from around the country and are perfect for mixing up behind the bar or in the comfort of your own home.

Furthermore, our selected four bartenders picked some of their favorite whiskeys, and we paired them up with premium cigars for your enjoyment.

Last, but not least, we included our bucket list of whiskeys. At one time or another, these extraordinary products graced our shelves and are a must try if you come across them. We hope that you enjoy this valuable resource, as we wanted to provide you with some material that you ordinarily might not see in a whiskey guide.

We rated each whiskey on a scale of 1-5 propellers. Keep an eye out for the lucky few with a golden propeller, meaning it's that exceptional that it earned all five.

Cheers,
Chad and Jeremy

OUR BARTENDERS

 ANNIE HOBBS

 JOHN WRIGHT

 JEFF DELOY

 BRANDON JOSEFOSKY

BOURBON

Bourbon is easily the most popular whiskey in America. Stroll into any bar in the country and order a whiskey and chances are the bartender is going to pour you a delicious amber-colored liquid that is made primarily from corn. Contrary to popular belief, bourbon can be produced anywhere in the United States. It must, however, be made from a grain mixture that is at least 51% corn. Other requirements include aging in new, charred oak barrels. It must be distilled no more than 160 proof or 80% alcohol by volume, and enter the barrel for aging at no more than 125 proof or 62.5% alcohol by volume. It also must be bottled at 80 proof or more (40% ABV). If the whiskey reads "straight bourbon," the whiskey must be aged at least two years. There can be no funny business of mixing in any coloring or adding flavor enhancers, so if you're looking for the real McCoy, make sure the label doesn't say "blended whiskey."

Kentucky produces over 90% of the bourbon on the market, but there are many great smaller craft distilleries across the country that are making a name for themselves by distilling quality whiskey. Many of them use organic products and take great pride in their "farm to bottle" small batch whiskeys. They are experimenting with different ages and styles that produce many different flavor profiles.

In this chapter we cover many of the most popular bourbons that you will find in your local whiskey bar, and we do our best to relay what the countless amounts of people who belly up to our copper bar top are saying about them as they sip away. So, whether you enjoy it straight up, on the rocks, mixed in your favorite cocktail, or even slammed into the back of your throat, we're sure we can help find the bourbon that's right for you! We welcome you to read the tasting notes from the bartenders, four professionals with very different palates who had absolutely no idea what the whiskey was as they tasted and commented on it. We held nothing back in the hopes of finding you some delicious bourbon to enjoy, for it truly is "America's Native Spirit."

ANCIENT AGE KENTUCKY STRAIGHT BOURBON WHISKEY

SUMMARY: This brand has been around 60 plus years offering up three whiskeys to choose from: Ancient Age, Ancient Age 10 Star and the much harder to find Ancient Age 10 Year. Distilled from corn, high rye and barley malt, it can be described as sweet. It's dry on the palate but has a pleasant burn. If you do add ice, we recommend only a cube or two as the whiskey is light not only in color but in flavor as well. It is one worthy of being on your shelf at home; just be sure the teenagers aren't adding any extra water!

FUN FACT: Ancient Age was the brand of choice for Kurt Dussander, fugitive Nazi war criminal and villain in Stephen King's *Apt Pupil*.

VARIETY/STYLE: Straight Bourbon

BARREL TYPE: New American Oak

AGE: 3 years

ORIGIN: Kentucky

BOTTLE: 750 ml, screw cap

ALCOHOL: 40%

PROOF: 80

PRICE: low-range

RELATED: Jim Beam, Wild Turkey, Fighting Cock, Old Crow, Old Taylor

PROPELLERS:

Age International, Inc., 229 West Main Street, Suite 202, Frankfort, KY 40601, (502) 223-9874, nknox@ageintl.com
Producer: Buffalo Trace Distillery, 113 Great Buffalo Trace, Franklin County, Frankfort, KY 40601, (800) 654-8471, info@buffalotrace.com, www.buffalotracedistillery.com

COMMENTS FROM THE BARTENDER:

ANNIE: Super sweet like sugar cookies.

JEFF: Nice sweet taste. That went down easy.

JOHN: Definite sugar, almond in the front with a nice finish.

BRANDON: Perfect for beginners. Soft and smooth with sweet caramel, oak in the finish.

ANGEL'S ENVY KENTUCKY STRAIGHT BOURBON WHISKEY

SUMMARY: The whiskey of angels. Born in 1938, Master Distiller Lincoln Henderson passed away in 2013. This family-run distillery continues the tradition of crafting premium bourbons. Angel's Envy is aged up to six years in charred white oak barrels and finished at least six months in ruby port wine casks. These hand-blended batches consist of eight to twelve barrels at a time. To keep up the family tradition and assure quality, each barrel is tasted throughout the process of distilling. Because of its intense maple, vanilla and dried fruit flavors, we often recommend this bourbon to the beginner who is ready to spend a little bit more to try a premium bourbon. It's great straight from the bottle to the glass. Try dipping the tip of a good cigar in to enhance the flavor of both.

FUN FACT: Unique tall sleek bottle, bearing angels wings

VARIETY/STYLE: Kentucky Straight Bourbon

BARREL TYPE: White Oak Barrels/Port Cask

AGE: 6 years

ORIGIN: Kentucky

BOTTLE: 750 ml, cork top

ALCOHOL: 43.3%

PROOF: 86.6

PRICE: mid-range

RELATED: Colorado Gold Bourbon, Eagle Rare 10 Year, Big Bottom Port Cask, Basil Hayden's, Elijah Craig 12 Year

PROPELLERS:

Louisville Distilling Company, LLC, 7204 Highway 329, Crestwood, KY 40014, (502) 241-6064, info@angelsenvy.com, www.angelsenvy.com

COMMENTS FROM THE BARTENDER:

ANNIE: Spice on the nose. Tastes fruity—like sugared apricots.

JEFF: This one seemed to have a little bitter taste that isn't suited for my palate. Dried fruit flavors were also noticeable.

JOHN: I definitely get fruit and leather. There's spice on the end. I love it and will recommend it to my lady!

BRANDON: Nose is sweet vanilla; it's unexpectedly spicy with a short bitter finish of dark fruit.

BAKER'S KENTUCKY STRAIGHT BOURBON WHISKEY

SUMMARY: Baker's is an award-winning small batch whiskey that is handcrafted in limited quantities dating back two centuries. According to Baker Beam, grandnephew of Jim Beam, Baker's Bourbon embodies over six generations of distilling experience and a tradition of putting their best secrets inside the bottle and not on the label. This bourbon has a pleasant start with aromas of vanilla and toffee. It continues on to give a combination of oak and vanilla sweetness and finishes fast with a rye bread, caramel flavor. It's a good, high-alcohol bourbon, but we generally recommend Booker's over Baker's because customers tend to prefer it.

FUN FACT: It's named after Baker Beam, the grandnephew of the distiller's namesake.

VARIETY/STYLE: Bourbon

BARREL TYPE: Oak

AGE: 7 years

ORIGIN: Kentucky

BOTTLE: 750 ml, cork top

ALCOHOL: 53.5%

PROOF: 107

PRICE: mid-range

RELATED: Michter's Small Batch Kentucky Straight Bourbon Whiskey, Bulleit 10 Year Kentucky Straight Bourbon Whiskey, Knob Creek Single Barrel Straight Bourbon, Pure Kentucky, Prichard's Double Barrel

PROPELLERS: ▲▲▲▲

Beam Suntory Inc., 222 W Merchandise Mart Plaza, Chicago, IL 60654, (312) 964-6999, info@jimbeam.com, www.beamglobal.com

COMMENTS FROM THE BARTENDER:

ANNIE: Big burn with great classic bourbon flavors. A real powerhouse whiskey.

JEFF: Can I get some cubes, please! Pretty alcohol forward with a nutty taste. Good for a sipper but not for an all-night event.

JOHN: It tastes just like it smells: delicious. A bit hot, I would prefer some water or ice.

BRANDON: The nose is that of a typical bourbon, but it's really full and robust. The finish is long and seems to hang out on the back of my tongue, and not disappointing at all.

BASIL HAYDEN'S KENTUCKY STRAIGHT BOURBON WHISKEY

SUMMARY: In 1796, Master Distiller Basil Hayden Sr. broke the rules by mixing small grains into the mash of a traditional corn base, which sprung what is now called Basil Hayden's Straight Bourbon. This small-batch Kentucky straight bourbon is known for being light bodied and easy to drink. It has a sweet corn start with a solid hint of peppercorn and a warm, smooth finish. Guests often use this as a reference point: "I like Basil Hayden, what else can you recommend?" People know the name for a reason; it's good.

FUN FACT: Basil Hayden's grandson, Raymond B. Hayden, founded a distillery and named it "Old Grand-Dad," after his grandfather. It's also James Bond's bourbon of choice in the novel *Carte Blanche*.

VARIETY/STYLE: Straight Bourbon

BARREL TYPE: New American Oak

AGE: 8 years

ORIGIN: Kentucky

BOTTLE: 750 ml, cork top

ALCOHOL: 40.0%

PROOF: 80

PRICE: mid-range

RELATED: Evan Williams Single Barrel, Eligah Craig, Knob Creek, Blanton's, Four Roses Small Batch

PROPELLERS: ▲▲▲▲▲

Beam Suntory Inc., 222 W Merchandise Mart Plaza, Chicago, IL 60654, (312) 964-6999, info@jimbeam.com, www.beamglobal.com

COMMENTS FROM THE BARTENDER:

ANNIE: This smells like a whiskey sour, but it tastes like pears and cinnamon. I'd drink this on Christmas with my Grandma.

JEFF: Fruity with a hint of spice. The fruit flavor hangs around.

JOHN: Nice spice! Long-lasting flavor. I would read a book by the fire with this one.

BRANDON: Smooth oak, cinnamon tastes not too robust, but delicious!

BELLE MEADE SOUR MASH STRAIGHT BOURBON WHISKEY

SUMMARY: This historical bourbon dates back nearly 100 years from the family of Charles Nelson. Prior to Prohibition, Belle Meade Bourbon was one of the most popular whiskeys in production. Known for its light color and body, this bourbon's old-school label tells a story. This small batch bourbon is high in rye and is known for its long legacy. They have plans on building their own distillery and producing some powerhouse whiskeys.

FUN FACT: The horses on the front label have a history that goes back to the days of the famous Belle Meade Plantation in Nashville, Tenn. The horse on the right-hand side of the label is Bonnie Scotland, one of Belle Meade's leading sires. Some of Bonnie Scotland's descendants include War Admiral, Man O' War, Seabiscuit and Secretariat, along with most of the horses that run in the Kentucky Derby today. Appropriately enough, one of Bonnie Scotland's fillies was named Bourbon Belle. The horse on the left-hand side of the label is Brown Dick, whose great-great-grand sire was simply named Whiskey.

VARIETY/STYLE: Bourbon

BARREL TYPE: Oak

AGE: 5½ and 7½ years, depending on the barrel chosen

ORIGIN: Tennessee

BOTTLE: 750 ml, cork top

ALCOHOL: 45.2%

PROOF: 90.4

PRICE: mid-range

RELATED: Blanton's, Berkshire Mountain Small Batch Bourbon, Angel's Envy, Fighting Cock, Buck Ranch Hand, Old Petrero

PROPELLERS:

Nelson's Green Brier Distillery, 1414 Clinton Street, Nashville, TN 37203, (615) 913-8800, andy@greenbrierdistillery.com charlie@greenbrierdistillery.com, www.greenbrierdistillery.com **Producer:** MGP Ingredients Inc., Cray Business Plaza, 100 Commercial Street, P.O. Box 130, Atchison, KS 66002, (800) 255-0302, www.mgpingredients.com

COMMENTS FROM THE BARTENDER:

ANNIE: Leather, oak and spices. Not overly complex. A solid juice!

JEFF: Vanilla on the nose. For sure, some woody notes like cedar planks with some nice sweetness.

JOHN: From the smell you'd think just another sweet whiskey, but the flavor is spicy and oaky. Too bad it fades fast.

BRANDON: There's definitely rye present on the nose and palate, but it's really well balanced with a little sweetness on the back end.

BERKSHIRE MOUNTAIN DISTILLERS BOURBON WHISKEY

SUMMARY: This New England–style bourbon is expertly crafted in small batches from locally grown ingredients. Berkshire Mountain Distillers Bourbon Whiskey is a balanced, harmonious spirit matured in virgin American white oak barrels. It has bright notes of spicy rye, vanilla and mature fruit. It ends with a lingering finish of caramel and toasted nut. Not much on this small distillery in Massachusetts, but definitely good bourbon for the novice of bourbon drinkers. Got to start somewhere!

FUN FACT: Berkshire Mountain Distillers is Massachusetts's first legal distillery since Prohibition.

VARIETY/STYLE: Bourbon

BARREL TYPE: American White Oak

AGE: N/A

ORIGIN: Massachusetts

BOTTLE: 750 ml, cork top

ALCOHOL: 43%

PROOF: 86

PRICE: low-range

RELATED: Bulleit, Acient Age, Cyrus Noble, Evan Williams Single Barrel

Berkshire Mountain Distillers, Inc., 356 South Main Street, Sheffield, MA 01257, (413) 229-0219, chris@berkshiremountaindistilleries.com, www.berkshiremountaindistillers.com

PROPELLERS:

COMMENTS FROM THE BARTENDER:

ANNIE: Nose of caramel and butter corn, tastes like caramel corn at the fair.

JEFF: Toasted and spicy in the beginning but ended with more of a caramel flavor.

JOHN: Dude, sweet all the way through, a guy could get used to this.

BRANDON: Complex, smooth finish; I recommend it if you want to try something different.

BIG BOTTOM AMERICAN STRAIGHT BOURBON WHISKEY

SUMMARY: Ted Pappas was inspired by the craft spirit movement in Oregon so much so he opened his own distillery in Hillsboro, Oregon, in 2010. Big Bottom produces a standard straight bourbon as well as some unique extra-aged expressions, including some bourbons doing time in port, cabernet and Zinfandel casks. The American straight bourbon whiskey consists of 36% rye and is proofed at 91. The whiskey has a cult-like following in the Pacific Northwest that is spreading fast. Guests visiting our San Diego watering hole are often asking us if we carry it. The answer, of course, is yes. It's a pretty reasonably priced craft whiskey that we suggest you try—to see if you agree with the hype.

FUN FACT: The Big Bottom name is a tribute to 128,000 acres on and around Mount Hood.

VARIETY/STYLE: Small Batch Straight Bourbon

BARREL TYPE: New Oak

AGE: 3 years

ORIGIN: Oregon

BOTTLE: 750 ml, cork top

ALCOHOL: 45.5%

PROOF: 91

PRICE: mid-range

RELATED: Angel's Envy, Hirsch, Cyrus Noble, Ballast Point, Wasmund's

PROPELLERS: !!!!

Big Bottom Whiskey, 21420 NW Nicholas Court, Suite D-9, Hillsboro, OR 97214, (503) 608-7816, info@bigbottomwhiskey.com, www.bigbottomwhiskey.com

COMMENTS FROM THE BARTENDER:

ANNIE: Alcohol burn first, baking spice, toasty and warming. Good for winter.

JEFF: This has a softer nose, good whiskey burn with all the usual flavors with no standouts.

JOHN: Very light burn. I would drink this all day. Mild, sweet; nice finish.

BRANDON: Smooth, easy sipper. Easy sell.

BIG BOTTOM AMERICAN STRAIGHT BOURBON WHISKEY PORT CASK FINISH

SUMMARY: This is our bestseller out of the Big Bottom distillery lineup. It spends another six months in 10-year tawny port barrels before reaching its beautifully labeled bottles. Distribution is limited because they are completely dependent on the wine industry. With an increase in demand for their whiskey, the squeeze is on to get the wine out of barrels and the bourbon into the still wet casks. This bourbon is a must try, especially if you like Angel's Envy. This is like its big brother.

FUN FACT: This whiskey has won a Gold Medal at the San Francisco World Spirits Competition and at the Micro Liquor Spirit Awards.

VARIETY/STYLE: Small Batch Straight Bourbon

BARREL TYPE: New Oak/Port Casks

AGE: 2 years

ORIGIN: Oregon

BOTTLE: 750 ml, cork top

ALCOHOL: 45.5%

PROOF: 91

PRICE: mid-range

RELATED: Angel's Envy, Wasmund's, Ballast Point, Anchor, High West, Prichard's

PROPELLERS: !!!!

Big Bottom Whiskey, 21420 NW Nicholas Court, Suite D-9, Hillsboro, OR 97214, (503) 608-7816, info@bigbottomwhiskey.com, www.bigbottomwhiskey.com

NOTES FROM THE BARTENDER:

ANNIE: A subtle vanilla. Pretty sweet and quietly complex. Some cereal, some sweet grain.

JEFF: Flavors on the nose are hard to read. Taste is dry and sweet somehow—a lot going on.

JOHN: No burning sensation! Sweet and grainy with no after taste.

BRANDON: No nose. Soft, sweet flavors with some funky oak flavors, craft whiskey for sure.

BIG BOTTOM AMERICAN STRAIGHT BOURBON WHISKEY ZINFANDEL CASK FINISH

SUMMARY: Big Bottom distillers are known for their cask finish bourbons, a process where whiskey is put into freshly emptied wine barrels for a further aging of around six months. There are many things that factor into doing this right, from the type of wine cask to the type of bourbon that needs to have high rye and wheat content. Scoring the winning combination is tedious and time-consuming, but I bet they had some fun, too. The ultimate goal is for the bourbon to soak into the casks, forcing the wine that is left over in the staves out into the bourbon. The Zinfandel finish is overshadowed by their port finish. Most of our customers only like experimenting with this, so it is rarely reordered.

FUN FACT: Ted Pappas served time in the Air Force and worked in the healthcare industry before moving his family to Oregon. He is currently serving as vice president of the Oregon Distillers Guild.

VARIETY/STYLE: Small Batch Straight Bourbon

BARREL TYPE: New Oak/Zinfandel Casks

AGE: N/A

ORIGIN: Oregon

BOTTLE: 750 ml, cork top

ALCOHOL: 45.5%

PROOF: 91

PRICE: mid-range

RELATED: Stein, High West, Angel's Envy, Cyrus Noble, Wasmund's, Wathen's

PROPELLERS: !!! !!!

Big Bottom Whiskey, 21420 NW Nicholas Court, Suite D-9, Hillsboro, OR 97214, (503) 608-7816, info@bigbottomwhiskey.com, www.bigbottomwhiskey.com

COMMENTS FROM THE BARTENDER:

ANNIE: Sugary and sweet. Lots of maple and toffee—candy whiskey!

JEFF: I know we're not doing flavored whiskeys but I think one may have snuck in.

JOHN: Yay for candy whiskey! Love it! Sweet, sweet candy.

BRANDON: This would make a great after-dinner sipper.

BLACK MAPLE HILL KENTUCKY STRAIGHT BOURBON

SUMMARY: You always want what you can't have. Van Winkle worked this marketing to perfection. Why not Black Maple Hill? Well, they're well on their way. We have a lot of people ask us if we have Pappy, and more often than not the answer is no. A very popular second choice has become Black Maple Hill. It's good bourbon with a lot of rich flavors of corn, fruits and vanilla, but it's often not picked first in our blind taste tests. The price per shot of Black Maple Hill keeps rising due to supply and demand, but we can honestly say that more guests than not are saying it's "Okay" or "Good" not "It's the best whiskey I've ever had."

FUN FACT: Black Maple Hill is an independent label owned by Paul Joseph who resides on the San Francisco Peninsula. The bourbon is blended at Kentucky Bourbon Distillers in Kentucky, then sent back to California where it's labeled.

VARIETY/STYLE: Small Batch Bourbon

BARREL TYPE: New American Oak

AGE: 8 years

ORIGIN: Kentucky

BOTTLE: 750 ml, cork top

ALCOHOL: 47.5%

PROOF: 95

PRICE: mid-range

RELATED: Maker's Mark 46, Woodford Reserve, Willett Family Estate 11 Year, Four Roses Single Barrel, Russell's Reserve

PROPELLERS: !!!! !!!!

CVI Brands, 1025 Tanklage Road, Suite F, San Carlos, CA 94070, (650) 595-1768, info@cvibrands.com, www.cvibrands.com

COMMENTS FROM THE BARTENDER:

ANNIE: Nose of honey, definitely on the sweet side with a mixed burn and a smooth finish. Burnt sugar cookies taste good finally.

JEFF: Honey was the flavor and smell that jumped off this one.

JOHN: A bit sweet, nice finish. Drink this one on a cold night with your lady.

BRANDON: Citrusy nose, long burning spicy finish. Could use some ice.

BLANTON'S THE ORIGINAL SINGLE BARREL BOURBON WHISKEY

SUMMARY: Blanton's The Original Single Barrel Bourbon was destined for greatness from the start. In 1881, Albert Bacon Blanton was born into one of the first known families of bourbon history. He grew up to be a pioneer in the whiskey world, working his way up to president by the age of 40. Albert Blanton, also known as Colonel Blanton, grew the brand from 44 to 144 buildings, becoming the largest distillery of its time. As you open your sense of smell to this fine whiskey, a soothing aroma of caramel and vanilla sets in. Blanton's well-balanced taste profile comes off with a burnt sugar, orange, citrus and nut flavor that will make you remember why you choose this bourbon time and time again. Blanton's amber-colored whiskey finishes soft with a nice medium body. This is a favorite of ours, as it is reasonably priced and well known, so it's offered by most watering holes. You can savor this bourbon on the rocks or simply enjoy neat.

FUN FACT: The tiny horse and jockey on the bottle is a recognized trademark of this single barrel bourbon. Acclaimed as one of the World's Top 10 Coolest Liquor Bottles, this bourbon's stopper is marked with a single barrel letter that spells out Blanton's when the set is complete. Rumor has it that if you send all eight stoppers back to Buffalo Trace Distillery, they will send you a free bottle and a limited edition collector's case displaying the horses in different strides.

PROPELLERS: !!!!!

"This is truly the coolest bourbon on the market."
—Jeremy LeBlanc, author of *The Best Craft Cocktails & Bartending with Flair*

Jim Murray's *Whisky Bible* voted Blanton's The Original Single Barrel Bourbon as "Liquid Gold."

VARIETY/STYLE: Single Barrel Bourbon

BARREL TYPE: White Oak

AGE: No age statement (best guess 12 to 14 years)

ORIGIN: Kentucky

BOTTLE: 750 ml, cork top

ALCOHOL: 46.5%

PROOF: 93

PRICE: mid-range

RELATED: Bulleit 10 Year Kentucky Straight Bourbon Whiskey, Four Roses Single Barrel Kentucky Straight Bourbon Whiskey, Jefferson's Reserve Straight Bourbon Whiskey Small Batch, Evan Williams Single Barrel

Age International, 229 West Main Street, Suite 202, Frankfort, KY 40601 (502) 223-9874, nknox@ageintl.com, www.blantonsbourbon.com **Producer:** Buffalo Trace Distillery, 113 Great Buffalo Trace, Franklin County, Frankfort, KY 40601, (800) 654-8471, info@buffalotrace.com, www.buffalotracedistillery.com

COMMENTS FROM THE BARTENDER:

ANNIE: I can't smell this one—is my nose okay? Tastes super sweet but pretty much a whiskey. Definitely sticks with you a while

JEFF: Didn't get a distinct taste from this one, just sweet the whole way through.

JOHN: It's very light at first and then I got hit by the burning finish!

BRANDON: Nose is sweet; strong charred oak finish. Would drink with a cube of ice.

BOOKER'S SMALL BATCH BOURBON

SUMMARY: This untouched, unfiltered small batch bourbon's personality stands out from the rest of all the Jim Beam brands, as it holds the highest alcohol content of the bunch. Jim Beam's grandson and Master Distiller Booker Noe originally bottled this bourbon straight from the barrel. Booker's is a full-body, full-oak bourbon with inviting sweetness of vanilla and orange notes. This Kentucky straight bourbon is smooth in a sense that it has no real harsh burn even through it's potent as hell. It's not hard to find as it is offered in most of your watering holes, but be careful after a couple of snorts of this fine whiskey—you might end up falling off your barstool. Not recommended for the beginner who is trying to break into the wonderful world of whiskey.

"One more drink and I'll be under the host." —Mae West

FUN FACT: Booker Noe first introduced this straight bourbon whiskey as Booker's True Barrel Bourbon. It reminds you of a time when drinkers would bring jugs to the distillery and have them filled up straight from the barrels for the price of 15 cents a quart.

VARIETY/STYLE: Small Batch Bourbon

BARREL TYPE: American White Oak

AGE: 7 years

ORIGIN: Kentucky

BOTTLE: 750 ml, cork top

ALCOHOL: 63.3%

PROOF: varies, between 127 and 129.2

PRICE: high-range

RELATED: Baker's Kentucky Straight Bourbon, Jefferson's Reserve Straight Bourbon, Noah's Mill, Rowan's Creek

PROPELLERS: ! ! ! !

Beam Suntory Inc., 222 W Merchandise Mart Plaza, Chicago, IL 60654, (312) 964-6999, info@jimbeam.com, www.beamglobal.com

COMMENTS FROM THE BARTENDER:

ANNIE: Fairly sweet and smooth as it goes down but ends on a huge spicy note. I'm liking the way this burns my throat. Great for a frosty day!

JEFF: I was not expecting the spice with how smooth this was. It kicked in halfway down my chest. Definitely warms the body up.

JOHN: Now we're talking. Pow, right in the kisser! Winner.

BRANDON: This one got under my tongue and just caught fire!

BREAKING AND ENTERING BOURBON WHISKEY

SUMMARY: The distillers at St. George pride themselves on their blending ability. To them it's a form of art, and they've had nearly 30 years of experience to prove it. They don't try to hide the fact that they carefully select and purchase bourbon barrels in Kentucky, then ship them to California where they blend and bottle them. Many brands on the market do the same thing, but they try very hard to play it down with a horse or cowboy or historical figure on the label. We like the fact that they are upfront about it and focus on the blending process. We love having it on the shelf because it has some very unique flavors of banana and black cherry that makes it an easy recommendation for someone looking for something a little different.

FUN FACT: This whiskey is said to be made from as many as 80 different bourbons, aged from five to seven years.

VARIETY/STYLE: Bourbon

BARREL TYPE: New American Oak

AGE: 5 to 7 years

ORIGIN: Kentucky

BOTTLE: 750 ml, cork top

ALCOHOL: 43%

PROOF: 86

PRICE: mid-range

RELATED: Woodford Reserve, Jefferson's, Buffalo Trace, Eagle Rare, Four Roses

PROPELLERS: ! ! ! !

St. George Spirits, 2601 Monarch Street, Alameda, CA 94501, (510) 769-1601, info@stgeorgespirits.com, www.stgeorgespirits.com

COMMENTS FROM THE BARTENDER:

ANNIE: Very soft oak with warm banana pudding and bread. If it were richer, it would be outstanding. Love the flavors.

JEFF: This one has a banana-nut bread nose. A nice mix of wood, toffee and a bit of honey on the palate.

JOHN: For me, this is middle of the road. I get the wood and sweetness, but the lack of finish makes it kind of weak.

BRANDON: I can't say I've every picked up banana on the nose of my whiskey, but there it was. It's definitely smooth and oaky, but it's a nice middle ground of sweetness.

BUCK 8 YEAR STRAIGHT BOURBON WHISKEY

SUMMARY: Buck 8 Year is fairly new to the market, and there's not a lot of information out there on this whiskey. What we do know is that it's made in Kentucky for a private party and then bottled independently. A lot of people agree that eight years is in the range of the "sweet spot," or best years for aging bourbon. This, of course, is a subject for debate, and we really don't pick up too much oak flavor from the barrel. It does, however, have some very easy-to-drink warm vanilla and toasted almond flavors with a hint of cherry cola. This whiskey is a no-brainer for recommending, and maybe the best bourbon you haven't tried yet, at least at that price range.

FUN FACT: The brand is a tribute to the spirit of the rodeo.

VARIETY/STYLE: Bourbon

BARREL TYPE: New American Oak

AGE: 8 years

ORIGIN: Kentucky

BOTTLE: 750 ml, cork top

ALCOHOL: 45%

PROOF: 90

PRICE: mid-range

RELATED: Bulleit, Knob Creek, Ancient Age, Eagle Rare, Fighting Cock

PROPELLERS: !!!!!

Frank-Lin Distillers, 2455 Huntington Drive, Fairfield, CA 94533, (800) 922-9363, www.frank-lin.com

COMMENTS FROM THE BARTENDER:

ANNIE: Lots of honey and fruit. Good flavor profile but lacks the oomph I like.

JEFF: A nutty taste that leads to a vanilla finish that complements it well. I could see myself enjoying this more often.

JOHN: This one is good; not great, but good. Warm vanilla with toasted almonds.

BRANDON: I really love a full-bodied bourbon that doesn't leave you questioning its own existence. It's sweet, nutty, oaky, notes of dry fruit with vanilla at the end.

BUFFALO TRACE KENTUCKY STRAIGHT BOURBON WHISKEY

SUMMARY: As the distillery's flagship brand, Buffalo Trace is made from the finest corn, rye and barley malt and is aged in century-old warehouses for eight years. This whiskey has a complex nose of vanilla, mint and molasses but isn't too sweet to the taste. The palate contains notes of brown sugar and spice that leads you in to the oak, toffee and dark fruit. The finish is long and smooth with excellent depth. It becomes obvious quickly why this bourbon has won over 50 awards from multiple spirits competitions since 2000.

FUN FACT: The company's first distillery was developed in 1858 by Daniel Swigert, making it one of America's oldest distilleries. Since then, what is now the Buffalo Trace Distillery has been home to many legends, such as George T. Stagg, William Larue Weller, Pappy Van Winkle, Albert B. Blanton and Elmer T. Lee.

VARIETY/STYLE: Straight Bourbon Whiskey

BARREL TYPE: New American Oak

AGE: 8 years

ORIGIN: Kentucky

BOTTLE: 750 ml, cork top

ALCOHOL: 45%

PROOF: 90

PRICE: mid-range

RELATED: Elmer T. Lee, Eagle Rare 10, Basil Hayden's, Blanton's, Rock Hill

PROPELLERS: !!!!

Buffalo Trace Distillery, 113 Great Buffalo Trace, Franklin County, Frankfort, KY 40601, (800) 654-8471, info@buffalotrace.com, www.buffalotracedistillery.com

COMMENTS FROM THE BARTENDER:

ANNIE: Pretty standard and boring. Burn is long when it finishes—but good.

JEFF: Smells wonderful! Sweet and oaky. The taste is much lighter than I expected, but great flavor all the way through.

JOHN: Good nose with a lot of aroma. Smooth with a good mix of spices. Not as sweet as I imagined.

BRANDON: Not very complex. Tastes high proof with an anise finish. Nice smooth whiskey all around.

BUFFALO TRACE SINGLE OAK PROJECT KENTUCKY STRAIGHT BOURBON WHISKEY (ASSORTED BARRELS)

SUMMARY: For over a century, Buffalo Trace Distillery has been a pioneering leader in quality and innovation. The Single Oak Project may be its most inventive undertaking yet, an industry first. It all started with 96 individually selected American oak trees carefully chosen with a special consideration for the thickness of the wood grain. They were made into single oak barrels. This is where Buffalo Trace looked outside the box. They filled the barrels with different whiskeys, altering the mash bill recipe and entry proof used. Stored in different locations, these barrels are aged and tested for their own uniqueness, hence creating what they call the Buffalo Trace Single Oak Project. A different taste with every barrel, but no matter which batch you try it will be sure to delight the pickiest of drinkers. Recommend serving straight from the bottle and at room temperature to maximize the full, rich tastes.

FUN FACT: Each barrel in the Single Oak Project is different from every other barrel in at least one aspect.

VARIETY/STYLE: Small Batch Bourbon

BARREL TYPE: American Oak Barrels, made into single oak barrels uniquely charred

ORIGIN: Kentucky

PROPELLERS: !!!!!

BOTTLE: 750 ml, cork top

ALCOHOL: varies from barrel to barrel

PROOF: varies from barrel to barrel

PRICE: high-range

RELATED: Woodford Reserve Double Oak, Basil Hayden's, Noah's Mill, Pure Kentucky, Black Maple Hill

Buffalo Trace Distillery, 113 Great Buffalo Trace, Franklin County, Frankfort, KY 40601, (800) 654-8471, info@buffalotrace.com, www.singleoakproject.com

COMMENTS FROM THE BARTENDER:

ANNIE: Alcohol and burn. Low sweetness. I'd drink this when I'm pissed off. Love it!

JEFF: A sweet nose that had a spicy beginning and end. Had a medium burn during the middle. Overall pretty tasty.

JOHN: Smoky sweet nose followed by a blast of oak and cinnamon spices. No need for any mixers!

BRANDON: Strong taste of oak and alcohol. This is for you if you love oak. Bit of a burn, but it's a short finish.

BULLEIT BOURBON 10 YEAR OLD KENTUCKY STRAIGHT BOURBON WHISKEY

SUMMARY: Same great bottle and label but with a better balance and less spice than the original Bulleit Bourbon. Tom Bulleit has aged this fine whiskey in charred American white oak barrels, which deliver a deep, rich, but level sipping experience. I would consider this a complex 10-year-old bourbon whiskey that is softer than the original but carries a heavier taste of fruit followed by a strong oak finish. With this being said, it is my recommendation that if you relish or appreciate the fruit and not so much of the spice, I would spend the extra money and purchase this great-tasting Kentucky bourbon; otherwise, save some dough and indulge in the original. You won't be disappointed either way.

FUN FACT: All Bulleit products have a rustic look and feel, but if you look carefully you will notice that the authentic paper label is intentionally corked to one side.

VARIETY/STYLE: Straight Bourbon

BARREL TYPE: American White Oak

AGE: 10 years

ORIGIN: Kentucky

PROPELLERS: !!!!

BOTTLE: 750 ml, cork top

ALCOHOL: 45.6%

PROOF: 91.2

PRICE: high-range

RELATED: Barrel Straight Kentucky Bourbon, Jefferson's Reserve Straight Kentucky Bourbon, Blaton's, E.H. Taylor, Four Roses Single

Diageo North America, 801 Main Avenue, Norwalk, CT 06851, (646) 223-2000, www.diageo.com, **Producer:** Four Roses Distillery, 1224 Hickory Grove Road, Lawrenceburg, KY 40342, (502) 839-3436, www.fourrosesbourbon.com

COMMENTS FROM THE BARTENDER:

ANNIE: Complex nose with a strong oak palate. Also getting raisins, fig and kind of like Dutch apple pie. It's good.

JEFF: Not super complex, with raisin and oak flavors coming through the most. Not a favorite but quite drinkable.

JOHN: I thought for sure I would love this after I smelled it, but it didn't have the big rich and oily flavors I'd hoped for.

BRANDON: Sweet nose with an oaky, nutty palate. Has a mature oaky, sweet finish.

BULLEIT KENTUCKY STRAIGHT BOURBON WHISKEY

SUMMARY: Tom Bulleit is a true "American" in every sense of the word. He is a Southern gentleman, a war veteran of Vietnam, a successful lawyer and the founder of Bulleit Bourbon. In 1987, Tom fulfilled a lifelong dream by rekindling an old family recipe (dating back nearly 200 years) and created the first batch of the modern-day Bulleit Bourbon. And so a product was born that helped define an era of American history. Bulleit Bourbon is distilled and aged in small batches and has become one of the most successful and award-winning whiskeys in the last two decades. One of the best noses I have smelled; one sniff of this fine Kentucky bourbon and your taste buds will be begging for a sip. Bulleit's well-balanced taste has hints of corn and vanilla with a gentle spiciness. Amber in color, this whiskey finishes smooth but packs a good punch. Easily one of the best bourbons for the price. The Bulliet bourbon and rye are very close to our biggest selling whiskeys under $10. Whether shooting, mixing or sipping, you can't go wrong.

FUN FACT: Tom Bulleit is married to the former Elizabeth Callaway Brooks, a descendent of frontier explorer Daniel Boone. And like any upright Southerner worth his salt, Bulleit has a true tale of adventure and mystery that comes with the family name.

PROPELLERS: ! ! ! !

VARIETY/STYLE: Small Batch Bourbon

BARREL TYPE: Oak

AGE: 6 years

ORIGIN: Kentucky

BOTTLE: 750 ml, cork top

ALCOHOL: 45%

PROOF: 90

PRICE: mid-range

RELATED: Fighting Cock, Eagle Rare, Four Roses, Buffalo Trace, Jim Beam

Diageo North America, 801 Main Avenue, Norwalk, CT 06851, (646) 223-2000, www.diageo.com **Producer:** Four Roses Distillery, 1224 Bonds Mill Road, Lawrenceburg, KY 40342, (502) 839-3436, www.bulleit.com

COMMENTS FROM THE BARTENDER:

ANNIE: No burn, super easy. Actually delicious on a second sip. I think this would make a good mixer. Medium burn that lasts for a hot minute but finishes warm and smooth.

JEFF: Once you get past that initial burn, you get that Charleston Chew vanilla candy taste.

JOHN: Ahh, this is good; doesn't blow me away . . . but it's nice Has just the right amount of all the flavors a good whiskey should have.

BRANDON: I get oak and vanilla up my nose. Initially burns but the finish is like candy!

CABIN STILL KENTUCKY STRAIGHT BOURBON WHISKEY

SUMMARY: Established in 1849 and now owned by Heaven Hill Distillery. There's not a ton of info to offer up on this whiskey. Alcohol forward with some faint smoke, it finishes fast. We don't recommend it over ice; water is not its friend. It's fine for a cocktail party that's mixing up drinks with pungent ingredients like ginger beer. Most people regard it as good bourbon for the price.

FUN FACT: Yellow label shows a nineteenth-century pot still.

VARIETY/STYLE: Straight Bourbon

BARREL TYPE: New White Oak

AGE: 4 years

ORIGIN: Kentucky

BOTTLE: 750 ml, screw cap

ALCOHOL: 40%

PROOF: 80

PRICE: low-range

RELATED: Old Fitzgerald 1849, Wild Turkey 101, Wild Turkey 81, Jim Beam 8 Star, Old Grand-Dad

Heaven Hill Distillery, P.O. Box 729, Bardstown, KY 40004, (502) 348-3921, www.heavenhill.com

PROPELLERS: !

COMMENTS FROM THE BARTENDER:

ANNIE: Candy corn and kettle corn. It's like Halloween and the Town Fair had a whiskey baby.

JEFF: Butterscotch jumps out at me paired up with a bit of a dried wood taste Almost no burn. I'd prefer something with more flavor for my money.

JOHN: I get a sweet caramel start with a slight burn. Really nice and mild

BRANDON: Slightly sweet and oaky but it lacks overall full palate It really tastes cheap even though it's smooth.

COLORADO GOLD STRAIGHT BOURBON WHISKEY

SUMMARY: We like this craft whiskey; it is very easy to drink. Lots of caramel candy and burnt sugar flavor. It is very rich, leaves the palate lingering of spice. In 2010 it was awarded fourth place by the American Distilling Institute in a blind taste test held in Kentucky. In 2012, they got the nod for Best in Class finish. This is a single barrel release; check your bottle for the number of your barrel. The bottle we tasted from was #14, barrel #15C.

FUN FACT: The distillery was founded by Austin, Texas, native Peter Cociola along with Master Distiller Mike Almy. They pride themselves on using clean, pure Rocky Top H_2O and locally grown grains.

VARIETY/STYLE: Bourbon

BARREL TYPE: White Oak

AGE: 3 years

ORIGIN: Colorado

BOTTLE: 750 ml, screw cap

ALCOHOL: 45%

PROOF: 90

PRICE: mid-range

RELATED: Angel's Envy, Ancient Age 10, Buck Ranch Hand, Eagle Ranch Hand, Eagle Rare 10

PROPELLERS:

Colorado Gold Distillery, 1290 S. Grand Mesa Drive, Cedaredge, CO 81413, (970) 856-2600, www.coloradogolddistillers.com

COMMENTS FROM THE BARTENDER:

ANNIE: This whiskey is like the perfect guest, quick and pleasant.

JEFF: A bit of pepper comes out in a short finish after a pretty balanced taste of vanilla and maple. Has a sweet nose but wasn't overly sweet in taste.

JOHN: Nice malts in this. It is very sugary and sweet. No finish. All in all very tasty.

BRANDON: This whiskey smells a bit malty but really turns out tasting like candy corn. Very short finish and limited flavor profile. Not bad, but not by any means is it great.

CORNER CREEK RESERVE BOURBON WHISKEY

SUMMARY: Corner Creek is another product from Willet Distilling Company, also known as Kentucky Bourbon Distillers. Most of their brands are considered premium whiskeys, but in our opinion the Corner Creek falls a little short. We've given this bourbon more than enough chances to sell at the Aero Club, but it has sadly faded away into the sea of bottles. The general comments from guests are that it's boring, dry and uncomplex; the bartenders were kind of on the fence. This is one you'll just have to try for yourself.

FUN FACT: Family owned and operated in the same location since 1935.

VARIETY/STYLE: Bourbon Whiskey

BARREL TYPE: American Oak

AGE: 8 years

ORIGIN: Kentucky

BOTTLE: 750 ml, cork top

ALCOHOL: 44%

PROOF: 88

PRICE: mid-range

RELATED: Old Bardstown, Wild Turkey, Jim Beam, Bulleit Bourbon, Four Roses

Kentucky Bourbon Distillers, 1869 Loretto Road, Bardstown, KY 40004, (502) 348-0899, kentuckybourbon@bardstown.com, www.kentuckybourbonwhiskey.com

PROPELLERS:

COMMENTS FROM THE BARTENDER:

ANNIE: Very dry with dried fruit chips and hard candies. This would be great with a splash of ginger ale.

JEFF: The nose doesn't lie. The dried fruit you smell comes out in the taste, along with a little toffee and oak. I just wish the flavors were a bit bigger.

JOHN: I think this is a spicy bourbon, not a rye. I like the spicy sweetness. I like this.

BRANDON: Wow! What a floral bouquet for a nose! The taste is warm, smooth and oaky with a dry finish. It reminds me of exploring the Carlsbad flower fields during the fall.

CYRUS NOBLE SMALL BATCH BOURBON WHISKEY

SUMMARY: Crafted in Nelson County, Kentucky, and bottled in San Francisco. We have a soft spot in our heart for this whiskey, not just because we're located in California, but because it's good! Its caramel and butter flavors make it easy to drink. We often recommend it as an after-dinner or last drink of the night with a splash of Amaretto over ice.

FUN FACT: Named after Cyrus Noble, a successful spirits distiller who became semi-famous for falling into a vat of his own whiskey.

VARIETY/STYLE: Straight Bourbon

BARREL TYPE: New American Oak

AGE: 5 years

ORIGIN: Kentucky Whiskey aged in San Francisco, CA

BOTTLE: 750 ml, synthetic cork top

ALCOHOL: 45%

PROOF: 90

PRICE: mid-range

RELATED: Heaven Hill, Elmer T. Lee, Eagle Rare, Buffalo Trace, Blanton's

PROPELLERS: !!!!!

Haas Brothers, 75 Broadway, Suite 258, San Francisco, CA 94111, (415) 282-8585, info@haas-brothers.com, www.haas-brothers.com **Producer:** Heaven Hill Distillery, P.O. Box 729, Bardstown, KY 40004, (502) 348-3921, www.heavenhill.com

COMMENTS FROM THE BARTENDER:

ANNIE: Breakfast flavors in a glass. Brown maple sugar, oatmeal, frosted vanilla flakes. Try this whiskey in a fat wash. Yummy!

JEFF: Heavy caramel and hazelnut flavors. The caramel kind of dominates the nose. Has a nice taste that I could enjoy through the night, as long as the price was right.

JOHN: I get hints of fruit that I almost never get from whiskey. It's nice and sweet. I will drink a lot of this.

BRANDON: Bitter, dry and malty but smooth. You know that grumpy old man that lives down your street? This is what he's drinking.

DEVIL'S SHARE CALIFORNIA SMALL BATCH BOURBON WHISKEY

SUMMARY: Ballast Point Distillery has a special place in our hearts. The distillery and brewery are located just 17 minutes north of the Aero Club up Interstate 15, and they recently opened a restaurant and brewery just one mile down the street in San Diego's Little Italy district. As you will notice from the empty bottles in our product shots, we sold out of all their whiskey days after it hit our shelves. When I explained to Skip Stegmair, Ballast Point's national sales manager, that I needed my bartenders to blind taste the whiskey before I could write the reviews, he didn't hesitate to offer up some of his secret stash and handed it over with total confidence. The bourbon was the first to sell out and we have a huge waiting list of people anxious for the next batch. Here is some of the info on the bourbon that Master Distiller Yuseff Cherney was nice enough to share. "We use 62% corn, 32% two-row malted brewer's barley and 6% malted wheat as the foundation of our bourbon. The grain is mashed and steeped in our brew house, just like our beer minus the addition of hops, and removed from the husk prior to fermentation. This lautering process produces a more refined whiskey with just the sweet barley malt being fermented in to our 'distiller's beer.' The beer is then distilled through our custom-built Vendome copper hybrid pot/column still. Only the hearts are kept and aged in virgin, heavily charred American oak barrels for a minimum of three years. Devil's Share Bourbon Whiskey is a celebration of history and a study in authenticity." The folks at Ballast Point take a lot of pride in their work; I've seen it firsthand. If you love whiskey, beer and sunshine, we highly recommend a trip to San Diego. Book a hotel in Little Italy and come see us.

PROPELLERS:

FUN FACT: When most distillers refer to "small batch," the definition is around 10 barrels; Ballast Point's first release of both bourbon and single malt were only two barrels each. Batch number two of Devil's Share Bourbon was three barrels.

VARIETY/STYLE: Small Batch Bourbon

BARREL TYPE: American Oak

AGE: 4 years

ORIGIN: California

BOTTLE: 750 ml, cork top

ALCOHOL: 46%

PROOF: 92

PRICE: high-range

RELATED: RoughStock, Corsair, Prichard's, Journeyman, Rogue

Ballast Point, 9045 Carroll Way, San Diego, CA 92131, (858) 790-6900, www.ballastpoint.com

COMMENTS FROM THE BARTENDER:

ANNIE: Cinnamon, brown sugar, toffee and vanilla. Bit of a bite, but it feels good. I really like this one a lot!

JEFF: Cinnamon, oak and a hint of tobacco. Perfect for a guys' night out.

JOHN: Really nice flavor! Definitely get tobacco and oak. The burn is short-lived, followed by a spice finish. We have a contender for my new fave.

BRANDON: Excellent nose on this whiskey! It's perfectly balanced between the sweetness and spice. It's not too complex, which is unnecessary because the oak, cinnamon and vanilla are a real treat!

EAGLE RARE SINGLE BARREL KENTUCKY STRAIGHT BOURBON WHISKEY

SUMMARY: Our biggest selling bourbon for under $10! Acquired in 1989 by the Sazerac Company and now distilled at Buffalo Trace, this is a well-rounded single barrel bourbon. We often have guests who are fairly new to the world of whiskey and they ask questions like "What's good?" Our question in return is "How much are you looking to spend?" If the answer is under $10, we often recommend Eagle Rare. We have served it countless times with the same reaction: "That's good!" Also check the section on Rare/Hard to Find Whiskeys for the Eagle Rare 17 Year. It's one of five bourbons included in the Award Winning Buffalo Trace Antique Collection.

FUN FACT: Between 2005 and 2010 Eagle Rare won a string of medals from the San Francisco Spirits Competition. They have a program called the Rare Life Award where you can submit a story as well as vote on others and Eagle Rare will donate $40,000 to the charitable organization of the winner's choice.

VARIETY/STYLE: Single Barrel Bourbon

BARREL TYPE: New American Oak

AGE: 10 years

ORIGIN: Kentucky

BOTTLE: 750 ml, cork top

ALCOHOL: 45%

PROOF: 90

PRICE: mid-range

RELATED: Benchmark 8, Ancient Age, Buffalo Trace, Wild Turkey 81, Bulleit

PROPELLERS:

Buffalo Trace Distillery, 113 Great Buffalo Trace, Franklin County, Frankfort, KY 40601, (800) 654-8471, info@buffalotrace.com, www.buffalotracedistillery.com

COMMENTS FROM THE BARTENDER:

ANNIE: This has almost no smell and is incredibly smooth. Low burn, super tasty. I'd drink this straight from the barrel.

JEFF: I really like this, soft flavors of honey and toffee.

JOHN: Nice and smooth. Very clean finish. Kind of forgot the taste already.

BRANDON: Great whiskey to drink straight. It's like smooth velvet on the palate.

ELIJAH CRAIG 20 YEAR SINGLE BARREL STRAIGHT BOURBON

SUMMARY: This award-winning, super-premium bourbon has its roots coming from the lineage of the man who discovered the way to make true Kentucky bourbon by aging whiskey in barrels that had been charred by a fire—Reverend Elijah Craig. Master Distillers Parker and Craig Beam select from one barrel bourbon that shows the aptitude and quality necessary for bottling. With balanced notes of vanilla, butterscotch and oak, this bourbon will slide down your throat with the luxury of a velvet slip and slide. Slight hints of citrus, pine and white pepper. This is technically bucket-list bourbon, as it is in very limited suppy, but we happened to have a bottle on the shelf and we were just dying to review it for you.

FUN FACT: This bourbon is named in honor of Reverend Elijah Craig.

VARIETY/STYLE: Single Barrel Straight Bourbon

BARREL TYPE: New American Oak

AGE: 20 years

ORIGIN: Kentucky

BOTTLE: 750 ml, cork top

ALCOHOL: 45%

PROOF: 90

PRICE: high-range

RELATED: Blanton's Single Barrel, Russell's Reserve Small Batch Single Barrel, Jefferson's Reserve Very Old Very Small Batch

PROPELLERS:

Heaven Hill Distilleries, P.O. Box 729, Bardstown, KY 40004, (502) 348-3921, www.heavenhill.com

COMMENTS FROM THE BARTENDER:

ANNIE: Sweet, rich nose that's very inviting. Coats the mouth with caramel and fresh-cut oak. No need for any mixer or even water.

JEFF: This delicious whiskey has a sweet caramel nose, and a tasty vanilla flavor. Drink up, my friends.

JOHN: Ahh yes, lots of dark cherry cola and dark fruits.

BRANDON: This is definitely an entertaining bourbon. From the perfectly sweet caramel nose to the long, complex finish, I'm very impressed.

ELIJAH CRAIG KENTUCKY STRAIGHT BOURBON WHISKEY 12 YEAR OLD

SUMMARY: This 12-year-old whiskey is among one of the all-time favorites of our staff. We have recommended this whiskey thousands of times and it's never let us down. Reverend Elijah Craig founded his distillery around 1789, and many say he's the first to use charred oak casks for aging. Essentially, this makes him the inventor of bourbon. We are not sure if that's true or not, but one thing that is for sure is this recipe is outstanding. Well done, Reverend Craig!

FUN FACT: The building where Craig stored his barrels caught fire and charred several of them. He decided to use them anyway and we're sure glad he did.

VARIETY/STYLE: Single Barrel Straight Bourbon

BARREL TYPE: New American Oak

AGE: 20 years

ORIGIN: Kentucky

BOTTLE: 750 ml, cork top

ALCOHOL: 45%

PROOF: 90

PRICE: high-range

RELATED: Blanton's Single Barrel, Russell's Reserve Small Batch Single Barrel, Jefferson's Reserve Very Old Very Small Batch, Four Roses Small Batch

PROPELLERS: !!!!!

Heaven Hill Distillers, P.O. Box 729, Bardstown, KY 40004, (502) 348-3921, www.heavenhill.com

COMMENTS FROM THE BARTENDER:

ANNIE: Super faint sugary nose. Big burn that lingers. I like the spice but honestly this is kind of boring. Maybe my taste was too small, but I could drink this all night, so I guess this wins.

JEFF: Not a strong nose but wonderful cherry cola flavors.

JOHN: Now we are talking. Beautiful smoke and light burn. Great aftertaste. Thick bourbon that you might save for a birthday!

BRANDON: The taste of an honest bourbon. Sweet caramel corn flavor with bite and a smooth finish.

ELMER T. LEE SINGLE BARREL SOUR MASH KENTUCKY STRAIGHT BOURBON

SUMMARY: Named after Master Distiller Elmer T. Lee, the man behind the single barrel bourbon. Mr. Lee was born in 1919 on a tobacco farm in Kentucky. He served in WWII as a radar bombardier. After the war, he returned to Kentucky and cut his teeth in whiskey at George T. Stagg Distillery, which is now Buffalo Trace. In 1984, he introduced Blanton's, the world's first single barrel bourbon. He passed away in July 2013 with a lifetime achievement award in the Whiskey Hall of Fame. His legend carries on, as his whiskey is often poured and enjoyed by our guests. It's like a sure thing among the mid-tier bourbons. It's got a little something for everyone—warm and spicy with cinnamon and raisin, it makes a great Egg White Whiskey Sour if you want to treat yourself.

FUN FACT: The bottles bear no age statement. Buffalo Trace honors the tradition that Lee used of picking the barrels when he thought they were ready, not how long they had aged.

VARIETY/STYLE: Straight Bourbon

BARREL TYPE: New American Oak

AGE: N/A

ORIGIN: Kentucky

BOTTLE: 750 ml, cork top

ALCOHOL: 45%

PROOF: 80

PRICE: mid-range

RELATED: Elijah Craig 12, Evan Williams Single Barrel, Blanton's, Booker's, Four Roses Single Barrel

PROPELLERS: !!!!!

Age International, Inc., 229 West Main Street, Suite 202, Frankfort, KY 40601, (502) 223-9874, nknox@ageintl.com
Producer: Buffalo Trace Distillery, 113 Great Buffalo Trace, Franklin County, Frankfort, KY 40601, (800) 654-8471, info@buffalotrace.com, www.buffalotracedistillery.com

COMMENTS FROM THE BARTENDER:

ANNIE: It's good, smooth, with honey and granola.

JEFF: Has a sweet smell and taste that would go great in a Manhattan.

JOHN: Ahh . . . one of those whiskeys that has hints of berry balanced with a long finish.

BRANDON: A nice nose of citrus and corn with a sweet, enjoyable honey and cocoa palate.

EVAN WILLIAMS SINGLE BARREL VINTAGE KENTUCKY STRAIGHT BOURBON WHISKEY

SUMMARY: Named for Evan Williams, who began distilling in 1783 near Louisville, Kentucky, after emigrating from Wales. Today each barrel of the whiskey is carefully hand-selected by Master Distillers Parker and Craig Beam at the Heaven Hill Distillery. It's really an art form to age and pick a single barrel of whiskey to achieve its maximum flavor profile. The main factor is its time and location in the rick house. Kentucky has extremely hot summers and bitter cold winters, so generally barrels from the upper levels are chosen, as they experience more of a rise and fall in temperatures. These are also referred to as the "honey barrels." There are people who will argue that blended whiskeys are better, that the blending takes the sharp edges off and smoothes out the whiskey. We say, "If it tastes good, drink it!" This is a great single barrel to try if you want to weigh in on the debate: great whiskey flavors and you can't beat the price.

FUN FACT: There are 10 other varieties of Evan Williams on the market, including everything from their standard black label brand to an eggnog whiskey.

VARIETY/STYLE: Single Barrel Bourbon

BARREL TYPE: New American Oak

AGE: 10 years

ORIGIN: Kentucky

BOTTLE: 750 ml, cork top

ALCOHOL: 43.3%

PROOF: 86.6

PRICE: mid-range

RELATED: Knob Creek, Four Roses, Blanton's, Elijah Craig, Russell's Reserve

PROPELLERS:

Heaven Hill Distillers, P.O. Box 729, Bardstown, KY 40004, (502) 348-3921, www.heavenhill.com

COMMENTS FROM THE BARTENDER:

ANNIE: Sweet and smooth, like it should be. Enough burn to please bourbon lovers.

JEFF: Nice! Sweet, smooth, caramel and some soft vanilla from the oak. This one's a sweet thing.

JOHN: Very sweet! Mild and easy-going. Really high sugar taste. I only get a slight taste of oak or wood, mostly in the finish.

BRANDON: This is evidence of a bourbon that has been bottled at its prime. It's sweet, smooth and overall just delicious!

EZRA BROOKS KENTUCKY STRAIGHT BOURBON WHISKEY

SUMMARY: Ezra Brooks is filtered with activated charcoal, which adds a charred character before barreling. This is not the same as the charcoal mellowing process that pulls out impurities after aging. Sadly, this bourbon doesn't get picked up off our shelves very often. Most of our beginner whiskey-drinking guests choose whiskey priced at around $5 a shot and prefer sweeter bourbon. Ezra Brooks tends to wrinkle the nose a little too much.

FUN FACT: The movie *The Sting* features a billboard for Ezra Brooks.

VARIETY/STYLE: Straight Bourbon Whiskey

BARREL TYPE: New American Oak

AGE: 7 years

ORIGIN: Kentucky

BOTTLE: 750 ml, cork top

ALCOHOL: 45%

PROOF: 90

PRICE: low-range

RELATED: Wild Turkey, Kentucky Gentleman, Cabin Still, Old Crow, Old Grand-Dad

Luxco, 1000 Clark Avenue, St. Louis, MO 63102, (314) 772-2626, contactus@luxco.com, www.luxco.com
Producer: Heaven Hill Distilleries, P.O. Box 729, Bardstown, KY 40004, (502) 348-3921, www.heavenhill.com

PROPELLERS:

COMMENTS FROM THE BARTENDER:

ANNIE: This smells a lot sweeter than it tastes but is definitely something I can get behind because of that.

JEFF: Interesting, light and clean.

JOHN: It tastes a bit like grass, kind of sweet but mostly it tastes green. Think farm.

BRANDON: Smells sweet and tastes of citrus. This would be good with a splash of Saint-Germain.

EZRA BROOKS SINGLE BARREL KENTUCKY STRAIGHT BOURBON WHISKEY

SUMMARY: Blended and bottled by Heaven Hill Distillery. This 12-year, 99-proof whiskey is interesting to say the least. We often recommend it when asked for a smoky or earthy whiskey, and guests are almost always happy with their purchase. Adding some ice doesn't seem to change it much. If you're in the mood for something a little different, tired of the same old thing, this may be what you're looking for, but we recommend tasting it at your local whiskey bar before you purchase.

FUN FACT: Ezra Brooks was introduced in 1960.

VARIETY/STYLE: Single Barrel Bourbon

BARREL TYPE: New American Oak

AGE: 12 years

ORIGIN: Kentucky

BOTTLE: 750 ml, cork top

ALCOHOL: 49.5%

PROOF: 99

PRICE: mid-range

RELATED: Old Crow Reserve, Old Forester, Knob Creek, Wild Turkey, Johnny Drum

PROPELLERS: ❗❗❗

Luxco, 1000 Clark Avenue, St. Louis, MO 63102, (314) 772-2626, contactus@luxco.com, www.luxco.com
Producer: Heaven Hill Distilleries, P.O. Box 729, Bardstown, KY 40004, (502) 348-3921, www.heavenhill.com

COMMENTS FROM THE BARTENDER:

ANNIE: Hmm . . . tastes thick and chewy, but also has a pretty good burn, I'm guessing it's high proof.

JEFF: Has a lot of oak, spice and burn.

JOHN: Chocolate, cola and maybe pecan pie? Great after dinner with a splash of Coke

BRANDON: This reminds me of one I used to sneak from my grandpa. Didn't like it then and still don't.

FIGHTING COCK KENTUCKY STRAIGHT BOURBON WHISKEY

SUMMARY: Do you want a bourbon with claws? Look no further. Fighting Cock shows its talons by bottling at 103 proof, making it one lean, mean bird. Aged six years with a little more rye in the mash bill, and as the distillers themselves say, "smoothes down the feathers." Upon opening, this spirit is actually inviting, a big whiff indicates little alcohol on the nose and some enticing vanilla/butterscotch spice notes. However, you are only one sip-n-swallow away from why this bourbon has "fighting" in its name. The pretty-smelling poultry packs a powerful punch, after all is said and done. Like a true frenemy, this bourbon will lure you in with niceties and finish you off like a trained world-class assassin (in a fairly pleasant way, I might add). Try this bourbon!

FUN FACT: Nicknamed "The Kick'n Chicken." It's self-labeled as "The Bad Boy of Bourbon."

VARIETY/STYLE: Straight Bourbon

BARREL TYPE: New American Oak

AGE: 6 years

ORIGIN: Kentucky

BOTTLE: N/A

ALCOHOL: 51.5%

PROOF: 103

PRICE: low-range

RELATED: Wild Turkey 101, Baker's, Booker's, Pure Kentucky, Noah's Mill

PROPELLERS: ❗❗❗❗❗

Heaven Hill Distilleries, P.O. Box 729, Bardstown, KY 40004, (502) 348-3921, www.heavenhill.com

COMMENTS FROM THE BARTENDER:

ANNIE: Maple syrup, corny, vanilla. Super sweet and drinkable. Would make a good Old Fashioned.

JEFF: One of the sweeter whiskeys that we carry, almost too sweet for me. Reminds me of kettle corn with a hint of maple. Try a few muddled lemons for a nice cocktail.

JOHN: Nice! Very sweet in the middle, good finish. Can I have more?

BRANDON: Such a sweet nose. Like maple, vanilla and corn. Little initial burn but a nice, smooth finish.

FOUR ROSES SINGLE BARREL KENTUCKY STRAIGHT BOURBON

SUMMARY: This premium single barrel uses one of Four Roses' 10 recipes. This bourbon is quite complex. On the nose it is fruity, spicy, floral with cocoa, maple syrup and a bit of oak. As a higher proof bourbon, the palate is robust, full bodied but mellow with hints of nutmeg, ripe plum and cherries. The finish is smooth and delicately long. Savor it while you drink; the bottle will be empty before you know it, especially in good company. Drink it straight up, on the rocks or with a splash of water. When serving premium whiskey like this, our cardinal rule is to never add anything but ice or water!

FUN FACT: In 1884, Paul Johnes Jr. moved his thriving business to Louisville, Kentucky, where he opened an office in a section of historic Main Street called "Whiskey Row." Four years later, he trademarked the name Four Roses, claiming production and sales back to the 1860s. In 1922, the Paul Johnes Company purchased the Frankfort Distilling Company, one of only six distilleries granted permission to operate through Prohibition to produce bourbon for medicinal purposes. In the years under Paul's direction, sales of the bourbon flourished and Four Roses grew to be a preeminent brand. Kirin Brewing bought the company and trademarked Four Roses Distillery LLC in 2002; it is earning its reputation as one of the finest names in the bourbon world.

VARIETY/STYLE: Single Barrel Straight Bourbon Whiskey

BARREL TYPE: New Charred Oak

AGE: 7 to 8 years

ORIGIN: Kentucky

BOTTLE: 750 ml, cork top

ALCOHOL: 50%

PROOF: 100

PRICE: mid-range

RELATED: Knob Creek, Basil Hayden's, Woodford Reserve, Pure Kentucky, Old Pogue

PROPELLERS:

Four Roses Distillery, 1224 Bonds Mill Road, Lawrenceburg, KY 40342, (502) 839-3436, www.fourrosesbourbon.com

COMMENTS FROM THE BARTENDER:

ANNIE: This smells like a man and then whiskey. Does not taste like a dude. Big burn.

JEFF: A sweet taste that disappears quickly. Would recommend to a virgin whiskey drinker.

JOHN: Very fast finish. It's there and then it's gone.

BRANDON: Sweet candy fruit nose, nutty finish, but long and smooth.

FOUR ROSES SMALL BATCH KENTUCKY STRAIGHT BOURBON

SUMMARY: Four Roses' Master Distiller selects four of their 10 recipes that mingle perfectly to create yet another fine bourbon. This small batch bourbon weighs in at 90 proof, providing your nose with little alcohol. More of the sweet oak, fruit, caramel and spice take over. The small batch is just as much a premium whiskey as their single barrel is. From 2008 to 2012, it won nine awards from the likes of the San Francisco World Spirits Competition and the World Whiskey Awards. It's rich, yet moderately sweet and with a warm oak taste. Leaves you nothing but satisfied! The finish is smooth and long. So please, "whiskey responsibly" and enjoy this bourbon neat, on the rocks or with just a splash of water.

FUN FACT: Bulleit Bourbon is also distilled at the Four Roses Distilling LLC.

VARIETY/STYLE: Small Batch Bourbon

BARREL TYPE: New Charred Oak

AGE: under 7 years

ORIGIN: Kentucky

BOTTLE: 750 ml, cork top

ALCOHOL: 45%

PROOF: 90

PRICE: mid-range

RELATED: Four Roses Single Barrel, Redemption High Rye, Bulleit, Fighting Cock, Basil Hayden's

PROPELLERS:

Four Roses Distillery, 1224 Bonds Mill Road, Lawrenceburg, KY 40342, (502) 839-3436, www.fourrosesbourbon.com

COMMENTS FROM THE BARTENDER:

ANNIE: Right off the bat, a classic bourbon burn with corn sweetness to balance. Medium-length finish with hints of corn syrup. Delicious and provoking.

JEFF: Sweet and simple with a traditional feel and taste. Caramel, oak and spice leave a pleasant taste in your mouth. Great way to get introduced to bourbon.

JOHN: No nose at all, but when it hits your lips—wow! So good! It has everything I like in a whiskey.

BRANDON: Here's a perfect example of a fine bourbon! You get a nice spicy kick in the back of your mouth with solid notes of oak, spice and caramel. Long, but somewhat dry finish.

FOUR ROSES YELLOW LABEL BOURBON

SUMMARY: Four Roses uses up to all 10 of their recipes to get their bourbon just where they want it to be. Their straight bourbon has a gentle nose with honey and spice but is fruity and floral as well. The taste is crisp and defined, but what stands out most often is the pear flavor. It's very enjoyable. The finish is smooth, so don't be afraid to throw this one back!

FUN FACT: You can get a bottle of this bourbon in Lawrenceburg, Kentucky, for less than $20!

VARIETY/STYLE: Straight Bourbon

BARREL TYPE: New Charred Oak

AGE: 7 years and under

ORIGIN: Kentucky

BOTTLE: 750 ml, screw cap

ALCOHOL: 40%

PROOF: 80

PRICE: low-range

RELATED: Basil Hayden's, Wild Turkey 101, Bulleit, Old Grand-Dad, Jim Beam Devil's Cut

Four Roses Distillery LLC, 1224 Bonds Mill Road, Lawrenceburg, KY 40342, (502) 839-3436, www.fourrosesbourbon.com

PROPELLERS:

COMMENTS FROM THE BARTENDER:

ANNIE: Spice city! A little bit of sweetness goes a long way. Super interesting and yummy, but surprising because the nose is so faint.

JEFF: No need to mix this one. A wonderfully complex combination that is very smooth and drinkable.

JOHN: I had a strange medicinal taste I need more for a definitive explanation. The finish is nice and smooth.

BRANDON: I got a nose full of fresh fruit and oak. Warmed me right up and numbed the inside of my mouth. There was a little burn, but the finish is long and complex. Serve neat.

HIRSCH SMALL BATCH RESERVE KENTUCKY STRAIGHT BOURBON WHISKEY

SUMMARY: Hirsh whiskey made its mark in 1974 when it was distilled at the Pennco Distillery in Schaefferstown, Pennsylvania, by Adolph Hirsch. The distillery closed down in the 1980s, leaving behind 16- and 20-year-old expressions that are almost impossible to find. The label now owned by Anchor Distilling is part of a group including Anchor Brewing, Berry Bros. and Rudd and Priest Imports in San Francisco. The new Hirsch whiskey is sourced from an unknown party. The bourbon sells well in part from its history as a quality A. H. Hirsch product and because it's good.

FUN FACT: Anchor Distilling Co. also produces some award-willing gins: Junipero and Genevieve.

VARIETY/STYLE: Small Batch Straight Bourbon Whiskey

BARREL TYPE: New American Oak

AGE: 4 to 6 years

ORIGIN: Kentucky

BOTTLE: 750 ml, cork top

ALCOHOL: 46%

PROOF: 92

PRICE: mid-range

RELATED: Four Roses Small Batch, Ballast Point, Wathen's, Temptation, Temperance Trader

PROPELLERS:

Anchor Distilling Co., 1705 Mariposa Street, San Francisco, CA 94107, (415) 863-8350, info@anchorsf.com, www.anchordistilling.com

COMMENTS FROM THE BARTENDER:

ANNIE: Smells grainy. Will give you "whiskey face." Not a huge fan, but I could drink it if I had to.

JEFF: Several different flavors fight to be noticed, but toffee wins the shouting match. Vanilla is the runner-up.

JOHN: Nice round full-flavor whiskey. Not very hot, more smooth. Would "like" on Facebook!

BRANDON: I would file this in the okay drawer. Has a kind of a medicinal taste, kind of earthy. Very influenced by the barrels.

JAMES E. PEPPER 100 PROOF STRAIGHT BOURBON

SUMMARY: The long history of the Pepper brand started with Elijah Pepper, master distiller from 1776–1838. Hailing from Culpeper, Virginia, Mr. Pepper settled in Old Pepper Springs, Kentucky, and by 1780 he was an established distiller in the area. Eventually, he would pass the family business on to his son, Oscar, who then passed it on to his grandson, James E. Pepper. In more recent years, the folks at Georgetown Trading Co. assumed stewardship of the brand and set out to produce whiskey that pays homage to the whiskey that was produced since the dawn of the American Revolution. Both the bourbon and the rye are said to be aged three to five years and sell pretty well, due mainly to a very good label. Most guests don't know the history, but after hearing the heritage, they enjoy this whiskey a little more.

FUN FACT: Today, the site where Elijah Pepper began distilling is a National Historic Landmark and home of the Woodford Reserve Distillery.

VARIETY/STYLE: Straight Bourbon Whiskey

BARREL TYPE: New American Oak

AGE: N/A

ORIGIN: Indiana

BOTTLE: 750 ml, cork top

ALCOHOL: 50%

PROOF: 100

PRICE: mid-range

RELATED: Bulleit, Buffalo Trace, Belle Meade, Elmer T. Lee, Evan Williams

PROPELLERS: !!!!!

Georgetown Trading Co., 4200 Cathedral Ave NW #711, Washington, DC 20016, (301) 518-1366, www.jamesepepper.com

COMMENTS FROM THE BARTENDER:

ANNIE: Super sweet and spicy. Pretty good balance; another good cocktail-maker.

JEFF: If I were a baker, I'd want my Christmas cookies to taste like this. A nice combination of honey, vanilla and spice.

JOHN: Sugar and spice and everything nice—that's what this is made of. Garnish this cocktail with a candy cane.

BRANDON: Easy drinker. The flavors all pop and are enjoyable—a solid purchase.

JAMES E. PEPPER 1776 15 YEAR STRAIGHT BOURBON WHISKEY

SUMMARY: Established in 1776 and distilled over three generations through 1958, the Pepper family is steeped in whiskey history, most notably Colonel James E. Pepper. Known to race thoroughbred horses and travel by private railcar, he is credited with making the Old Fashioned cocktail famous. Today this cocktail is the holy grail of any good whiskey bar. There are many subtle versions of this classic drink and every bartender in a vest or suspenders claims to have the best. This 15-year-old selection may be a little too pricey to mix up, but if you are looking to try bourbon that has sat a spell, this may be the one for you.

FUN FACT: Pepper nicknamed his whiskey "Old 1776" and proudly used his grandfather's original Revolutionary-era recipes.

VARIETY/STYLE: Straight Bourbon Whiskey

BARREL TYPE: New American Oak

AGE: 15 years

ORIGIN: Indiana

BOTTLE: 750 ml, cork top

ALCOHOL: 46%

PROOF: 92

PRICE: high-range

RELATED: Bulleit 10 year, Elijah Craig, George T. Stagg Jr., Willett, Booker's

PROPELLERS: !!!

Georgetown Trading Co., 4200 Cathedral Ave NW #711, Washington, DC 20016, (301) 518-1366, www.jamesepepper.com

COMMENTS FROM THE BARTENDER:

ANNIE: Vanilla and toffee smells. Burns the back of the throat.

JEFF: Not a lot for me to say about this one. Some cinnamon and nutmeg comes through with a medium burn, but no wow factor.

JOHN: Cinnamon sticks and spices. If you like that, this is for you.

BRANDON: Very light nose, very mild flavor that fades fast, almost like it's watered down too much.

JEFFERSON'S KENTUCKY STRAIGHT BOURBON WHISKEY VERY SMALL BATCH

SUMMARY: Jefferson's standard offering is another good whiskey from the collection offered up by Trey Zoeller and friends. Using blended barrels of 8- to 12-year-old whiskey, this is a solid choice on any day. You probably won't "wow" your guests, but you won't disappoint them either. It's an easy up-sell for a mixed cocktail but a little too pricey for an everyday mixer.

FUN FACT: Jefferson's uses barrels, new and aged, from established distillers who have spent hundreds of years perfecting their art.

VARIETY/STYLE: Straight Bourbon

BARREL TYPE: New American Oak

AGE: N/A

ORIGIN: Kentucky

BOTTLE: 750 ml, cork top

ALCOHOL: 41.15%

PROOF: 82.3

PRICE: mid-range

RELATED: Knob Creek, Four Roses, Michter's, Elijah Craig, Elmer T. Lee

PROPELLERS: !!!!

Castle Brands Inc., 122 East 42nd Street, Suite 5000, New York, NY 10168, (800) 882-8140, info@castlebrands.com, www.castlebrands.com

COMMENTS FROM THE BARTENDER:

ANNIE: Light, creamy vanilla with a woody finish. Not much burn, and I like a good burn.
JEFF: Nose is sweet. Flavors that are very elegant and enjoyable, with a constancy I enjoy.
JOHN: Nothing wrong with this; sip away!
BRANDON: Easy drinker with soft vanilla and all spice.

JEFFERSON'S RESERVE VERY OLD KENTUCKY STRAIGHT BOURBON WHISKEY VERY SMALL BATCH

SUMMARY: Upon first opening this bourbon and wafting it from a Glencairn glass, I found it to be initially overwhelming on the alcohol side, but given a small amount of time, notes of raisin and maple come through in a very satisfactory way. Founder and master bourbon maker Trey Zoeller consistently tries to make the best, albeit unique, bourbons in the world. From ocean aging to extremely small batches, these bourbons are definitely what I would call craft distillates. Although the distiller's description of this bourbon falls under "unforgettable," given the price per bottle, I would say it is something that you would really have to like to buy again (I would!). Granted a 94 point score from *Wine Enthusiast* never really hurts your brand! From ancient barrels found in the reserve to aging bourbons on the bows of ships going around the world, this distillery is definitely on the cutting edge of bourbon creation.

FUN FACT: Very small batch, indeed. Each bottling contains no more than 8 to 12 barrels, compared to the normal 200 to 300 barrels.

VARIETY/STYLE: Bourbon

BARREL TYPE: American oak

AGE: N/A

ORIGIN: Kentucky

BOTTLE: 750 ml, cork top

ALCOHOL: 45.1%

PROOF: 90.2

PRICE: high-range

RELATED: Woodford Reserve, James E. Pepper, Russell's Reserve, Booker's, Bulleit 10 Year

PROPELLERS: !!!!

Castle Brands Inc., 122 East 42nd Street, Suite 5000, New York, NY 10168, (800) 882-8140, info@castlebrandsinc.com, www.castlebrandsinc.com

COMMENTS FROM THE BARTENDER:

ANNIE: Big spice. So much on the front that I actually just sneezed. I'm a big spice fan, so keep this one coming.
JEFF: Nothing but spice. So much that it had a bit of a burn in my mouth. Spicy-food lovers should give this a shot.
JOHN: Spice, spice, baby . . . spice, spice, baby. Rolling in my 5.0, rag top down so my hair can blow.
BRANDON: This whiskey has flavors that would be perfect after dinner with a piece of Julian apple pie.

JIM BEAM BLACK KENTUCKY STRAIGHT BOURBON WHISKEY

SUMMARY: Proudly displaying a label on its bottle reading: "The Highest Rated North American Whiskey." Jim Beam Black is aged eight years, twice as long as the signature Jim Beam White Label Bourbon. Beam is striving to create a full-bodied flavor with smooth caramel and warm oak. In our opinion they did a good job. When a guest requests a whiskey to sip on in the $5 to $10 range, the Black is a solid pick. We usually let them get a few sips in before asking, "What do ya think?" The response is often, "It's pretty good. I like it, what is it?" When we reveal that it's Jim Beam Black, the response is often, "Really? Wow!" It's a solid choice, especially in its price range.

FUN FACT: Beam Double Black is well known at the San Francisco Spirits Competition, earning Gold Medals in 2005, 2007 and Double Gold in 2009.

VARIETY/STYLE: Straight Bourbon

BARREL TYPE: New Oak

AGE: 8 years

ORIGIN: Kentucky

BOTTLE: 750 ml, screw cap

ALCOHOL: 43%

PROOF: 86

PRICE: low-range

RELATED: Woodford Reserve, Ridgemont Reserve, Knob Creek, Benchmark 8, Old Forester

PROPELLERS: ♜♜♜♜♜

Beam Suntory Inc., 222 W Merchandise Mart Plaza, Chicago, IL 60654, (312) 964-6999, www.jimbeam.com

COMMENTS FROM THE BARTENDER:

ANNIE: Kind of like a date with the guy who's in the friend zone. Rather have the rock star!

JEFF: I wish the taste would have lasted the whole way through. A good taste but finished fast.

JOHN: Good sipping whiskey. Solid oak and toffee. A good daily drinker—not that I do that.

BRANDON: Sweet butterscotch nose. Short, soft palate that's easy to drink. Not too bad.

JIM BEAM BOURBON

SUMMARY: The Beam family has been making bourbon for over 200 years with seven generations of family sticking together through the Great Depression, major wars and, oh yeah—Prohibition. Even if you've never had a drop of whiskey in your life, you most likely know the name and product. In 1856, David M. Beam moved his family distillery to Nelson County, a key location with vital railway lines providing easier distribution to the north and south. Today, Beam boasts a wide variety of products, but they are best known for their signature White Label Bourbon. There's a good chance most people reading this have had a Beam and Coke, and why not, it's an amazing combination. The trouble with this bourbon is that in a whiskey bar with a large selection most people pass it over when looking to enjoy something straight or on the rocks; either way, it's a must-have whiskey for any bar.

FUN FACT: Fred Noe, Jim Beam seventh-generation master distiller, was inducted into the Kentucky Bourbon Hall of Fame on September 20, 2013.

VARIETY/STYLE: Straight Bourbon

BARREL TYPE: New American Oak

AGE: 4 years

ORIGIN: Kentucky

BOTTLE: 750 ml, screw cap

ALCOHOL: 40%

PROOF: 80

PRICE: low-range

RELATED: Bulleit, Wild Turkey, Old Grand-Dad, Ten High, Old Crow

PROPELLERS: ♜♜

Beam Suntory Inc., 222 W Merchandise Mart Plaza, Chicago, IL 60654, (312) 964-6999, www.jimbeam.com

COMMENTS FROM THE BARTENDER:

ANNIE: Alcohol-forward nose. Sweet, springy, burns the back of the throat. Finishes kind of long. Easy to drink. Caramel.

JEFF: Besides the taste of malt, I got nothing from this. Pretty bland and not interesting at all.

JOHN: Can't say this is one of my favorites. My guess is it's from the bottom shelf. Some mild plum and pepper notes. Definitely a mixer!

BRANDON: Not a very big nose. Smooth but not robust at all. Malty but not very good.

JIM BEAM CHOICE KENTUCKY STRAIGHT BOURBON WHISKEY CHARCOAL FILTERED

SUMMARY: According to the Jim Beam website, this is the whiskey that Jim Beam would choose. Also known as Green Label, it's charcoal filtered before bottling, the only Beam product to do so. This process is designed to remove impurities from the whiskey. Mellow is the word best used to describe this 5-year-old bourbon. It makes a good mixer or novelty bottle to have at your bar, but we recommend pouring the Beam Black Double Aged if you want to keep your guests happy.

FUN FACT: The Beam family has played a major role in the Heaven Hill Distillery. All of the master distillers at Heaven Hill since its founding have been members of the Beam family.

VARIETY/STYLE: Straight Bourbon

BARREL TYPE: New American Oak

AGE: 5 years

ORIGIN: Kentucky

BOTTLE: 750 ml, screw cap

ALCOHOL: 40%

PROOF: 80

PRICE: low-range

RELATED: Jack Daniel's, Bulleit, Wild Turkey, Old Crow, Ancient Age

PROPELLERS:

Beam Suntory Inc., 222 W Merchandise Mart Plaza, Chicago, IL 60654, (312) 964-6999, www.jimbeam.com

COMMENTS FROM THE BARTENDER:

ANNIE: Smells like Corn Chex. Tastes sweet with no burn. Super good for mixing.

JEFF: A sweet nose with an oaky taste. Has a medium burn to it. Not bad if you are looking for something less complex.

JOHN: Has a toasty sweet nose. Very mild. This would make a great well whiskey.

BRANDON: Simple. Just tastes like your run of the "still" whiskey . . . ha, ha. Not much of a nose or much flavor.

JIM BEAM DEVIL'S CUT 90 PROOF KENTUCKY STRAIGHT BOURBON WHISKEY

SUMMARY: As bourbon ages, a certain percentage (3%) evaporates, which is gone forever. This is referred to as the angel's share. Some of the whiskey stays trapped in the wood; this is what Jim Beam calls the devil's share. After the barrels are emptied, springwater is added and shaken in the barrels. The water pulls out some of the whiskey from the wood. The water is then blended with the aged whiskey and bottled at 90 proof. The result from the masses seems to be a definite strong oak flavor with some sweet dark fruit, but the burn of the 90 proof often prevents a second round. However, it does make a great Manhattan.

FUN FACT: In January 2014, Jim Beam was sold to the Japanese company Suntory Holdings, LTD.

VARIETY/STYLE: Straight Bourbon

BARREL TYPE: New White Oak

AGE: N/A

ORIGIN: Kentucky

BOTTLE: 750 ml, screw cap

ALCOHOL: 45%

PROOF: 90

PRICE: low-range

RELATED: Old Forester, Cabin Still, Buck, Corner Creek, Bench Mark

PROPELLERS:

Beam Suntory Inc., 222 W Merchandise Mart Plaza, Chicago, IL 60654, (312) 964-6999, www.jimbeam.com

COMMENTS FROM THE BARTENDER:

ANNIE: Very rich nose, warm and fruity. Too much burn for whiskey drinkers still on training wheels.

JEFF: A strong oak taste that helps cover up the alcohol, which is fairly noticeable all the way through.

JOHN: This is a good recommendation for the spice drinker. It would make a great Manhattan.

BRANDON: Smells like sweet, dark fruit. Has a burn from start to finish and very oaky. Not a personal favorite.

JIM BEAM SIGNATURE CRAFT SMALL BATCH BOURBON

SUMMARY: If you're already a Jim Beam fan, you will love this signature craft bourbon. Focusing on wood management and barrel selection, the folks at Beam are striving for elegance and balance. We have trouble selling a Jim Beam whiskey in the mid to upper price range, but on the occasion guests allow us to choose for them, they are often surprised to be enjoying a Beam 12-year bourbon. Not as complex as most of its competitors, but a solid choice nonetheless. We recommend drinking it straight for maximum flavor.

FUN FACT: Jim Beam also offers up a Signature Craft rare Spanish brandy bourbon. It's a limited-edition bourbon made by adding a small amount of brandy, giving it sweet notes of date and fig.

VARIETY/STYLE: Small Batch Bourbon

BARREL TYPE: New White Oak

AGE: 12 years

ORIGIN: Kentucky

BOTTLE: 750 ml, cork top

ALCOHOL: 43%

PROOF: 86

PRICE: mid-range

RELATED: Knob Creek, Old Pogue, Russell's Reserve, Four Roses Small Batch, Elmer T. Lee

PROPELLERS:

Beam Suntory Inc., 222 W Merchandise Mart Plaza, Chicago, IL 60654, (312) 964-6999, www.jimbeam.com

COMMENTS FROM THE BARTENDER:

ANNIE: Smells like Grandma after baking all day (in a good way . . . vanilla, brown sugar). Tastes good, sweet and slightly burny.

JEFF: Very mild, but great flavor: cola and toffee, sugar and spice . . . very nice.

JOHN: Smells great. Taste is very mild, almost no finish. Great starter for a night of whiskey.

BRANDON: Smells wonderful. Has a complex taste of mild vanilla and shortbread. Great after a steak dinner!

JOHNNY DRUM PRIVATE STOCK KENTUCKY BOURBON

SUMMARY: Johnny Drum doesn't get pulled from the shelf very often, mainly because we just forget about it. The whiskey starts sweet with people calling out many flavors like cherry, vanilla and even banana. Its price is reasonable, around $30 a bottle, so you can mix it and not feel embarrassed at the bar. Maybe it's time to give it a second chance.

FUN FACT: Johnny Drum 101 Private Stock won Double Gold at the San Francisco World Spirits Competition in 2010.

VARIETY/STYLE: Straight Bourbon Whiskey

BARREL TYPE: New American Oak

AGE: N/A

ORIGIN: Kentucky

BOTTLE: 750 ml, screw cap

ALCOHOL: 50.5%

PROOF: 101

PRICE: mid-range

RELATED: Four Roses Small Batch, Elijah Craig 12 Year, Pure Kentucky, Kentucky Vintage, Ridgemont Reserve 1792

Kentucky Bourbon Distillers, 1869 Loretto Road, P.O. Box 785, Bardstown, KY 40004, (502) 348-0899, (502) 348-5539, kentuckybourbon@bardstown.com, www.kentuckybourbon.com

PROPELLERS:

COMMENTS FROM THE BARTENDER:

ANNIE: Almost no smell. Super sweet, corny and smooth.

JEFF: Has a long-lasting bitter finish, with little burn. Not one of my favorites.

JOHN: I liked this one after the first impression. It has a crazy, zesty grass flavor that I love.

BRANDON: Sweet caramel nose, unexpected complex finish.

JOSHUA BROOK KENTUCKY STRAIGHT BOURBON WHISKEY

SUMMARY: This may be our least interesting review of the book, simply because there's not much information out there on it and we just don't ever pour it. Once a week it gets picked up and dusted off, but that's about it. There's a lot of mystery around where the whiskey comes from: most think Heaven Hill Distillery, or possibly multiple places. Either way, there's not a lot of buzz around it. It's hard to recommend it when there are so many other great whiskeys in the same price range.

FUN FACT: Joshua Brook offers up a 4-year bourbon in a plastic 750 ml bottle.

VARIETY/STYLE: Straight Bourbon

BARREL TYPE: New White Oak

AGE: 8 years

ORIGIN: Kentucky

BOTTLE: 750 ml, screw cap

ALCOHOL: 43%

PROOF: 86

PRICE: low-range

RELATED: Wild Turkey, Old Grand-Dad, Kentucky Gentleman, Cabin Still, Early Times

Frank-Lin Distillers, 2455 Huntington Drive, Fairfield, CA 94533, (800) 922-9363, www.frank-lin.com

PROPELLERS:

COMMENTS FROM THE BARTENDER:

ANNIE: Warming burn with some enjoyable honeycomb and ginger spice. Rich smooth flavor.

JEFF: You wouldn't guess it from the nose, but this has a good amount of spice right in the beginning. It then calms down to maple and vanilla notes. Quite tasty.

JOHN: A really sweet nose that smelled like candy caramel, honey and vanilla. The palate is enjoyable and smooth with a finish that leaves you questioning whether or not you are drinking whiskey.

BRANDON: Faint sweetness, very soft flavors of ginger and vanilla. Seems young—a few more years in the barrel and this would be a fantastic whiskey.

JOURNEYMAN FEATHERBONE ORGANIC BOURBON WHISKEY

SUMMARY: Bill Welter, founder of Journeyman Distillery, claims this is fairly traditional wheated bourbon with a mash bill of 70% corn, 20% wheat and just a bit of barley and rye. A young whiskey, it's aged one year in new charred white oak barrels. The flavors tend to reflect that: soft and a little sweet with a clean finish. It doesn't get picked very often from our selection of wheated bourbons; people almost always order Maker's Mark or Old Weller Antique. Oh, and they are cheaper.

FUN FACT: A true grain to grass distillery. All of their products are certified organic by the Midwest Organic Services Association.

VARIETY/STYLE: Organic Bourbon

BARREL TYPE: New American Oak

AGE: N/A

ORIGIN: Michigan

BOTTLE: 750 ml, cork top

ALCOHOL: 45%

PROOF: 90

PRICE: mid-range

RELATED: W.L. Weller 12 Year, Lion's Pride, Maker's Mark, Rebel Yell

Journeyman Distillery, 109 Generations Drive, Three Oaks, MI 49128, (269) 820-2050, info@journeyman.com, www.journeymandistillery.com

PROPELLERS:

COMMENTS FROM THE BARTENDER:

ANNIE: What is this? Smelled light and tasted light. Good for a beginner to ease into whiskey.

JEFF: Didn't care for this and is one that I would avoid for myself.

JOHN: Just smelled it . . . can't put my finger on it . . . tasting . . . nice, clean and sweet whiskey.

BRANDON: Based on the nose, I wasn't thrilled to taste this one but the finish is clean.

KENTUCKY GENTLEMAN KENTUCKY BOURBON WHISKEY

SUMMARY: This whiskey has a bad rap among many bourbon enthusiasts due to its mash content. We do sell a lot of it but only because everyone's 21 once and it's only $4 a shot. It can make a decent well mixer with Coke and ginger beer (Kentucky Kernal), but we strongly discourage it straight or even on the rocks.

FUN FACT: Kentucky Gentleman just makes the cut as bourbon with a mash of 51% straight Kentucky bourbon and 49% natural grain spirits.

VARIETY/STYLE: Straight Bourbon Whiskey

BARREL TYPE: New American Oak

AGE: N/A

ORIGIN: Kentucky

BOTTLE: 750 ml, screw cap

ALCOHOL: 40%

PROOF: 80

PRICE: low-range

RELATED: Wild Turkey, Old Grand-Dad, Jim Beam, Cabin Still, Old Williamsburg

Barton 1792 Distillery, 300 Barton Road, Bardstown, KY 40004, (502) 348-3991, www.1792bourbon.com

PROPELLERS:

COMMENTS FROM THE BARTENDER:

ANNIE: Weak, not one of my favorites at all.

JEFF: Mild sweetness that disappears to a bitter taste. Nothing remarkable.

JOHN: It's got some heat that quits pretty fast, nice aftertaste.

BRANDON: Sweet dark fruit on the nose, hot corn on the palate, with a nice bittersweet finish.

KENTUCKY VINTAGE STRAIGHT KENTUCKY BOURBON WHISKEY

SUMMARY: Probably the hardest to find and least popular among our guests of the four small batch bourbons from Kentucky Bourbon Distillers (others being Pure Kentucky XO, Noah's Mill and Rowen's Creek). It starts with some sweet notes and finishes with wood, spice and even a little mint. This would be good bourbon to muddle up a Mint Julep.

FUN FACT: Kentucky Vintage won Double Gold in 2005 and Silver in 2012 at the San Francisco World Spirits Festival.

VARIETY/STYLE: Kentucky Straight Bourbon

BARREL TYPE: New American Oak

AGE: N/A

ORIGIN: Kentucky

BOTTLE: 750 ml, screw cap

ALCOHOL: 45%

PROOF: 90

PRICE: mid-range

RELATED: Temptation, Rock Hill Farms, Noah's Mill, Knob Creek, Jim Beam 8 Year

Kentucky Bourbon Distillers, 1869 Loretto Road, P.O. Box 785, Bardstown, KY 40004, (502) 348-0899, (502) 348-0899, kentuckybourbon@bardstown.com, www.kentuckybourbon.com

PROPELLERS:

COMMENTS FROM THE BARTENDER:

ANNIE: Yikes, this has got to be high octane, on the cubes for sure!

JEFF: Smells sweeter than it actually tasted, smooth with a mild burn.

JOHN: I do not like this burning feeling going down my throat.

BRANDON: Nice nose of sweet corn, tastes best after sitting in the glass for a minute, long finish with a great burn. I like it.

KNOB CREEK SINGLE BARREL RESERVE KENTUCKY STRAIGHT BOURBON WHISKEY

SUMMARY: In 2010, Knob Creek introduced a single barrel reserve bourbon. It's an even bigger expression of their signature flavor. It is 120 proof, so instead of blending barrels the way most bourbons are made, Beam handpicks and ages its barrels of brown water for nine years. Admittedly this process allows for slight variations in the taste, color and aroma, depending on the rack placement. This bourbon really benefits from adding a little water. It has a wide range of flavors from the heavy charred oak and long aging time. You will get everything from rich chocolate to nutmeg and charred oak. It's a solid selection.

FUN FACT: The Knob Creek bottle was designed after the turn-of-the-century bourbon bottles sold throughout Kentucky. The labels were inspired by the decades-old custom of wrapping finished bottles in newspaper at the distillery.

VARIETY/STYLE: Small Batch Straight Bourbon

BARREL TYPE: New American Oak

AGE: 9 years

ORIGIN: Kentucky

BOTTLE: 750 ml, screw cap

ALCOHOL: 60%

PROOF: 120

PRICE: mid-range

RELATED: Kentucky Vintage, Rowan's Creek, Black Maple Hill, Booker's, Baker's

PROPELLERS:

Beam Suntory Inc., 222 W Merchandise Mart Plaza, Chicago, IL 60654, (312) 964-6999, www.beamglobal.com
Producer: Jim Beam American Stillhouse, 526 Happy Hollow Road, Claremont, KY 40110, (502) 543-9877

COMMENTS FROM THE BARTENDER:

ANNIE: Apricot and vanilla on the nose; lots of chocolate and spicy rye flavors. Needs water.

JEFF: Fruity apricot nose, but no real wow factor. Not going to make my recommendation list.

JOHN: I kind of taste apple pie? Burnt sugars and fruits. Its color is nice and dark too. It's gotta be old I like it.

BRANDON: Ripe fruit nose, but it burns. Just give me some ice for this one, and we can have a good time.

KNOB CREEK SMALL BATCH KENTUCKY STRAIGHT BOURBON WHISKEY

SUMMARY: Knob Creek Small Batch is one of four in the small batch collection from Jim Beam, the others being Booker's, Baker's and Basil Hayden's. It has a very dark brown color that the company says is due to its longer aging process. This 100-proof bourbon was voted Double Gold at the San Francisco World Spirits Competition and rightfully so. It has great flavors of malt, chocolate and big oak. You can really get creative in mixing this bourbon in general cocktails.

FUN FACT: This whiskey was named after the small stream that flows through the childhood home of Abraham Lincoln.

VARIETY/STYLE: Small Batch Straight Bourbon

BARREL TYPE: New American Oak

AGE: 9 years

ORIGIN: Kentucky

BOTTLE: 750 ml, screw cap

ALCOHOL: 50%

PROOF: 100

PRICE: mid-range

RELATED: Booker's, Baker's, Basil Hayden, Four Roses, Pure Kentucky

PROPELLERS:

Beam Suntory Inc., 222 W Merchandise Mart Plaza, Chicago, IL 60654, (312) 964-6999, www.beamglobal.com
Producer: Jim Beam American Stillhouse, 526 Happy Hollow Road, Claremont, KY 40110, (502) 543-9877

COMMENTS FROM THE BARTENDER:

ANNIE: Kind of sweet, kind of malty and corn-cereal flavored. This went down super easy but tastes like alcohol for sure.

JEFF: Strong alcohol burn covered up the sweet malty taste that I was looking forward to off the nose. The flavor returned late and kind of reminds me of Whoppers from the movies, minus the chocolate.

JOHN: I could sip this on the porch with a good pipe full of Black Cavendish. Some burn at first but great malty, oaky flavors.

BRANDON: I love the milk chocolate nose. Can't say I feel the same way about the hot charred-oak taste! Put this bad boy on the rocks?

LEXINGTON FINEST KENTUCKY BOURBON WHISKEY

SUMMARY: Lexington is a new whiskey that hit the market in 2012. This bourbon-rye-barley mix is a product of Western Spirits Company, which is based in Wyoming, with its principal office in Kentucky. The whiskey is sourced from a larger producer, even though the label leads you to believe everything about the bottle and what's inside is pure Kentucky. Even the inspiration for the whiskey is horseracing's most successful thoroughbred series. You would think they have been distilling and bottling this for years. The marketing seems to be working. We've had numerous guests ordering it because of the pretty horsey on the label. When asked if they like it . . . the answer is almost always yes, and that's good enough for us. If oak or vanilla are flavors you love, give this a try.

FUN FACT: Lexington Bourbon received a 95 by *Tasting Panel* magazine.

VARIETY/STYLE: Bourbon

BARREL TYPE: New American Oak

AGE: N/A

ORIGIN: N/A

BOTTLE: 750 ml, cork top

ALCOHOL: 43%

PROOF: 86

PRICE: mid-range

RELATED: Michter's, Jefferson's, Jim Beam, Bulleit, Eagle Rare

PROPELLERS:

Western Spirits, 220 Lapsley Lane, Bowling Green, KY 42103, (270) 796-5851, info@westernspirits.com, www.westernspirits.com

COMMENTS FROM THE BARTENDER:

ANNIE: Burnt wood, vanilla cookies, kind of tastes like those Cow Tail candies cooked over an oak fire.

JEFF: I pick up a sweet nose with some vanilla in it. The taste provides more of oaky vanilla notes. I'll take a few cubes to open it up a bit.

JOHN: This has some funny woody flavor with some vanilla that makes me wonder about what type of barrel was used for aging.

BRANDON: This is a nice, sweet whiskey. Heavy notes of vanilla and butterscotch. In between your first taste and the long finish, it reminds you it is really full-flavored with a little smack in the mouth.

MAKER'S 46 KENTUCKY BOURBON WHISKY

SUMMARY: Maker's Mark is one of the few distilleries to rotate its barrels from the upper to the lower levels of the aging warehouse. This is said to even out the temperatures as upper levels tend to age faster at warmer temperatures. This rotation ensures the barrels have the same quality of taste. Maker's 46 is the same whiskey as the standard Maker's Bourbon, but what makes it unique is the adding of charred French oak staves. The barrels are then aged another six weeks. The result is a slightly woodier flavor. It's also bottled at a slightly higher ABV. So, expect a little more burn, but it's subtle.

FUN FACT: Maker's Mark holds a U.S. Trademark on the wax seal on their bottle. T. William Samuels's wife Marjorie gave the whiskey its name, drew up the label and thought up the idea of the wax dripping that gives the bottle its signature look.

VARIETY/STYLE: Bourbon

BARREL TYPE: New American Oak

AGE: N/A

ORIGIN: Kentucky

BOTTLE: 750 ml, cork top

ALCOHOL: 47%

PROOF: 94

PRICE: mid-range

RELATED: Old Rip Van Winkle, Old Weller Antique, W.L. Weller 12 Year, Old Fitzgerald, Virginia Gentleman

PROPELLERS:

Beam Suntory Inc., 222 W Merchandise Mart Plaza, Chicago, IL 60654, (312) 964-6999, www.beamglobal.com

COMMENTS FROM THE BARTENDER:

ANNIE: Sugar and spice and everything nice . . . that's what this bourbon is made of.

JEFF: This grainy whiskey has a cinnamon nose and a spicy, caramel, wheat flavor. I could drink this every night.

JOHN: It's hot, maybe a little too hot for me. Same old flavors of spice and oak. I like whiskey that's a little more complex.

BRANDON: A wonderful nose of spice. It has a sweet finish, but I wouldn't buy a bottle for home.

MAKER'S MARK KENTUCKY STRAIGHT BOURBON WHISKY

SUMMARY: Production for Maker's Mark started in 1954 after its originator T. William "Bill" Samuels Sr. purchased the Burks Distillery. The first bottle hit shelves in 1958. Since then the Maker's Mark label has been sold a few times, to Hiram Walker and Sons in 1981, then to Allied Domecq in 1987 and then to Fortune Brands in 2005. In 2011, Fortune Brands split, its drinks division became Beam Suntory Inc., and for many years production has been overseen by Bill Samuel Jr. In 2011, he announced his retirement. His son Rob Samuels succeeded him in April 2011. The Maker's Mark recipe was developed by baking bread—lots and lots of bread—and using different combinations of wheat, rye, and barley. Along with considerable influence from his friend Julian Van Winkle II, Samuels chose a mash bill consisting of corn, red winter wheat and barley. The result is a delicious rich vanilla bourbon with favors of cream corn and even some hints of mint. Most people find enough oak to keep them happy, and you can't beat the consistency. For all of this we've chosen Maker's as the whiskey we pour when someone orders a house Manhattan.

FUN FACT: Each bottle is stamped with "S IV." The S stands for the Samuels family name, the IV signifies Bill Samuels Sr.'s place in the family line of distillers.

VARIETY/STYLE: Straight Bourbon

BARREL TYPE: New American Oak

AGE: N/A

ORIGIN: Kentucky

BOTTLE: 750 ml, screw cap

ALCOHOL: 45%

PROOF: 90

PRICE: mid-range

RELATED: Old Weller Antique, Larceny, Old Rip Van Winkle, W.L. Weller Reserve, Rebel Yell

PROPELLERS:

Beam Suntory Inc., 222 W Merchandise Mart Plaza, Chicago, IL 60654, (312) 964-6999, www.beamglobal.com

COMMENTS FROM THE BARTENDER:

ANNIE: Smells sweeter than it tastes. Syrupy rich with a big burn.

JEFF: Came on with a prominent burn that slightly overpowered a mild vanilla flavor. Has a rich, thick texture.

JOHN: Very good—soft flavors of creamy vanilla wafers with a little peppermint. Would make a great Mint Julep.

BRANDON: The nose has some vanilla, oaky sweet palate I wouldn't mind mixing it in a cocktail.

MCAFEE'S BENCHMARK OLD NO. 8 BRAND KENTUCKY STRAIGHT BOURBON WHISKEY

SUMMARY: Benchmark isn't a bad bourbon, but it rarely finds it's way off our wall of whiskey. Most of our guests are reluctant to try something they've never heard of at such a low price. I even had someone comment that it tastes like a burnt Cheez Its. We're not too sure about that, but what we do know is that the bartenders seem to like it. If you're a fan of vanilla and spice, this whiskey is for you.

FUN FACT: Named after the McAfee brothers who surveyed a site just north of Frankfort in the late 1700s, this rye recipe bourbon is yet another label that honors the storied history of the distillery and the land it sits on.

VARIETY/STYLE: Straight Bourbon

BARREL TYPE: New Oak

AGE: 8 years

ORIGIN: Kentucky

BOTTLE: 1.75 liter, screw cap

ALCOHOL: 40%

PROOF: 80

PRICE: low-range

RELATED: Jim Beam Black, Old Grand-Dad, Wild Turkey, Fighting Cock, Old Ezra

PROPELLERS:

Buffalo Trace Distillery, 113 Great Buffalo Trace, Franklin County, Frankfort, KY 40601, (800) 654-8471, info@buffalotrace.com, www.buffalotracedistillery.com

COMMENTS FROM THE BARTENDER:

ANNIE: It smells like birthday cake! Super clean, no burn. It's tasty.

JEFF: It had a lasting vanilla flavor. I'd add maybe one cube. A great first whiskey to try.

JOHN: This tastes so good. No finish, no burn. I could drink this every day.

BRANDON: It has a nose of vanilla and caramel. Finished long and spicy. Good if you like malty bourbon.

MICHTER'S SMALL BATCH BOURBON

SUMMARY: The history of the Michter name goes back to the Michter's Distillery in Pennsylvania. In 1951 Louis Forman, along with his master distiller Everett Beam, distilled the first batch of Michter's using an old-fashioned pot still. The Michter's name came from combining Louis's two sons' names, Michael and Peter. Struggling over the years to keep control of and run a successful business, the distillery finally closed in 1989 after declaring bankruptcy. Today the distillery is recognized as a national historic landmark and the Michter's name, now owned by Chatham Imports, sources their whiskey from premium stock. We love their whole lineup of whiskey, and they never disappoint the guest. For this they sit in the first row, eye level, on our back bar.

FUN FACT: Master Distiller Everett Beam hails from the famous "Jim Beam" family.

VARIETY/STYLE: Bourbon

BARREL TYPE: New White Oak

AGE: N/A

ORIGIN: Kentucky

BOTTLE: 750 ml, cork top

ALCOHOL: 45.7%

PROOF: 91.4

PRICE: mid-range

RELATED: Knob Creek, Bulleit 10 Year, Four Roses Small Batch, Eagle Rare 10 Year

PROPELLERS: ⚜⚜⚜⚜⚜

Chatham Imports, 245 Fifth Avenue, New York, NY 10016, (212) 473-1100, info@michters.com, www.michters.com
Producer: Kentucky Burnon Distillers, 1869 Loretto Rd., Bardstown, KY 40004, (502) 561-1001, kentuckyburbon@bardstown.com, www.kentuckyburbonwhiskey.com

COMMENTS FROM THE BARTENDER:

ANNIE: Dry oat with warm fruit and spice, some cherry cola and raisin—very good

JEFF: The nose lets you know that you can expect some fruit out of this one, mainly apricot. The honey note in the taste was a nice addition. Will warm your body on those cold nights.

JOHN: I like the zestfulness and aftertaste I can taste dark fruits and vanilla I want some more, please

BRANDON: It's like taking a big whiff of a bouquet, but grainy and peppery. It's not a very complex palate, but its notes of dry fruit and oak stand out. It's warm and leaves my mouth dry.

NOAH'S MILL GENUINE BOURBON WHISKEY

SUMMARY: One of four in the small batch line from Kentucky Bourbon Distillers. This bourbon has a higher proof than its brothers (Rowan's Creek, Pure Kentucky XO and Kentucky Vintage), coming in at 114.3. It's a blend of whiskeys aging from four to 20 years from no more than 20 barrels. It needs some ice or water to really open it up. There are some nutty and fruity flavors but overall just an average whiskey.

FUN FACT: San Francisco World Spirits Competition Double Gold Winner 2011.

VARIETY/STYLE: Straight Bourbon

BARREL TYPE: New American Oak

AGE: N/A

ORIGIN: Kentucky

BOTTLE: 750 ml, cork top

ALCOHOL: 57.15%

PROOF: 114.3

PRICE: high-range

RELATED: Rowan's Creek, Knob Creek, Kentucky Vintage, Willett 6 Year, James E. Pepper 1776

Kentucky Bourbon Distillers, 1869 Loretto Road, P.O. Box 785, Bardstown, KY 40004, (502) 348-0899, (502) 348-5539, kentuckyburbon@bardstown.com, www.kentuckyburbon.com

PROPELLERS: ⚜⚜⚜⚜

COMMENTS FROM THE BARTENDER:

ANNIE: Smells nice, was surprised with a sudden burn. Finished nice, not bad!

JEFF: Filled my nose with a sweet smell while having notes of dried berries.

JOHN: I want to climb right in this bottle. Not too sweet and just the kind of burn I like.

BRANDON: Really sweet nose, complex, warm palate, short tasty finish.

OLD BARDSTOWN ESTATE BOTTLED KENTUCKY STRAIGHT WHISKEY

SUMMARY: This Kentucky Straight Bourbon is well known to the Willet family. Old Bardstown Estate Bottle is 100% old fine sour mash Kentucky bourbon. This award-winning whiskey was recognized as "Outstanding," the highest award category rated by North American whiskeys in the International Competition held in London in 1996. This high-quality rated bourbon is known as a "sour mash," which means the yeast they use in fermentation is the same from batch to batch. The Estate Bottle has an auburn color with a strong sense of intensity to the nose, with a robust note of sweet corn. This bourbon delivers some earthy and leathery tones with a hint of nutmeg. This whiskey has a unique taste that's not for everyone.

FUN FACT: The horse on the label was a world-class racing horse known as Bardstown. He was bred and raced by Calumet Farm of Lexington, Kentucky, who named him for the city of Bardstown in Nelson County, Kentucky. Due to ankle and hip joint problems, Bardstown did not race until age four but then competed for four years and became one of the top older horses of his time.

VARIETY/STYLE: Small Batch Straight Bourbon

BARREL TYPE: American White Oak

AGE: 10 years

ORIGIN: Kentucky

BOTTLE: 750 ml, cork top

ALCOHOL: 50.5%

PROOF: 101

PRICE: low-range

RELATED: Old Williamburg, Jim Beam, Old Grand-Dad, Kentucky Gentleman

PROPELLERS:

Kentucky Bourbon Distilleries, 1869 Loretto Road, Bardstown, KY 40004, (502) 348-0899, kentuckybourbon@bardstown.com, www.kentuckybourbonwhiskey.com

---

COMMENTS FROM THE BARTENDER:

ANNIE: Smells like straight up vanilla. Hot burn up front that goes away as quickly as it comes.

JEFF: The sweet vanilla nose covers up the bitter taste of oak and pepper. I'm kind of glad the taste didn't linger.

JOHN: Great nose, not a fan of the taste. Very grain forward. I really didn't like the aftertaste.

BRANDON: The soft nose opened up a little with a drop of water. Became a bit grainy and tasted quite bitter. I'm not selling this as a recommendation.

OLD BARDSTOWN KENTUCKY STRAIGHT BOURBON WHISKEY

SUMMARY: Named after the famous town in Nelson County, Kentucky, Old Bardstown has a smell of pralines, oak and vanilla. Its rough but peppery components finish dry with a touch of sweet caramel. Made by Kentucky Bourbon Distilleries, the label offers 90- and 101-proof varieties. Old Bardstown is known in the whiskey world as relatively cheap bourbon that is suitable for dirty mixing, and would not be considered a sipping whiskey.

FUN FACT: The well-known label with the horse (Bardstown) has made this a widely recognized brand. Bardstown's exercise and lifetime rider, Tony Beneivenga, together earned a total of $628,752, which is over $19 million in today's dollars, and he was pensioned at Calumet Farm, where he died in 1972. The legend lives on through the brand.

VARIETY/STYLE: Small Batch Straight Bourbon

BARREL TYPE: American White Oak

AGE: 10 years

ORIGIN: Kentucky

BOTTLE: 750 ml, cork top

ALCOHOL: 43%

PROOF: 86

PRICE: low-range

RELATED: Old Crow, Kessler American Blended Whiskey, Kentucky Gentleman, Old Williamsburg

PROPELLERS:

Kentucky Bourbon Distillers, 1869 Loretto Road, Bardstown, KY 40004, (502) 348-0899, kentuckybourbon@bardstown.com, www.kentuckybourbonwhiskey.com

---

COMMENTS FROM THE BARTENDER:

ANNIE: Tons of hay and spice that just can't save this very mild whiskey. This would be a solid go-to as a gift to the in-laws.

JEFF: The caramel and straw nose was very misleading. The taste was definitely more of a wood and corn mix with a lot of peppery spice. This won't be a name I toss out to customers.

JOHN: I don't hate it. It actually has a nice youthful flavor. I bet this is young; I would like to age this in my own barrel.

BRANDON: Someone out there may enjoy this whiskey. Personally, it made me frown.

OLD CROW KENTUCKY STRAIGHT BOURBON

SUMMARY: First produced by Dr. James C. Crow in 1835, inventor of the sour mash process, this historic bourbon has been a favorite of many great American leaders and icons. Known during the Civil War, regiments from both North and South received rations of bourbon to keep morale up and Old Crow was definitely on the menu. General Ulysses S. Grant was a drinker and his drink of choice was Old Crow. Legend has it that after the battle of Shiloh, in which the Union suffered staggering losses, Grant's critics came out in legion and went to President Lincoln and demanded Grant's head, charging that he lacked leadership and drank too much. Lincoln, always a Grant supporter, was reported to have said, "Find out what kind of whiskey he drinks, and send a barrel to my other generals."

Old Crow has not changed its recipe in over 175 years, and once you are over the burn you can taste a sense of sweet candy corn and fruit. It's a well-balanced whiskey ending with a slight caramel flavor that finishes on your palate. As far as price goes, this is a good whiskey that tastes best when you mix with cola or ginger beer.

FUN FACT: Old Crow's logo, a crow perched atop grains of barley, is rumored to stem as a symbol bridging the North and South during the Civil War.

Old Crow is said to be the favorite bourbon of American writers Mark Twain and Hunter S. Thompson. Twain reportedly visited the distillery in the 1880s, and Old Crow advertised this heavily; John C. Gerber sees in this commercial exploitation a sign of Twain's continuing popularity.

VARIETY/STYLE: Small Batch Straight Bourbon

BARREL TYPE: Charred White Oak

AGE: 3 years

ORIGIN: Kentucky

BOTTLE: 750 ml, screw top

ALCOHOL: 40%

PROOF: 80

PRICE: low-range

RELATED: Wild Turkey 81, Evan Williams, Buffalo Trace, Jim Beam

PROPELLERS:

James B. Distilling Company, 526 Happy Hollow Road, Clermont, KY 40110, (502) 215-2295, www.americanstillhouse.com

COMMENTS FROM THE BARTENDER:

ANNIE: This smells outrageous, but tastes slightly more mellow. Good spice, cinnamony. The more I drink, the more I like

JEFF: Smells like rubbing alcohol, but tastes like good bourbon. Would make a good hot toddy.

JOHN: Pretty pleasing. Not too much burn, and it has a nice sweetness—not too sweet, though.

BRANDON: Soft nose, mellow palate. I would pick up a bottle of this to bring to a friend's house party.

OLD CROW RESERVE KENTUCKY STRAIGHT BOURBON WHISKEY

SUMMARY: A standard upgrade from the original Old Crow, with an extra year added. Its aroma is of sweet corn, vanilla and light caramel, like the original, and finishes smooth with a slight grainy taste. Excellent for mixing and is recommended for an Old Fashioned or a Mint Julep because it is made from a 100% sour mash.

FUN FACT: The term "sour mash" is frequently misunderstood. "Sweet" mash whiskey is produced by using fresh water to begin the fermentation, while "sour" mash includes the addition of the mash from a previous distillation. This results in a slightly sweeter and heavier bodied whiskey; it is not at all sour as the term suggests. —Jim Beam website

VARIETY/STYLE: Small Batch Straight Bourbon

BARREL TYPE: Charred White Oak

AGE: 4 years

ORIGIN: Kentucky

BOTTLE: 750 ml, screw cap

ALCOHOL: 43%

PROOF: 86

PRICE: low-range

RELATED: Wild Turkey 81, Evan Williams, Buffalo Trace, Jim Beam, Old Grand-Dad

James B. Distilling Company, 526 Happy Hollow Road, Clermont, KY 40110, (502) 215-2295, www.americanstillhouse.com

PROPELLERS:

COMMENTS FROM THE BARTENDER:

ANNIE: Super smooth, easy drinker. No real power flavors, just a good basic, I'm guessing bourbon.

JEFF: Pretty sweet, hardly any oak or wood flavors. Good, but not very complex at all.

JOHN: Oooh! So good! I love the sweet middle and spicy finish!

BRANDON: I loved the charred-oak and berry notes. It's hot but in a good way! This one could really get me going!

OLD FITZGERALD 1849 KENTUCKY STRAIGHT BOURBON WHISKEY

SUMMARY: Old Fitzgerald 1849 originated in the mid-1800s. It had originally been called Weller 1849, from one of the founding fathers of W.L. Weller and Sons. Old Fitz 1849's bottle and label sure dates itself and just by one look at the bottle, it will assure you of its authenticity. The labeling of this authentic bourbon dates as far back as the whiskey. The black, gold and red color scheme along with its old-style script is different from all other brands. The 1849 numbering has some old floral accents in between each number. As you begin to open this bottle, you will get hit with one of the strongest open bottle smells. This simple but pleasant bourbon has accents of rich caramelized apples with strong tastes of vanilla and oaks. Its medium finish ends with lingering flavors of coffee, tobacco and dried fruit, which seem to fade into dryness at the back of the mouth. This is damn good bourbon for the price, highly recommend as a cost-efficient choice for a Kentucky straight bourbon.

FUN FACT: The block text of this bourbon sits on the front of the label, whereas most bourbon usually displays its description on the back of the bottle. It's also the same bottle as W.L. Weller Antique.

VARIETY/STYLE: Straight Bourbon

BARREL TYPE: Charred White Oak

AGE: 4 years

ORIGIN: Kentucky

BOTTLE: 750 ml, screw cap

ALCOHOL: 45%

PROOF: 90

PRICE: low-range

RELATED: Old Grand-Dad Bonded, Old Crow, Rebel Yell, Old Bardstown, Evan Williams, Eagle Rare

PROPELLERS:

Heaven Hill Distillers, P.O. Box 729, Bardstown, KY 40004, (502) 348-3921, www.heavenhill.com

COMMENTS FROM THE BARTENDER:

ANNIE: Almost no nose, faint burnt sugar taste. A little burn. Sweet on first taste and finishes with a pleasant sweetness and burn.

JEFF: Light nose, you don't really pick up much. Nice flavor of grain and cinnamon apples.

JOHN: Has a nice burn. Has dark, earthy flavor. A nice whiskey neat.

BRANDON: Mild flavors with medium burn. Not my favorite combo.

OLD FITZGERALD ORIGINAL SOUR MASH KENTUCKY BOURBON WHISKEY

SUMMARY: Old Fitzgerald is another iconic American whiskey dating back over 120 years. After changing hands many times, Pappy Van Winkle eventually acquired the brand and introduced the signature wheat-heavy mash bill, and started selling it to the public. Made with a "Whisper of Wheat," instead of the more traditional rye grain. Old Fitzgerald, aka "Old Fitz," offers a smooth taste that has hints of corn and vanilla ending with caramel apples.

FUN FACT: John E. Fitzgerald was among the first to sell his selection of bourbon as "private label," according to the *Book of Bourbon*. Fitzgerald sold exclusively to steamships and railways.

VARIETY/STYLE: Small Batch Bourbon

BARREL TYPE: Charred White Oak

AGE: 4 years

ORIGIN: Kentucky

BOTTLE: 750 ml, screw cap

ALCOHOL: 50%

PROOF: 100

PRICE: low-range

RELATED: Old Forester, Fighting Cock, Blanton's, Michter's, Evan Williams

PROPELLERS:

Heaven Hill Distillers, P.O. Box 729, Bardstown, KY 40004, (502) 348-3921, www.heavenhill.com

COMMENTS FROM THE BARTENDER:

ANNIE: The flavor came and went so fast it's hard to describe. Hope we're not charging too much for this.

JEFF: For sure it has a flavor of vanilla, and you get some hint of the charred oak.

JOHN: Big, Big, BIG front! Settles nicely into a bright vanilla. Then it's just gone; nothing left.

BRANDON: Smells great, sweet and corny. But it malted my mind!

OLD FORESTER KENTUCKY STRAIGHT BOURBON WHISKEY

SUMMARY: Old Forester is known to be one of the greatest brands in bourbon distilling history. This twice-distilled whiskey, introduced in the 1870s by George Galvin Brown, has an interesting past behind its bottling. Known to be popular back in the day with doctors and pharmacists alike, for being the first sealed bottles to protect the authenticity and assurance of quality of the bourbon, its innovative bottles started a trend that was fueled further by emerging advances in mass production. Not only is the bottle notorious, but so is the bourbon. Old Forester delivers spice, cinnamon and caramel aromas that truly provide your palate with some intense taste. This complex and extensive finish offers notes of toffee and a slight hint of apple. It's one of the best-priced bourbons on the market, so if you haven't tried this one you are truly missing out on a legendary Kentucky straight bourbon.

FUN FACT: Old Forester is officially the longest running bourbon on the market to date. This 143-year-old whiskey was the first bourbon sold exclusively in sealed bottles.

VARIETY/STYLE: Straight Bourbon

BARREL TYPE: American White Oak

AGE: N/A

ORIGIN: Kentucky

BOTTLE: 750 ml, cork top

ALCOHOL: 43.5%

PROOF: 86

PRICE: low-range

RELATED: Knob Creek Single Barrel, Basil Hayden's, Early Times 354, Joshua Brook, Rebel Yell

PROPELLERS:

Brown-Forman Distillery, 850 Dixie Hwy, Louisville, KY 40210, (502) 774-2960, Brown-Forman@b-f.com, www.brown-forman.com

COMMENTS FROM THE BARTENDER:

ANNIE: Smells homey and sweet. Alcohol forward but finishes fairly sweet. With its vanilla and corn sweetness, this would make a good Old Fashioned.

JEFF: Almost no burn. Very grassy to drink. Sweet almond and nut flavors.

JOHN: Nice and mild. Kind of too sweet for me, but we are still friends.

BRANDON: This would be a great whiskey to use in bacon fat washing cocktails. Very rich maple and molasses flavors.

OLD GRAND-DAD 114 PROOF BOURBON WHISKEY

SUMMARY: Old Grand-Dad 114 Proof produced by Jim Beam is a high-rye mash bill that contains around 27% rye and has an exceptionally high ABV content. The bottle has a unique look to it other than the portrait of the Grand-Dad on the label. This 114-proof bourbon is packaged in an elegant bottle that illustrates the deep copper tones of this pleasant bourbon. Unlike its predecessors, it has a cork top that makes the presentation much more enjoyable as you get your first aromas. This bourbon contains the same spicy rye and sweet vanilla notes but carries an intense heat. Old Grand-Dad 114 Proof might express a tad bit more oak and leather flavors along with a bold rye that takes over the palate. Finishing long and smooth, this extraordinary bourbon should not be rushed when consumed, as it is recommend for sipping. Big taste, big flavor with a high octane, it's my kind of bourbon!

FUN FACT: Old Grand-Dad 114 Proof and Basil Hayden's share the distinction of being distilled to 127°F (53°C) and watered down to 125°F (52°C) for barreling, which is the barreling proof for all Beam bourbons.

VARIETY/STYLE: Small Batch Bourbon

BARREL TYPE: Charred White Oak

AGE: 7 to 8 years

ORIGIN: Kentucky

BOTTLE: 750 ml, cork top

ALCOHOL: 57%

PROOF: 114

PRICE: mid-range

RELATED: Booker's 7 Year, Baker's 7 Year, Basil Hayden's, Blanton's Single Barrel

PROPELLERS:

James B. Distilling Company, 526 Happy Hollow Road, Clermont, KY 40110, (502) 215-2295, www.mericanstillhouse.com

COMMENTS FROM THE BARTENDER:

ANNIE: Sweet smooth vanilla custard, butterscotch and cream. It's good, but thin for my taste.

JEFF: Reminds me of a vanilla wafer, but bitter instead of sweet. Not a fan.

JOHN: Reminds me of my grandpa's liquor cabinet, and he didn't have the most expensive stuff. This is average whiskey.

BRANDON: Vanilla on my nose, oak on the palate. Hot with a smooth finish. This is a real whiskey!

OLD GRAND-DAD BONDED KENTUCKY STRAIGHT BOURBON WHISKEY

SUMMARY: Raymond B. Hayden created this brand as a tribute to his grandfather, Basil Hayden Sr., who is known for using a higher percentage of rye in the mash bill for his bourbon whiskey. The first impression coming from the nose of Old Grand-Dad is the high-rye smell of corn and hay. Once sipped, its buttery, vanilla and citrus fruit flavors stimulate the palate. Old Grand-Dad finishes soft with a medium baked-pie flavor that ends with a smoky spice. The "Olds" are legendary products coming from a time when America was just being formed and changes were happening. Nothing has changed here; they are still fine bourbons that most just don't consider anymore. I would give Old Grand-Dad another chance.

FUN FACT: When bourbon sales collapsed in the 1970s and '80s, brands whose names start with "Old" took the biggest hit. It remains conventional wisdom among producers that legacy brands, especially the Olds, deserve only minimal support, as they are only bought by longtime fans and aren't capable of attracting significant numbers of new consumers.

VARIETY/STYLE: Small Batch Straight Bourbon

BARREL TYPE: Charred White Oak

AGE: 8 years

ORIGIN: Kentucky

BOTTLE: 750 ml, screw cap

ALCOHOL: 50%

PROOF: 100

PRICE: low-range

RELATED: Wild Turkey 81, Evan Williams, Buffalo Trace, Jim Beam, Old Crow

PROPELLERS:

James B. Distilling Company, 526 Happy Hollow Road, Clermont, KY 40110, (502) 215-2295, www.americanstillhouse.com

COMMENTS FROM THE BARTENDER:

ANNIE: Sweet, light nose. Interesting first taste, tangy with a hint of fruit, maybe some cloves or cinnamon. Some burn. Doesn't linger long; has almost a wine-like tannins feel afterward.

JEFF: Very peppery. So much that it covers up the flavor notes that I was expecting to come across from the sweet corn and honey nose.

JOHN: Really, really, really mild. Love the taste; sweet, no burn.

BRANDON: This smells, tastes and feels like Christmas! I can hear the sleigh bells now!

OLD GRAND-DAD WHISKEY

SUMMARY: This bourbon dates back to 1882. It was created by Raymond B. Hayden, in honor of his grandfather, Basil Hayden Sr. A pioneer bourbon, Old Grand-Dad was distilled with a higher percentage rye mash bill, and his grandson Raymond preserved this preference in this bourbon. Known by many for its realistic picture of his grand-pappy, it has preserved a spot in American bourbon history. It became a Beam brand when the two companies merged in 1987. Of the many bourbons Beam acquired in that transaction, the original recipe was retained for only one: Old Grand-Dad. The rest (Old Crow, Old Taylor, etc.) became Beam juice. The Old Grand-Dad recipe was retained because its mash bill contains about twice as much rye as Jim Beam and other standard bourbons, and a consequently smaller proportion of corn. It was also, at the time, commanding a premium price, so the higher cost of preserving its integrity was deemed acceptable. The Old Grand-Dad recipe is also used for Basil Hayden's bourbon.

FUN FACT: During Prohibition, Old Grand-Dad was produced by a pharmaceutical company, the American Medicinal Spirits Co., and was one of the few distilled spirits permitted to be prescribed as medicine.

VARIETY/STYLE: Straight Bourbon

BARREL TYPE: Charred White Oak

AGE: 8 years

ORIGIN: Kentucky

BOTTLE: 750 ml, screw cap

ALCOHOL: 43%

PROOF: 86

PRICE: low-range

RELATED: Wild Turkey 81, Evan Williams, Buffalo Trace, Jim Beam, Old Crow

PROPELLERS:

James B. Distilling Company, 526 Happy Hollow Road, Clermont, KY 40110, (502) 215-2295, www.mericanstillhouse.com

COMMENTS FROM THE BARTENDER:

ANNIE: Tastes like it's already been sitting in the melting ice, no predominant flavors.

JEFF: This would be like driving a Ford Pinto: probably get you where you wanna go, but not too fun to drive.

JOHN: Very mild. Nice and cool, no heat. It would make a great summer cooler.

BRANDON: I like this mellow whiskey. On the rocks with a little citrus would do a lot for this one.

OLD POGUE MASTER'S SELECT KENTUCKY STRAIGHT BOURBON WHISKEY

SUMMARY: "Pogue: A good old Kentucky name that means good old Kentucky bourbon." Just one of many slogans for many brands over many years in the whiskey business dating back to 1876, when Henry Edgar Pogue purchased the Old Time Distillery. The distillery became the Kentucky Registered Distillery No. 3 in Maysville, Mason County, Kentucky. Prohibition took its toll on the Old Pogue Distillery, and it closed its doors on August 10, 1926. After Prohibition in 1935, the distillery was sold to Rose of Chicago, who renovated it and added three 10,000-barrel warehouses. They then sold it to Shenley in 1942, who operated it through the war for defense purposes; but shortly after, its doors closed once again. Now with a new distillery, fourth and fifth generations of Pogues are making whiskey fashioned from the original recipes. This is good whiskey to try if you want to broaden your horizons from the standard bourbon flavors. Most find dried fruits of raisins, prunes and apricots, and almost always oak, but it's the burn you gotta look out for.

FUN FACT: H. E. Pogue I died in a work-related accident in 1890. He was succeeded by his son, H. E. Pogue II, until 1918 when he, too, passed away in an accident in the granary.

VARIETY/STYLE: Straight Bourbon

BARREL TYPE: New American Oak

AGE: 9 years

ORIGIN: Kentucky

BOTTLE: 750 ml, cork top

ALCOHOL: 45%

PROOF: 90

PRICE: mid-range

RELATED: Blanton's, Basil Hayden's, Bulleit 10 Year, Rock Hill Farms, Rowan's Creek

PROPELLERS:

Old Pogue Distillery, 716 West 2nd Street, Maysville, KY 41056, (317) 697-5039, info@oldpogue.com, www.oldpogue.com

COMMENTS FROM THE BARTENDER:

ANNIE: Super alcohol forward, but easy to drink. Pretty standard, but solid. No single flavor stood out. Average?

JEFF: Warmed my body the whole way down. Has an oaky taste that comes through once you get past the alcohol.

JOHN: Maybe add a little maple sugar and lemon-lime? It will blow your hair back if you drink it straight.

BRANDON: A nose of alcohol. Tastes like alcohol, and I hope no animals were harmed in the charring of the oak. It works much better over ice.

OLD RIP VAN WINKLE HANDMADE BOURBON

SUMMARY: One of the true great pioneers of bourbon, Julian P. "Pappy" Van Winkle Sr. began his career as a traveling salesman for W.L. Weller and Sons wholesale house in Louisville, Kentucky. Pappy and close friend Alex Farnsley purchased the A. PH. Stitzel Distillery, which started producing bourbon for Weller. Eventually, the two companies merged and became the Stitzel-Weller Distillery, where Pappy had heavy influence on the daily operations until his death at the age of 91. Pappy's son, Julian Jr., soon assumed the role of his late father and was forced to sell to stockholders in 1972. After selling the distillery, Julian Jr. resurrected a pre-Prohibition label, the only one to which Van Winkle kept the rights, called Old Rip Van Winkle. The brand continued the Van Winkle tradition, producing the highest quality wheated bourbon. In the 1980s the company was sold to Buffalo Trace Distillery but continues the same strict guidelines the family has followed in order to produce this fine Kentucky bourbon. These bourbons are special for many reasons—all the Van Winkle bourbons are made with corn, wheat and barley instead of corn, rye and barley. This high wheated whiskey produces a much softer, smoother taste and texture that allows the whiskey to age more gracefully.

Old Rip Van Winkle Handmade Bourbon 107 Proof is the only Van Winkle bourbon that we are reviewing simply because it is the only one we can keep on our shelf for more than a couple of days, and frankly because it has such a cult following that if it were to blind taste poorly, we would have a riot on our hands. Don't get us wrong, we love all their products, but this book is about finding whiskeys that you can go out and enjoy, and frankly their stuff is just too darn hard to find. So we chose to review our old friend Rip. This high-proof wheated bourbon is full of intense flavors. Van Winkle's high octane has a ton of alcohol that needs to be aired out. After the burn settles, you can start to pick up a robust sense of sweet vanilla with hints of caramel, pecan and cinnamon. This handmade bourbon has strong notes of toffee and oak wood that tickles your palate. Old Rip Van Winkle finishes with a nice spice that you get from well-aged bourbon; one taste is just not enough.

PROPELLERS:

FUN FACT: Pappy Van Winkle and all of his expressions have become extremely rare these days. With the explosion of bourbon taking place over the last couple of years, it has become so sought after that enthusiasts have created a "Pappy Tracker," which is solely dedicated to finding Pappy Van Winkle products. This has started a frenzy across the nation, which has gained cult status. Find any Van Winkle spirits and you better keep it quiet because this fine bourbon is liquid gold!

"We make fine bourbon. At a profit if we can, at a loss if we must, but always fine bourbon."
—"Pappy" Van Winkle

VARIETY/STYLE: Small Batch Bourbon

BARREL TYPE: White Oak

AGE: 10 years

ORIGIN: Kentucky

BOTTLE: 750 ml, cork top

ALCOHOL: 53.3%

PROOF: 106.6

PRICE: high-range

RELATED: Rebel Yell Reserve, Old Weller Antique, Larceny, Maker's Mark, W.L. Weller 12 Year

Buffalo Trace Distillery, 113 Great Buffalo Trace, Franklin County, Frankfort, KY 40601, (800) 654-8471, www.buffalotrace.com

COMMENTS FROM THE BARTENDER:

ANNIE: I taste burnt orange, vanilla, butter and molasses.

JEFF: Toasty, alcohol forward. Sweet smell and finish.

JOHN: Soft bite with a clean finish. Great for someone new to whiskey or maybe an Irish whiskey drinker.

BRANDON: Nose is sweet, but it has a hot burn I didn't enjoy.

OLD TAYLOR KENTUCKY STRAIGHT BOURBON WHISKEY

SUMMARY: Buffalo Trace acquired the Old Taylor label as well as its barrel inventory in a deal with Beam Global Group (Jim Beam) in 2009. In the exchange Beam acquired the Effen Vodka Brand from Buffalo Trace. This is another whiskey that the general consensus is that it's just okay—smooth and easy to drink but no wow factor. We often hear terms like buttery, corn, soft and sweet. In the world of lower-tier whiskeys it stands out as one we would recommend to a novice, maybe with a splash of ginger ale.

FUN FACT: Colonel E.H. Taylor Jr. established Old Taylor Distillery in 1887. Taylor started and owned seven different distilleries in his career. The price and quality go up if you want to explore their E.H. Taylor Jr. Collection. Look into their small batch, single barrel, straight rye, old-fashioned sour mash.

VARIETY/STYLE: Straight Bourbon Whiskey

BARREL TYPE: New American Oak

AGE: N/A

ORIGIN: Kentucky

BOTTLE: 750 ml, screw cap

ALCOHOL: 40%

PROOF: 80

PRICE: low-range

RELATED: Jim Beam, Henry McKenna, Four Roses, Evan Williams, Ancient Age, Heaven Hill

PROPELLERS:

Buffalo Trace Distillery, 113 Great Buffalo Trace, Franklin County, Frankfort, KY 40601, (800) 654-8471, info@buffalotrace.com, www.buffalotracedistillery.com

COMMENTS FROM THE BARTENDER:

ANNIE: Lots of cereal flavors that mix well with candy corn. Too bad it's so light.

JEFF: I could recommend this with a straight face, but as a lower-end pour. It's a little thin but overall pleasant with nice oak.

JOHN: I'll tip my hat to this pretty lady. Good whiskey. Some leather and tobacco notes that remind me of my old cowboy way back in Boston.

BRANDON: Super smooth, I taste a lot of corn. As it lingers around my mouth, some black cherry flavors show up.

OLD WELLER ANTIQUE ORIGINAL 107 BRAND KENTUCKY STRAIGHT BOURBON

SUMMARY: The Weller lines of bourbons were named after William Larue Weller (1825–1899), who was a bourbon whiskey distiller in the early days of Kentucky. He was supposedly the first to produce straight bourbon using wheat instead rye in the mash bill. His Wheated Bourbon was first produced in 1848. Our favorite of the three Weller brands on the market is the Old Weller Antique 107. Working in a whiskey bar that boasts a selection of over 900 choices, we bartenders pour this one often. It's a warm whiskey that we recommend over ice. A little water opens the door to fantastic flavors of fruit and Tahitian vanilla. Easily one of our favorites!

FUN FACT: We put this in our blind tastings and it often wins!

VARIETY/STYLE: Bourbon/Wheated

BARREL TYPE: American Oak

AGE: 7 years

ORIGIN: Kentucky

BOTTLE: 750 ml, screw cap

ALCOHOL: 53.5%

PROOF: 107

PRICE: mid-range

RELATED: W.L. Weller Special Reserve, W.L. Weller 12 Year, Rebel Reserve, Old Rip Van Winkle, Maker's Mark 46, William Larue Weller 12 Year

PROPELLERS:

Buffalo Trace Distillery, 113 Great Buffalo Trace, Franklin County, Frankfort, KY 40601, (800) 654-8471, info@buffalotrace.com, www.buffalotracedistillery.com

COMMENTS FROM THE BARTENDER:

ANNIE: Sweet fruitiness on the nose. Some good burn up front, spicy and sweet. Definitely a full-bodied bourbon.

JEFF: This should be in everyone's liquor cabinet. Caramel and vanilla up front, with a bit of spice lingering on the back of the tongue.

JOHN: Man, so good! Full-flavor bourbon, this has got to be high-end. Nice and sweet with a slight burn, sugary finish.

BRANDON: What a powerful whiskey! Damn good, I really love it.

OLD WILLIAMSBURG KENTUCKY STRAIGHT

SUMMARY: There's not much to say about this whiskey featuring the Brooklyn Bridge on the label. Old Williamsburg is a bottom-shelf kind of selection that is certified kosher. I guess what that really means is that a rabbi has taken notice of this bourbon and given it his approval. When tasting this thin, amber-colored bourbon it was harsh on my palate. It had some taste of grass and some hints of pepper, but the overall taste really took my mind to another place where all I was thinking of is to add some mix to it. It's much better with ginger ale or cola.

FUN FACT: This bourbon is made in Kentucky but is owned by the Royal Wine Corporation of New Jersey. I guess that's where the Brooklyn Bridge photo comes from.

VARIETY/STYLE: Small Batch Bourbon

BARREL TYPE: White Oak

AGE: N/A

ORIGIN: Kentucky

BOTTLE: 750 ml, screw cap

ALCOHOL: 40%

PROOF: 80

PRICE: low-range

RELATED: Old Crow, Kentucky Gentleman, Old Bardstown Kentucky Straight Bourbon Whiskey, Jim Beam 8 Star

Heaven Hill Distillery, P.O. Box 729, Bardstown. KY 40004, (502) 348-3921, www.heavenhill.com

PROPELLERS: !

COMMENTS FROM THE BARTENDER:

ANNIE: Strong nose of straw. Very light flavors of grain, finishes very quick. I'm guessing it's very young.

JEFF: Smells and tastes like water from the fields.

JOHN: Okay, I kind of have to say this tastes like cow shit on the farm.

BRANDON: After tasting this whiskey, my new cheesy pickup line to use when serving this is, "How 'bout a roll in the hay?"

PRICHARD'S DOUBLE BARREL BOURBON WHISKEY

SUMMARY: Phil Prichard runs his distillery with a very un-corporate feel. The whole family pitches in, operating out of the old school house and community center buildings in Kelso, Tennessee. Their double barrel bourbon sees multiple new oak casks. It sits at full proof for seven years in new charred oak. After that it is brought to 92 proof and stored in different oak casks for another two to four years. The result is a big bourbon with sweet, warm flavors.

FUN FACT: Prichard's Distillery represents the first legal distillery to be built in Tennessee in nearly 50 years.

VARIETY/STYLE: Bourbon

BARREL TYPE: New American Oak

AGE: 9 years

ORIGIN: Tennessee

BOTTLE: 750 ml, cork top

ALCOHOL: 45%

PROOF: 90

PRICE: mid-range

RELATED: Blanton's, Four Roses Small Batch, Noah's Mill, Woodford Reserve Double Oaked, Ridgemont Reserve

Prichard's Distillery, 4125 Whites Creek Pike, Nashville, TN 37189, (615) 724-1600, www.prichardsdistillery.com

PROPELLERS: !!!!!

COMMENTS FROM THE BARTENDER:

ANNIE: Soft oak and spice. Not much burn at all. It's probably low proof. A solid recommendation.

JEFF: The spicy vanilla flavor goes down easy. With its smoothness, it could easily make my recommendation list.

JOHN: Very spicy and what I've come to think of as zest! Nice clean finish.

BRANDON: Perfect Christmas whiskey: cinnamon, apples, spice and fig. I'll leave this for Santa instead of milk.

PURE KENTUCKY XO KENTUCKY STRAIGHT BOURBON WHISKEY

SUMMARY: This is the biggest seller of the four small batch bourbons from Kentucky Bourbon Distillers. (The other three are Kentucky Vintage, Noah's Mill and Rowan's Creek.) It's a blend of whiskey with an average age believed to be around 12 years. It has a cream corn flavor with hints of vanilla that most people seem to enjoy. It sits in the front row of our upper shelves and is poured often. That may be because of its location, because it's not usually ordered a second time.

FUN FACT: Kentucky Bourbon Distillers considers this their Masterpiece Bourbon.

VARIETY/STYLE: Straight Bourbon Whiskey

BARREL TYPE: New American Oak

AGE: N/A

ORIGIN: Kentucky

BOTTLE: 750 ml, screw cap

ALCOHOL: 53.5%

PROOF: 107

PRICE: mid-range

RELATED: Maker's Mark 46, Baker's, Booker's, Willet 6 Year, Rowan's Creek

PROPELLERS:

Kentucky Bourbon Distillers, 1869 Loretto Road, P.O. Box 785, Bardstown, KY 40004, (502) 348-0899, (502) 348-5539, kentuckybourbon@bardstown.com, www.kentuckybourbon.com

COMMENTS FROM THE BARTENDER:

ANNIE: Maple! (nose). Tastes like alcohol but finishes nice and warm, but not on fire.

JEFF: Alcohol forward with subtle tastes. The nose has more scents than tastes.

JOHN: This has got to be cask strength. It is a bit rough but in a good way. Clean finish.

BRANDON: Sweet nose. But it's all alcohol all the way.

REBEL RESERVE KENTUCKY STRAIGHT BOURBON WHISKEY

SUMMARY: This is a true Kentucky straight wheated bourbon. It is steeped in tradition with a recipe that was first bottled in 1849 by the W.L. Weller family, the first distillers to produce straight bourbon whiskey using wheat instead of rye in the mash bill. This whiskey is crafted in select small batches from a Weller family recipe over 150 years old. This whiskey is not overly complex, but the wheat really comes through. If you like a softer bourbon with flavors of sweet corn and vanilla, this may be for you.

FUN FACT: The rebel yell was the war cry used by Confederate soldiers to instill fear while engaging in battle.

VARIETY/STYLE: Straight Wheated Bourbon

BARREL TYPE: New American Oak

AGE: N/A

ORIGIN: Kentucky

BOTTLE: 750 ml, cork top

ALCOHOL: 45.3%

PROOF: 90.6

PRICE: mid-range

RELATED: Larceny, Maker's Mark, Old Weller Antique 107, W.L. Weller, W.L. Weller 12 Year

PROPELLERS:

Luxco, 1000 Clark Avenue, St. Louis, MO 63102, (314) 772-2626, contactus@luxco.com, www.luxco.com
Producer: Heaven Hill Distillers, P.O. Box 729, Bardstown, KY 40004, (502) 348-3921, www.heavenhill.com

COMMENTS FROM THE BARTENDER:

ANNIE: Rich, fruity and sweet nose I thought of a fresh-baked cobbler. Definite burn, very fruity and sweet. It's good!

JEFF: If you want citrus in your whiskey, but don't want to deal with cutting up fresh fruit, this is the answer. The fruit helps tone down what could have been a strong burn to a medium one.

JOHN: Oh! I get orange and fruits. A wine finish. I would say this is very bright. It is the sun! And Juliet is the stars. I like it; very fruit-forward.

BRANDON: Very aromatic and a little sweet. It tastes quite wheat-y and candied. It left my mouth a little dry but I could recommend this one.

REBEL YELL KENTUCKY STRAIGHT BOURBON WHISKEY

SUMMARY: Steeped in history (almost using it as a crutch/wheelchair), this bourbon is your bottom dollar pleaser. It is light on the nose and light on the palate with a warm finish that is sure to please anyone who is just stepping into the whiskey scene. As for a more experienced/demanding connoisseur, this bourbon will only regale you with its historical flamboyances and alliterated references. However, there is something that is somewhat interesting about smooth bourbon that prefers a complement of wheat instead of rye in the mash bill. This obviously young bourbon comes off with soft caramel fumes, a semi-sweet soft body and a finish that is like your tongue is snuggled in a soft fleece blanket. It's soft. If that sounds pleasant or desirable, then you only have to skip lunch one day to afford a bottle.

FUN FACT: Billy Idol's hit song and album "Rebel Yell" was named after a night out with Rolling Stones' members Keith Richards, Mick Jagger, and Ron Wood—all drinking Rebel Yell!

VARIETY/STYLE: Straight Bourbon

BARREL TYPE: White Oak

AGE: N/A

ORIGIN: Kentucky

BOTTLE: 750 ml, screw cap

ALCOHOL: 40%

PROOF: 80

PRICE: low-range

RELATED: Maker's Mark, Maker's Mark 46, Old Weller Antique 107, Larceny, W.L. Weller Reserve

PROPELLERS:

Luxco, 1000 Clark Avenue, St. Louis, MO 63102, (314) 772-2626, contactus@luxco.com, www.luxco.com
Producer: Heaven Hill Distilleries, P.O. Box 729, Bardstown, KY 40004, (502) 348-3921, www.heavenhill.com

COMMENTS FROM THE BARTENDER:

ANNIE: Sweet and oak-y, warming, toasty. A good camping whiskey. I bet this would be good with apple pie. Pie and whiskey; I think I just came up with a new bar concept.

JEFF: This whiskey has a nice light fruit nose. These flavors get mostly covered up by vanilla, but came through a little on the finish. I'm thinking apple and yellow raisin.

JOHN: Super mild, easy to drink but not much to say, honestly. Was this watered down?

BRANDON: It's smooth and tasty, so enjoy it neat.

RED/BLUE STATE STRAIGHT BOURBON WHISKEY

SUMMARY: Politics and booze, I get it. What political gathering couldn't be improved with a few bottles of bourbon? In January 2012, Heaven Hill launched a bourbon that was bottled with red and blue state labels. They wanted to make a fun bourbon that would be the life of both parties. You could show your patriotic spirit and track the bottle sales as an indicator of how the election would go. In 2012, we had a pretty good run with it, but the whiskey just wasn't exciting enough to get people to reorder it. The bottles have become more of a novelty item, maybe because of the strict rule that most bartenders enforce: "No talk of religion or politics at the bar!" There's never a winner in those arguments.

FUN FACT: While the labels are different, the bourbon inside is exactly the same.

VARIETY/STYLE: Bourbon

BARREL TYPE: New American Oak

AGE: N/A

ORIGIN: Kentucky

BOTTLE: 750 ml, screw cap

ALCOHOL: 40%

PROOF: 80

PRICE: low-range

RELATED: Old Crow, Jim Beam, Old Grand-Dad, Fighting Cock, Wild Turkey

PROPELLERS:

Heaven Hill Distillery, P.O. Box 729, Bardstown, KY 40004, (502) 348-3921, www.heavenhill.com

COMMENTS FROM THE BARTENDER:

ANNIE: Toffee, spice and strong oak—good earthy flavors.

JEFF: I was fooled by the nose. Expected some sweetness and ended up with a slightly bitter wood taste.

JOHN: I like flavors that are bitter and dry. This has some good leathery, sawdust flavors. Nice to have something a little different.

BRANDON: This whiskey is a little strange by the way the palate differs so much from the nose. It smells sweet and fruity but finishes really bitter. I'm gonna need a full glass and some ice.

REDEMPTION HIGH-RYE STRAIGHT BOURBON WHISKEY

SUMMARY: With a mash bill approaching the upper limit of allowable rye grain in a bourbon mash, redemption rye mixes it up with 38.2% rye, 1.8% barley and 60% corn. The goal is to balance the sweetness of the corn with the dry spiciness of the rye. This is a young, vibrant whiskey that should be enjoyed earlier in the night, maybe before dinner, and it's affordable enough not to feel guilty if used as a mixer.

FUN FACT: This whiskey is distilled in Indiana and bottled in Kentucky.

VARIETY/STYLE: Straight Bourbon

BARREL TYPE: New American Oak

AGE: 2 years plus

ORIGIN: Indiana

BOTTLE: 750 ml, screw cap

ALCOHOL: 46%

PROOF: 92

PRICE: mid-range

RELATED: Basil Hayden's, Bulleit, Booker's, Willett, Baker's

Bardstown Barrel Selection, 1050 Withrow Court, Bardstown, KY 40004, (502) 348-4448, ds@redemptionrye.com,. www.redemptionrye.com **Producer:** MGP Ingredients, Inc., Cray Business Plaza, 100 Commercial Street, P.O. Box 130, Atchison, KS 66002, (800) 255-0302, www.mgpingredients.com

PROPELLERS: ! ! ! !

COMMENTS FROM THE BARTENDER:

ANNIE: Standard whiskey. Super easy and drinkable.

JEFF: I want to turn this into a Manhattan. Sweet caramel, like a bourbon but infused with the spice of a rye.

JOHN: Nice spice up front! Mild burn. I like it.

BRANDON: This is nice—spicy fig pie, yep, spicy fig pie

RIDGEMONT RESERVE 1792 KENTUCKY STRAIGHT BOURBON WHISKEY

SUMMARY: Named after the year Kentucky came to statehood, this rye recipe bourbon is handcrafted in small batches, aged for eight years and bottled at 93.7 proof. The Barton Distillery operates on the site of the historic Tom Moore Distillery, established in 1879. Today, the distillery operates on 192 acres and is home to many historic buildings, including their well-known warehouse Z. In 2010, Jim Murray's *Whiskey Bible* gave 1792 a 92.5 rating and described it as spicy up front with delicate flavors of custard, cream and apple finishing with oak, licorice and coffee. It's a big bourbon that we recommend trying if your palate is looking to kick it up a notch.

FUN FACT: Ridgemont Reserve Barrel Select is the official toasting bourbon of the Kentucky Bourbon Festival.

VARIETY/STYLE: Straight Bourbon

BARREL TYPE: New American Oak

AGE: 8 years

ORIGIN: Kentucky

BOTTLE: 750 ml, cork top

ALCOHOL: 46.85%

PROOF: 93.7

PRICE: mid-range

RELATED: Hirsch, Jefferson's, Knob Creek, Russell's Reserve, Woodford Reserve

Barton 1792 Distillery, 300 Barton Road, Bardstown, KY 40004, (502) 348-3991, info@bartonbrands.com, www.1792bourbon.com

PROPELLERS: ! ! ! !

COMMENTS FROM THE BARTENDER:

ANNIE: Smells like maple. Sweet at first with a solid burn in the back of the throat.

JEFF: A great burn the whole way down. Lots of good flavors that show up. I give it a B+.

JOHN: Pretty sweet, very mild burn. Nice and sugary.

BRANDON: It smells like brown sugar. Rich juice that covers the palate. Toasted honey, yum!

ROCK HILL FARMS SINGLE BARREL BOURBON WHISKEY

SUMMARY: Rock Hill Farms is a single barrel bourbon distilled at Buffalo Trace using their high rye mash bill and is named after an area not far from the distillery. The label is now owned by a Japanese company named Age International and is produced under contract by Buffalo Trace. This is a big, well-balanced bourbon that's hard to find. We usually sell out pretty quickly, and the supply and demand have caused the price to rise. The Rock Hill loyals don't seem to mind, but most will choose from the many other wonderful whiskeys in this family for a lot less dough (see related whiskeys below).

FUN FACT: Within the past decade, Buffalo Trace has won more awards than any other distillery in the world.

VARIETY/STYLE: Single Barrel Straight Bourbon

BARREL TYPE: New American Oak

AGE: 4 years

ORIGIN: Kentucky

BOTTLE: 750 ml, cork top

ALCOHOL: 50%

PROOF: 100

PRICE: high-range

RELATED: Buffalo Trace, Blanton's, Elmer T. Lee, Wild Turkey Rare Breed, Basil Hayden's

PROPELLERS: 🎖🎖🎖🎖🎖

Age International, Inc., 229 West Main Street, Suite 202, Frankfort, KY 40601, (502) 223-9874, **Producer:** Buffalo Trace Distillery, 113 Great Buffalo Trace, Frankfort, KY 40601, (502) 696-5926, info@buffalotrace.com, www.buffalotrace.com

COMMENTS FROM THE BARTENDER:

ANNIE: Very toasted nuts and spicy flavors at first, followed by sweeter vanilla and honeycomb, with a peppery finish.

JEFF: Wonderful nose, complex flavors of chile pepper, oak and raisins. I love it!

JOHN: This is not your everyday whiskey; this has to be pricey. There's a lotta love in this one.

BRANDON: Very rich, with a wonderful pepper burn that's just right. Lots of dark fruits like raisin and plum.

ROUGHSTOCK STRAIGHT BOURBON

SUMMARY: RoughStock Distillery is the first to legally produce whiskey in Montana in more than 100 years, and the first to ever make straight bourbon in Montana. Their brown water is a vatted mix of four different in-house bourbon recipes with varying corn, wheat, rye and malt content. The whiskey is handcrafted in small batches in Bozeman, Montana. The words "Kentucky" and "bourbon" go together like peas and carrots, but if you go adventuring outside the Bluegrass State, we recommend the mountains of Montana.

FUN FACT: RoughStock double distills their mash on the grains in custom copper pot stills.

VARIETY/STYLE: Straight Bourbon

BARREL TYPE: New Charred Oak

AGE: N/A

ORIGIN: Montana

BOTTLE: 750 ml, cork top

ALCOHOL: 45%

PROOF: 90

PRICE: mid-range

RELATED: Berkshire Mountain, Ballast Point, Journeyman, Temperance Trader, Stein

RoughStock Distillery, this distillery is now permanently closed

PROPELLERS: 🎖🎖🎖

COMMENTS FROM THE BARTENDER:

ANNIE: Alcohol smell. Wood. Smoke. No burn. No finish. Super simple.

JEFF: From the nose to the finish, both smoke and oak are present. A little caramel helps round it out. I would prefer this in a cocktail rather than neat.

JOHN: Nice sweet caramel and rye flavor. No burn at all as well as no finish. Very nice. I would mix this, maybe a Sazerac.

BRANDON: The nose full of malt is pleasant but the bitter taste of dirty wet socks overwhelms my palate.

ROWAN'S CREEK STRAIGHT KENTUCKY BOURBON WHISKEY

SUMMARY: Named after a creek near the distillery that carries limestone-filtered springwater. Rowan's Creek is one of four small batch bourbons at 90-plus proof produced by Kentucky Bourbon Distillers. Others include Noah's Mill, Pure Kentucky XO and Kentucky Vintage. All four of these sell well, especially to advanced whiskey drinkers. About Rowan's Creek, the masses seem to agree on one thing, it's hot and spicy. The kind of whiskey that will warm you right up!

FUN FACT: San Francisco World Spirits Competition Gold Medal Winner 2011.

VARIETY/STYLE: Straight Kentucky Bourbon

BARREL TYPE: New American Oak

AGE: 12 years

ORIGIN: Kentucky

BOTTLE: 750 ml, cork top

ALCOHOL: 50.05%

PROOF: 101.1

PRICE: mid-range

RELATED: Noah's Mill, Pure Kentucky XO, Kentucky Vintage, Four Roses Single Barrel, Kentucky Spirit

PROPELLERS: !!!
!!!

Kentucky Bourbon Distillers, 1869 Loretto Road, P.O. Box 785, Bardstown, KY 40004, (502) 348-0899, (502) 348-5539, kentuckybourbon@bardstown.com, www.kentuckybourbon.com

COMMENTS FROM THE BARTENDER:

ANNIE: Smells like a dog rolled in sugar. Tastes super intensely like alcohol with a sweet finish. Not a big fan.

JEFF: Dried fruit carries through this one with a mild burn.

JOHN: It's making my tongue buzz! I like it, though—just the right amount of sweetness.

BRANDON: For those who like hot, oaky bourbons.

RUSSELL'S RESERVE SMALL BATCH SINGLE BARREL KENTUCKY STRAIGHT BOURBON WHISKEY

SUMMARY: Wild Turkey Master Distiller Jimmy Russell II and his son, Eddie, select "A Groups" of barrels from what they call the center cut. This area in the aging storage somewhere in the middle section is said to have the most consistent flavor profile. Whiskey ages slightly faster in the upper row at the warmer temperatures and slower in the lower cooler, damper rows. The barrels have the deepest #4 char. This heavy charring will cause cracks in the surface of the oak, allowing easier penetration by the spirit and gives this whiskey a wonderful cinnamon butter-toasted flavor. This is one of our favorite whiskeys, especially at the price. Try this ASAP!

FUN FACT: Russell's Reserve Bourbon has had three different labels since its release in the early 2000s.

VARIETY/STYLE: Small Batch Straight Kentucky Bourbon

BARREL TYPE: New American Oak

AGE: 10 years

ORIGIN: Kentucky

BOTTLE: 750 ml, cork top

ALCOHOL: 45%

PROOF: 90

PRICE: mid-range

RELATED: Four Roses Small Batch, Prichard's Double Barrel, Bulleit 10 Year, Willet, Blanton's

PROPELLERS: !!!!!
!!!!!

Beam Suntory Inc., 222 W Merchandise Mart Plaza, Chicago, IL 60654, (312) 964-6999, www.jimbeam.com

COMMENTS FROM THE BARTENDER:

ANNIE: No sweetness in the smell . . . I smell wood and spice. At first taste, I get burn and cinnamon with toasty oak. Yum.

JEFF: Fresh fruits and hard candy with a refreshing cinnamon finish. Very enjoyable.

JOHN: I like it. It has no nose, but I love the burn and sweetness.

BRANDON: The nose is light and floral. This is what bourbon should taste like.

SPRING MILL BOURBON
INDIANA STRAIGHT BOURBON WHISKEY

SUMMARY: Matt Colglazier and Stuart Hobson, the distillers behind Sorgrhum American Spirits, released their bourbon in 2012. It's distilled, aged and bottled in Indiana. They take the original bourbon, which has been aged at least four years, and rebarrel it in a new set of charred, American oak barrels for bit of further maturation. The secondary maturation is meant to mellow and round out the flavor profile. Unlike many large manufacturers, Heartland Distillers uses large copper stills, claiming the copper acts on the mash to create a clean, smooth finish. This Hoosier State whiskey can be called bourbon, as it meets all the legal requirements. It comes off the still at no more than 160 proof and is stored in new charred oak barrels.

FUN FACT: The bourbon is bottled in a vintage ceramic bottle.

VARIETY/STYLE: Straight Bourbon

BARREL TYPE: New American Oak

AGE: 4 plus years

ORIGIN: Indiana

BOTTLE: 750 ml, cork top

ALCOHOL: 45%

PROOF: 90

PRICE: mid-range

RELATED: Temptation, Wathen's, Berkshire, Cyrus Noble, Breaking and Entering

PROPELLERS: !!!!

Colglazier & Hobson Distilling Company, Heartland Distillers, 9402 Uptown Drive, Suite 1000, Indianapolis, IN 46256, (317) 714-4138, stuart@heartlanddistillers.com, matt@heartlanddistillers.com, www.springmillbourbon.com

COMMENTS FROM THE BARTENDER:

ANNIE: Almost no nose. Sweet start and finishes smooth and tasty, just like a good soul singer should be.

JEFF: This seems like it's probably not spent too much time in the barrel. Very light. A good summer whiskey.

JOHN: I would say this whiskey has zest. Clean finish.

BRANDON: Some mild citrus notes: orange and dried fruits. This would be great with a little Saint-Germain on the rocks.

STEIN STRAIGHT BOURBON SMALL BATCH WHISKEY

SUMMARY: In 2009, Austin and Heather Stein constructed their distillery and began production on their 150-acre farm in Oregon. Their straight bourbon has a mash bill of 75% corn and 25% unmalted barley. This is a two-year-old expression that is priced around $40, which makes it a tough sale for most of our guests who are unfamiliar with it. The high barley produces powerful grainy flavors that most people either love or hate. Definitely try this at your favorite whiskey bar before purchasing a bottle.

FUN FACT: In late 2014, they will release a five-year-old expression of their bourbon and rye.

VARIETY/STYLE: Small Batch Straight Bourbon

BARREL TYPE: New American Oak

AGE: 2 years

ORIGIN: Oregon

BOTTLE: 750 ml, cork top

ALCOHOL: 40%

PROOF: 80

PRICE: mid-range

RELATED: Temptation, Belle Meade, Bench Mark 8, Ballast Point, Temperance Trader

PROPELLERS: !!!!

Stein Distillery, P.O. Box 200, Joseph, OR 97846, (541) 432-2009, whiskey@steindistillery.com, www.steindistillery.com

COMMENTS FROM THE BARTENDER:

ANNIE: Maple, vanilla, nutty and toffee. Super smooth with a tiny burn. I like this, plain and simple.

JEFF: The vanilla nose and maple, toffee taste doesn't make this whiskey stand out from the pack. Definitely drinkable, though, as long as you don't want anything complex.

JOHN: I get some heat and spice. I think I would drink this as an Old Fashioned. The finish is great.

BRANDON: Great flavor of graham cracker; thanks for the childhood flashback. Good stuff.

TEMPERANCE TRADER STRAIGHT BOURBON WHISKEY

SUMMARY: In 2010, Bull Run Distillery was founded by Lee Medoff and Patrick Bernards, operating out of a 1950s warehouse in northwest Portland, Oregon. The whiskey in the Temperance Trader bottle is sourced from a nondisclosed source in Kentucky, but don't let that detour you from trying it. Truth is, there are some pretty exceptional barrels out there from very notable producers who can't use all the whiskey they produce. This is a high rye whiskey with a mash bill of 60% corn, 35% rye and 5% barley malt. The guys are very excited about the bourbon they chose for their first release and it sells well. It's often described as toasty warm bourbon.

FUN FACT: In the early days, the area where the distillery is located was called Slab Town, due to the legends that if you dared visit, you were most likely to leave on a slab.

VARIETY/STYLE: Straight Small Batch Bourbon

BARREL TYPE: New Oak

AGE: 4 years

ORIGIN: Kentucky

BOTTLE: 750 ml, cork top

ALCOHOL: 43.11%

PROOF: 86.22

PRICE: mid-range

RELATED: Redemption, High West, Breaking and Entering, Ballast Point

PROPELLERS: !!!

Bull Run Distilling Co., 2259 NW Quimby St., Portland, OR 97210, (503) 224-3483, spirits@bullrundistillery.com, www.bullrundistillery.com/Temperance-Trader.html

COMMENTS FROM THE BARTENDER:

ANNIE: Thin alcohol smell. I wasn't too stoked on trying this, but it tastes much better than it smells: hot and spicy, makes me very nicey!

JEFF: This starts slow, but the flavors come out in the finish: oak and caramel with a dash of spice to kick it up a notch.

JOHN: Very mild in the front, sweet middle, with a hot finish. Kind of spicy. Also, I might be crazy, but I get some smoke.

BRANDON: Damn! This one really burned my tongue! The long finish is worth it, though. Pleasant taste of nutmeg, caramel and oak.

TEMPTATION STRAIGHT BOURBON WHISKEY

SUMMARY: Temptation Bourbon has a mash bill consisting of 75% corn, 20% rye and 5% barley. It is aged for three plus years in new charred American oak barrels. The high corn provides some sweet notes, but like its brothers, Redemption Rye and Redemption High-Rye, they are good but rarely cause that wide eyed, big smile reaction that bartenders love to see.

FUN FACT: Temptation is "straight" bourbon, meaning it has sat in new charred oak barrels for at least two years.

VARIETY/STYLE: Straight Bourbon

BARREL TYPE: New American Oak

AGE: 3 plus years

ORIGIN: Indiana

BOTTLE: 750 ml, screw cap

ALCOHOL: 41%

PROOF: 82

PRICE: mid-range

RELATED: Blanton's, Berkshire, Elmer T. Lee, Basil Hayden's, Wild Turkey Rare Breed

PROPELLERS: !!

Bardstown Barrel Selection, 1050 Withrow Court, Bardstown, KY 40004, (502) 348-4448, ds@redemptionrye.com, www.redemptionrye.com **Producer:** MGP Ingredients, Inc., Cray Business Plaza, 100 Commercial Street, P.O. Box 130, Atchison, KS 66002, (800) 255-0302, www.mgpingredients.com

COMMENTS FROM THE BARTENDER:

ANNIE: Tastes like grains and grass. Initial burn that dissipates quick and spicy.

JEFF: Concentrated corn nose. Soft burn with toasted corn and sugar cubes.

JOHN: I get spicy burn at first, but now it coated my tongue with a thick heaviness.

BRANDON: Not my favorite by far. Flavors are mild and boring; tastes very young. Mix it up!

TEN HIGH STRAIGHT BOURBON WHISKEY

SUMMARY: Ten High began production in the 1930s and was a leading brand until the late 1960s, when the whiskey market went through some tough times. The brand has jumped around to a few different distilleries over the years and is now owned by Sazerac and is produced in Bardstown, Kentucky. The recipe has also changed from straight Kentucky bourbon to blended bourbon with a mash now containing some neutral-grain spirits, at least in some bottlings. The change was made to create an inexpensive, mass-produced whiskey for mixing. Mission accomplished.

FUN FACT: The name Ten High refers to its barrel location in the rick house, an optimal location with warmer temperatures and a faster maturation rate. Whether the barrels all truly come from there is a subject of debate.

VARIETY/STYLE: Straight Bourbon, but some bottles are Blended Straight Bourbon

BARREL TYPE: New American Oak

AGE: N/A

ORIGIN: Kentucky

BOTTLE: 1 liter, screw cap

ALCOHOL: 40%

PROOF: 80

PRICE: low-range

RELATED: Old Crow, Kessler's, Jim Beam 8 Star, Kentucky Gentleman, Early Times

PROPELLERS: ❗

Sazerac Company, 3850 N. Causeway Boulevard, Suite 1695, Metairie, LA 70002, (866) 729-3722, info@sazeraz.com, www.sazerac.com **Producer:** Barton 1792 Distillery, 300 Barton Road, Bardstown, KY 40004, (502) 348-3991, www.1792bourbon.com

COMMENTS FROM THE BARTENDER:

ANNIE: Outdoors-y and earthy—mountain man material.

JEFF: Very woods-y taste, like wet wood or wool. Like sucking the snow off your winter mittens. A little cinnamon at the end to look forward to.

JOHN: Easy on the nose but pretty harsh taste I think this is best for ice fishing. It will warm you up but not very high-quality.

BRANDON: Well, this one doesn't taste as good as it smells. I'm sure it's cheap. Pick it up if you're trying to save money but said you'd bring a bottle to the party.

TRAVERSE CITY STRAIGHT BOURBON WHISKEY

SUMMARY: The story of Traverse City dates back to the beginning of the twentieth century when an accomplished brew master named John Silhavy emigrated from Czechoslovakia and settled in Michigan. The family would develop a passion for distilling spirits and create recipes that would be passed down through generations. The folks at Traverse City will have a brand-new facility opening in the summer of 2014 and have been planting corn, barley and rye to reconstruct their masterpiece. As for what's in the bottle now, they say they had their master distiller match up the bourbon as close as he could. We're excited to see Traverse City grow. And if the next generation stuff is even better than this, they're gonna be very successful.

FUN FACT: It's common for Michiganaders to use their left hand as a map. You can find Traverse City up in the pinky making whiskey.

VARIETY/STYLE: Straight Bourbon

BARREL TYPE: New American Oak

AGE: 4 years

ORIGIN: Michigan

BOTTLE: 750 ml, cork top

ALCOHOL: 43%

PROOF: 86

PRICE: mid-range

RELATED: RoughStock, Ballast Point, Big Bottom, Stein, Cyrus Noble

PROPELLERS: ❗❗❗❗

Traverse City Whiskey Company, 201 E 14th Street, Traverse City, MI 49684, (231) 922-8292, info@tcwhiskey.com, www.tcwhiskey.com

COMMENTS FROM THE BARTENDER:

ANNIE: Super sweet on first taste but it burns on contact too. Nice contrast and throat burn. Good Old-Fashioned or Horse Feather material.

JEFF: Brings a bit of heat once it gets halfway down the throat. More of a grain taste rather than the typical sweet caramel or vanilla. Was a refreshing change of pace.

JOHN: It melts on the tongue like orange chicken. I love the citrus flavor.

BRANDON: This guy really wants to be a big bad bourbon. It has a little pinch of bitterness in the middle but is much softer than most other bourbons—it's not a bad thing.

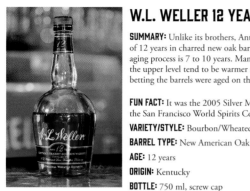

W.L. WELLER 12 YEAR KENTUCKY STRAIGHT BOURBON WHISKEY

SUMMARY: Unlike its brothers, Antique 107 and Special Reserve, this wheated whiskey is aged a minimum of 12 years in charred new oak barrels. Most bourbon drinkers agree the prime age or sweet spot for the aging process is 7 to 10 years. Many elements affect the aging process. In the warehouse, the barrels on the upper level tend to be warmer and therefore age faster. This is a toasty whiskey with a spicy finish. I'm betting the barrels were aged on the bottom shelves.

FUN FACT: It was the 2005 Silver Medal winner at the San Francisco World Spirits Competition.

VARIETY/STYLE: Bourbon/Wheated

BARREL TYPE: New American Oak

AGE: 12 years

ORIGIN: Kentucky

BOTTLE: 750 ml, screw cap

ALCOHOL: 45%

PROOF: 90

PRICE: mid-range

RELATED: Van Winkle Reserve 12 Year, Very Very Old Fitzgerald 12 Year, Maker's Mark, Larceny, Virginia Gentleman, Old Rip Van Winkle Handmade Bourbon

PROPELLERS: !!!!!

Buffalo Trace Distillery, 113 Great Buffalo Trace, Franklin County, Frankfort, KY 40601, (800) 654-8471, info@buffalotrace.com, www.buffalotracedistillery.com

COMMENTS FROM THE BARTENDER:

ANNIE: Crème brulée, anyone? Tasty stuff.

JEFF: This reminds me of vanilla wafers. This is a smooth and tasty bourbon with no bitterness. No need to add anything to this.

JOHN: Delicious! This is right up my alley. Vanilla and graham cracker with a spicy burn finish.

BRANDON: Really rich and toasty body that's absolutely delightful. Give me the bottle!

W.L. WELLER SPECIAL RESERVE KENTUCKY STRAIGHT BOURBON WHISKEY

SUMMARY: Often referred to as a cheaper Van Winkle, it makes sense. Julian "Pappy" Van Winkle bought the Weller brand and offered us up some great wheated bourbon. After his passing, his son, Julian Jr., operated the distillery until 1972, when the company closed its doors. Today, it's owned by the Sazerac Company and distilled at Buffalo Trace. We don't pour the special reserve very often, as we've seen too many novice drinkers squint their nose and roll their eyes. Don't let that discourage you if you like a little flavor of charred oak, grain and a little toffee. This bourbon gets our third place ribbon out of the three Wellers.

FUN FACT: When we put this in our blind tests it never wins.

VARIETY/STYLE: Bourbon/Wheated

BARREL TYPE: New American Oak

AGE: 7 years

ORIGIN: Kentucky Straight Bourbon

BOTTLE: 750 ml, screw cap

ALCOHOL: 45%

PROOF: 90

PRICE: mid-range

RELATED: Rebel Yell, Maker's Mark 46, Larceny, W.L. Weller 12 Year, Old Weller Antique 107, Old Fitzgerald

PROPELLERS: !!!!

Buffalo Trace Distillery, 113 Great Buffalo Trace, Franklin County, Frankfort, KY 40601, (800) 654-8471, info@buffalotrace.com, www.buffalotracedistillery.com

COMMENTS FROM THE BARTENDER:

ANNIE: Almost no smell. Super light and fruity. Think apricots and citrus with a lingering slight burn on the tongue. So delicious, drink this straight.

JEFF: Sweet caramel and a smooth palate. Almost want to say a little burnt orange too. This is great on it's own, but I'm more inclined to make a Manhattan with it.

JOHN: Sweet nose like caramelized sugar. Spicy and sweet with a bit of a burn and a smooth finish.

BRANDON: It might be best if you mixed this one in your favorite whiskey cocktail. It just didn't have the very strong whiskey flavor that I was hoping for.

WATHEN'S SINGLE BARREL KENTUCKY BOURBON

SUMMARY: The Wathens and Medleys are two well-known and respected families in the bourbon world, with eight generations of master distillers operating on the site of the Green River Distillery, established in 1885. In 1937, the Medley family began directing operations and producing Kentucky sour mash. The site ownership changed hands a few times but always maintained its ties to the Medley family, until 2007, when it was sold to Angostura. They never reopened the distillery. Today, the whiskey is sourced from an undisclosed location, though the label on the bottle will lead you to believe otherwise. This whiskey sells okay, but there are definitely some better picks in this price range.

FUN FACT: The Medleys and the Wathens came together by marriage around 1900. Over the last 200 years, the families have owned no less than a half-dozen distilleries.

VARIETY/STYLE: Single Barrel Straight Bourbon

BARREL TYPE: New American Oak

AGE: N/A

ORIGIN: Kentucky

BOTTLE: 750 ml, cork top

ALCOHOL: 47%

PROOF: 94

PRICE: mid-range

RELATED: Old Forester, Old Bardstown, Ridgemont Reserve, Old Crow Reserve, Bulleit

PROPELLERS:

Charles Medley Distillery, 10 Distillery Road, Owensboro, KY 42301, (270) 691-9001, info@wathens.com, www.wathens.com

COMMENTS FROM THE BARTENDER:

ANNIE: Smells grainy and tastes oat-y. Pretty taste and good for sipping.

JEFF: I picked up a nice clean nose full of citrus. It wasn't until the taste did I notice some vanilla and cherries, which then evolved again into a spicy finish. I think each sip might uncover something new.

JOHN: That's creamy! Full mouthfeel—easy to drink. Go for it!

BRANDON: Not too often can you predict what a whiskey will taste like from the nose. From start to finish this is clearly a bourbon done right.

WILD TURKEY 81 KENTUCKY STRAIGHT BOURBON WHISKEY

SUMMARY: Associate Master Distiller Eddie Russell was inducted into the Bourbon Hall of Fame in 2010. The son of Master Distiller Jimmy Russell, Eddie joined the Wild Turkey family in 1981, working as a relief operator. In 2011, he brought us Wild Turkey 81 proof. The classic high-rye mash is used, and it is aged six to eight years. It's a solid product from a great company. It's a little milder than the 101, so you may be let down if that's what you're used to, but it makes a solid mixer in any bar.

FUN FACT: Wild Turkey Bourbon has been featured in many films, including *Rambo*, *Mystic River*, *In the Heat of the Night*, *Silver Bullet*, *The Color of Money* and *Thelma and Louise*, just to name a few.

VARIETY/STYLE: Straight Bourbon

BARREL TYPE: New American Oak

AGE: 6 to 8 years

ORIGIN: Kentucky

BOTTLE: 1 liter, cork top

ALCOHOL: 40.5%

PROOF: 81

PRICE: low-range

RELATED: Russell's Reserve, Ridgemont Reserve, Four Roses Yellow Label, Cabin Still, Ancient Age

PROPELLERS:

Austin, Nichols Distilling Co., 1535 Tyrone Road, Lawrenceburg, KY 40342, (502) 839-4544, wildturkey@qulitycustomercare.com, www.wildturkey.com

COMMENTS FROM THE BARTENDER:

ANNIE: Sweet corn, toffee and a large burn. Super good for a Whiskey Sour. I'm actually digging this afterburn in my throat. Not too complex but definitely good.

JEFF: A floral bouquet and sweet corn make up the nose. Had a pretty high burn. I'd put a couple of cubes in this to tone it down and release a few more notes.

JOHN: I get the sweet candy flavor, but I would say this is mild with some light smoke, almost like sweet pipe tobacco.

BRANDON: This has a real cherry, leathery thing going on. Would make a great whiskey Cherry Coke.

WILD TURKEY 101 KENTUCKY STRAIGHT BOURBON WHISKEY

SUMMARY: In 1855, Austin Nichols started selling spirits as a wholesale grocer; he would eventually source and sell whiskey from the Ripy family, who had built a distillery in Tyrone, Kentucky, near Lawrenceburg in 1869. The Austin Nichols Company would grow and eventually purchase the Ripy Distillery. It would changed hands two more times, purchased by Pernod Ricard in 1980 and is currently owned by the Compare Group. Through all this, tons of good whiskey has been produced, but the best known is probably their Wild Turkey 101 proof. A marriage of primarily six-, seven- and eight-year-old bourbons, this bourbon has a bad rap for being considered a lower-end drink of choice, but let me tell you, the whiskey is good.

FUN FACT: In 1893, the Ripy Brother's Bourbon represented Kentucky at the World Fair.

VARIETY/STYLE: Straight Bourbon

BARREL TYPE: New American Oak

AGE: 8 years

ORIGIN: Kentucky

BOTTLE: 1 liter, cork top

ALCOHOL: 50.5%

PROOF: 101

PRICE: low-range

RELATED: Basil Hayden's, Booker's, Baker's, Pure Kentucky, Kentucky Vintage

PROPELLERS:

Austin, Nichols Distilling Co., 1535 Tyrone Road, Lawrenceburg, KY 40342, (502) 839-4544, wildturkey@ qulitycustomercare.com, www.wildturkey.com

COMMENTS FROM THE BARTENDER:

ANNIE: This smells like cherry-almond hand lotion. It does not taste like lotion. I actually really like it: cherry and nuts.

JEFF: Sweet smell with rich almond and cola flavors. Tasty.

JOHN: Full-bodied whiskey. It's all up front, and the finish is mild. Must be a high proof.

BRANDON: This whiskey tastes very familiar. I'm guessing it's a big producer. Whatever it is, it's good.

WILD TURKEY KENTUCKY SPIRIT SINGLE BARREL STRAIGHT BOURBON WHISKEY

SUMMARY: Master Distiller Jimmy Russell personally selects each barrel for bottling. Single barrel bourbon means that all the whiskey in the bottle came from one barrel, instead of being mixed from different barrels. Serious distillers will put information on the label, such as the date it was bottled, the barrel number and where it was stored in the warehouse. The bottle we reviewed was barrel #35, bottled 9-20-12, warehouse "M" on deck #1. This is a big, dry bourbon that you got to be in the mood for. Too dry for some, and too much bite for others, but if you are looking to enjoy explosive flavors of heavy rye, charred oak and a little peppery hard candy, we say dive in. Try this one with a piece of good chocolate. It's fantastic!

FUN FACT: Bourbon is America's only native spirit and 95% of it comes from Kentucky.

VARIETY/STYLE: Single Barrel Straight Bourbon

BARREL TYPE: New American Oak

AGE: 8½ to 9½ years

ORIGIN: Kentucky

BOTTLE: 750 ml, cork top

ALCOHOL: 50.5%

PROOF: 101

PRICE: high-range

RELATED: Pure Kentucky, Knob Creek Single Barrel, Rowan's Creek, Kentucky Vintage, Woodford Reserve

PROPELLERS:

Austin, Nichols Distilling Co., 1535 Tyrone Road, Lawrenceburg, KY 40342, (502) 839-4544, wildturkey@qualitycustomercare.com, www.wildturkey.com

COMMENTS FROM THE BARTENDER:

ANNIE: SPICE! And also whiskey flavor.

JEFF: This is a spicy little number that's ready for the dance; the burn is not for everyone.

JOHN: Another smooth and sweet whiskey. It is very mild. Reminds me of Irish whiskey.

BRANDON: The sweet caramel-y nose tells me it's obviously bourbon, but the spiciness of some rye comes in hot for a minute. Not my choice.

WILD TURKEY RARE BREED KENTUCKY STRAIGHT BOURBON WHISKEY BARREL PROOF

SUMMARY: It is said that Jimmy Russell keeps his rare breed in the freezer so he doesn't have to add ice, which would dilute the flavor. Not a bad idea if you are looking for a big, robust whiskey to warm up your insides. However, we highly recommend drinking it with some ice or cold water. The whiskey is barrel proofed, meaning no water is added after it's been distilled, so put the kids to bed, sit down, strap in and get ready to enjoy big, Old West-style flavors of leather, tobacco, molasses and brown sugar.

FUN FACT: In May 2009, a seven-story warehouse burned to the ground, spilling thousands of gallons of whiskey into the Kentucky River, killing a lot of fish. The company paid a quarter of a million dollars to help restore the fish population.

VARIETY/STYLE: Barrel Proof Straight Bourbon

BARREL TYPE: New American Oak

AGE: A mixture of 6, 8 and 12 year

ORIGIN: Kentucky

BOTTLE: 750 ml, cork top

ALCOHOL: 54.1%

PROOF: 108.2

PRICE: high-range

RELATED: Pure Kentucky, Kentucky Vintage, Rowan's Creek, Booker's, Baker's

PROPELLERS: !!!!

Austin, Nichols Distilling Co., 1535 Tyrone Road, Lawrenceburg, KY 40342, (502) 839-4544, wildturkey@qualitycustomercare.com, www.wildturkey.com

COMMENTS FROM THE BARTENDER:

ANNIE: This tastes like pepper beef jerky dipped in maple syrup. Too harsh to enjoy straight. I bet this would really shine with some cool water.

JEFF: Has rustic flavors of spice and tobacco. A little sweetness balances out the smoky flavor that would be great while sitting back enjoying a nice cigar.

JOHN: I hear the Rolling Stones' "Brown Sugar." Very sweet sugar with a versatile finish.

BRANDON: Smells sweet and sugary, but it's not as nice when it goes down. Numbed my tongue and burned as it traveled to my gut. But the warmth is nice afterward.

WILLETT FAMILY ESTATE SINGLE BARREL 4 YEAR

SUMMARY: The Willett brand is now owned by Even Kulsveen and his family. Their company is called Kentucky Bourbon Distillers. They offer up some great whiskeys and are currently distilling at the newly renovated Willett Distillery. This is a truly family-run operation. From the gift shop to the assembly line, the folks at Willett are very passionate about their products and at the same time down-to-earth and helpful. They make you want to sell their whiskey. This 4 Year expression definitely has a burn, but it's a controlled burn. We recommend a cube or two when serving.

FUN FACT: Other KBD brands include Rowan's Creek, Noah's Mill and Kentucky Vintage.

VARIETY/STYLE: Single Barrel Straight

BARREL TYPE: New American Oak

AGE: 4 years

ORIGIN: Kentucky

BOTTLE: 750 ml, cork top

ALCOHOL: 56.5%

PROOF: 113

PRICE: mid-range

RELATED: Rowan's Creek, Black Maple Hill, Pure Kentucky, Kentucky Vintage, Noah's Mill

PROPELLERS: !!!

Kentucky Bourbon Distillers, 1869 Loretto Road, Bardstown, KY 40004, (502) 348-0899, kentuckybourbon@bardstown.com, www.kentuckybourbonwhiskey.com

COMMENTS FROM THE BARTENDER:

ANNIE: Burny, but not in a gross way. Mostly just tastes like whiskey, and whiskey is good!

JEFF: This whiskey has a big burn, and not enough flavors get through for me to recommend it. Straight, a little water goes a long way.

JOHN: Another high-alcohol whiskey. These are not for beginners. A seasoned drinker such as myself loves it.

BRANDON: This is another of those high-proof bourbons that is not for the faint of heart. I'm sure it's barrel strength, but it's short-lived.

WILLETT FAMILY ESTATE SINGLE BARREL 6 YEAR

SUMMARY: Kentucky Bourbon Distillers owns and operates Willett Distilling Company. This family operation produces various brands of bourbon and rye, and most of the brands are considered to be in the premium category with a wide range of ages. The five expressions that we currently carry are all well over 100 proof (except the Pot Still), making them not for everyone. We like to talk with our guests a little bit to find out what they're looking for. If it's big, spicy bourbon with excellent wood flavors, the choice is easy: Willett 6 Year it is.

FUN FACT: The company has remained under family ownership and operation in the same area since 1935.

VARIETY/STYLE: Single Barrel Straight Bourbon

BARREL TYPE: New American Oak

AGE: 6 years

ORIGIN: Kentucky

BOTTLE: 750 ml, cork top

ALCOHOL: 58.5%

PROOF: 117

PRICE: mid-range

RELATED: Kentucky Spirit, Booker's, Noah's Mill, Rowan's Creek, Baker's

PROPELLERS: !!!!! !!!!

Kentucky Bourbon Distillers, 1869 Loretto Road, Bardstown, KY 40004, (502) 348-0899, kentuckybourbon@bardstown.com, www.kentuckybourbonwhiskey.com

COMMENTS FROM THE BARTENDER:

ANNIE: Grainy and wood-flavored. No extra sugar but a fair amount of spice. I'm digging the afterburn.

JEFF: This one's nose is filled with notes from the wood barrel. Has a nice, lasting finish, but it kicks in late after a more prominent burn.

JOHN: Turn it up to high! Very spicy with a really nice finish. Is it me or is this delicious?

BRANDON: Tastes very similar to a few we've had. Bet I could guess it. Bites up front and finishes like a champ.

WILLETT FAMILY ESTATE STRAIGHT BOURBON 9 YEAR

SUMMARY: The Willett family has a distinguished history not only as distillers but also as war veterans and farmers who proudly served our country and worked the land to provide for their families. Times were harder back then for sure, and we believe this 9 Year, 125-proof whiskey would have been much appreciated. Today, however, it's a very hard sell due to the burn. Occasionally, you get the guy who just wants to shoot it for the effect, but trust me, you don't need that guy in your bar.

FUN FACT: Willett founder John David Willett served as master distiller for five plants in Kentucky, even though he was handicapped with failing eyesight.

VARIETY/STYLE: Straight Bourbon/Single Barrel

BARREL TYPE: New Oak

AGE: 9 years

ORIGIN: Kentucky

BOTTLE: 750 ml, cork top

ALCOHOL: 62.55%

PROOF: 125.1

PRICE: high-range

RELATED: Kentucky Spirit, Rowan's Creek, Baker's, Noah's Mill, Pure Kentucky

PROPELLERS: !

Kentucky Bourbon Distillers, 1869 Loretto Road, Bardstown, KY 40004, (502) 348-0899, kentuckybourbon@bardstown.com, www.kentuckybourbonwhiskey.com

COMMENTS FROM THE BARTENDER:

ANNIE: Alcohol! Woo! This maybe put hair on my chest. Give this to your nephew on his bar mitzvah.

JEFF: Do not drink this while smoking! Call the Culligan Man. This needs water.

JOHN: I felt like I was using a vaporizer! Way too much alcohol. Pretty damn good, though—once you get past the vapor.

BRANDON: It's funny how much your nose differs from your palate. I expected a sweet candy-corn bourbon but it felt like a lit sparkler in my mouth.

WILLETT POT STILL RESERVE

SUMMARY: Shortly after the Civil War, John David Willett began the Willett distilling tradition in Kentucky. He developed mash bills that would later be used by the Willett Distilling Company. His son, Aloysius Lambert Willett, worked closely with his father, learning the trade and earning the respect of his peers. In 1936, at the age of 27, he and his brother Johnny opened the Willett Distilling Company. On July 1, 1984, Even G. Kulsveen, son-in-law to Thompson Willett, purchased the property and formed Kentucky Bourbon Distillers. Even and family continue to operate the facility today. We currently carry five Willett whiskeys, with more on the way upon release. The biggest seller is the Pot Still Reserve. The bottle is simple and gorgeous, and we proudly display it in the front row. This is a great bourbon that really opens up with a little water.

FUN FACT: During Prohibition, Lambert raised hogs and cattle on his farm in Bardstown, Kentucky.

VARIETY/STYLE: Straight Bourbon/Single Barrel

BARREL TYPE: New American Oak

AGE: N/A

ORIGIN: Kentucky

BOTTLE: 750 ml, cork top

ALCOHOL: 47%

PROOF: 94

PRICE: mid-range

RELATED: Pure Kentucky, Rowan's Creek, Noah's Mill, Kentucky Vintage, Booker's

PROPELLERS:

Kentucky Bourbon Distillers, 1869 Loretto Road, Bardstown, KY 40004, (502) 348-0899, kentuckybourbon@bardstown.com, www.kentuckybourbonwhiskey.com

COMMENTS FROM THE BARTENDER:

ANNIE: Smells like corn; tastes like corn; must be bourbon. Anyway, super smooth and tasty.

JEFF: Once I got past the high burn, I found notes of vanilla, cinnamon and something else—I want to say sawdust.

JOHN: This must be what bourbon was like during the Prohibition era. We've come a long way in creating better flavor profiles. Order this when you're feeling nostalgic. Next!

BRANDON: Lots of burn! Sugary goodness with a great zesty finish. It's got to be a high proof.

WOODFORD RESERVE DISTILLER'S SELECT KENTUCKY STRAIGHT BOURBON WHISKEY

SUMMARY: This is bourbon that has a rich and enduring past as flavorful as the bourbon itself. Produced on a site that has been distilling since 1780, Woodford Reserve is bred for success. A dram that leans heavy on corn (72%) and rye (18%), this bourbon has classic style wrapped up with a win-place-show mentality. Sweet cornbread and toffee nose, gives way to a mouth-sucking spicy finish that leaves you with warm tobacco and clove to enjoy before the next mouthful. With an emphasis on being unique and discriminating through Woodford's five stages of production—from limestone-filtered water to their own cooperage on site—this bourbon is carefully handled and deliciously enjoyable.

FUN FACT: Nicknamed "The Thoroughbred of Bourbons," Woodford Reserve is the official bourbon of The Kentucky Derby and The Breeder's Cup.

VARIETY/STYLE: Straight Bourbon

BARREL TYPE: New White Oak

AGE: N/A

ORIGIN: Kentucky

BOTTLE: 750 ml, cork top

ALCOHOL: 45.2%

PROOF: 90.4

PRICE: mid-range

RELATED: Blanton's, Elmer T. Lee, Eagle Rare 10 Year, Basil Hayden's

PROPELLERS:

Woodford Reserve Distillery, 7855 McCracken Pike, Versailles, KY 40383-9781, (859) 879-1812, info@woodfordreserve.com, www.woodfordreserve.com

COMMENTS FROM THE BARTENDER:

ANNIE: Vanilla and toffee with wood. Good camping whiskey for people who appreciate subtle and smooth drinks.

JEFF: I would recommend all whiskey drinkers give this a try. Caramel and vanilla nose with a nice balance of caramel, toffee and oak. I'll take mine neat, please.

JOHN: God, I know I keep saying this, but damn this one's good, too! Well balanced and just straight good.

BRANDON: This one is a bit dry for my palate. It's pretty boozy with long notes of anise and oak.

WOODFORD RESERVE DOUBLE OAKED KENTUCKY STRAIGHT BOURBON WHISKEY

SUMMARY: The man responsible for creating Woodford Reserve's award-winning taste is Master Distiller Chris Morris. Chris is just the seventh master distiller in Brown-Forman Corporation's 140-year history. Chris and his team grabbed a Louisville slugger and hit one out of the park with this whiskey. Twice matured in separate charred oak barrels, the second deeply toasted before a light charring, this whiskey has a wonderful, sweet, soft oak character. Hundreds of our guests agree: It's very good!

FUN FACT: The Woodford Reserve website has a 10-question quiz to see whether you're a bourbon master. Check it out.

VARIETY/STYLE: Straight Bourbon

BARREL TYPE: New American Oak/Twice Barreled

AGE: N/A

ORIGIN: Kentucky

BOTTLE: 750 ml, cork top

ALCOHOL: 45.2%

PROOF: 90.4

PRICE: high-range

RELATED: Buffalo Trace Single Oak Project, Black Maple Hill, Wild Turkey Rare Breed, Prichard's Double Oaked, Knob Creek Small Batch

PROPELLERS: !!!!!

Woodford Reserve Distillery, 7855 McCracken Pike, Versailles, KY 40380-9781, (859) 879-1812, info@woodfordreserve.com, www.woodfordreserve.com

COMMENTS FROM THE BARTENDER:

ANNIE: Smells of cereal and maple—maple brown sugar oatmeal. But when you drink it, it melts your lips off! How deceiving! Finishes with lots of wood flavor.

JEFF: You can sum this one up with two words: maple and oak. No need to cut this with anything.

JOHN: Although lacking a little citrus and fruit that I like, this is a sure thing for anyone who loves whiskey. Well done.

BRANDON: Oh, baby Jesus, I love this one! I really enjoy the sweet, chocolaty nose. And I love the maple, brown sugar granola bar taste.

TENNESSEE

If the thought of your favorite bourbon being slowly filtered through a thick layer of sugar-maple charcoal before it enters the cask for aging sounds good to you, then it may be time to try Tennessee whiskey.

Tennessee whiskey is basically straight bourbon that's produced in Tennessee. What really separates most of them from other whiskeys is what's called the "Lincoln County Process." In this process, the whiskey slowly passes through the hard maple charcoal shortly after distillation. This extra filtering process is designed to remove impurities and fusel oils that are hanging out in the whiskey, but the main thing that happens is that the whiskey takes on a character and flavor that is unique and delicious. While Tennessee whiskeys meet the other legal requirements of bourbon—at least 51% corn, aged in new charred oak barrels and limits on alcohol by volume concentration for distillation, aging and bottling—the flavor profile is undeniably Tennessee. In the past few years, there have been heated legal debates on laws trying to require all whiskey made in Tennessee to use the Lincoln County Process; as of now, it is not legally required. With laws changing to allow more counties to distill in Tennessee, you're sure to see more new whiskeys hitting the shelves of your favorite whiskey bar.

We review for you the Tennessee whiskeys that we currently carry. Some we're sure you will know by heart (Jack Daniel's), and one of our favorites that doesn't use the Lincoln County Process (Prichard's). Welcome to the wonderful world of Tennessee whiskey.

GENTLEMAN JACK

SUMMARY: Gentleman Jack is the perfect whiskey to try if you want to experience the true benefits of the charcoal filtration process (or the Lincoln County Process). The whiskey is passed through large vats of charcoal that's pressed between large wool blankets to filter out impurities. Gentleman Jack goes through this process twice, with the goal of achieving the smoothest, cleanest whiskey possible. We often recommend guests order a "flight," or four tasters of different whiskeys, when they're having trouble deciding what they want to order. We often slip this one in when they allow us to choose for them, and more often than not, it's picked as their favorite. A blind tasting is a great way to discover flavors you may like without being influenced by the label. Gentleman Jack is a great whiskey to relax and sip on.

FUN FACT: Frustrated that he couldn't open the safe in his office, Mr. Jack kicked it and broke his toe. Infection set in and led to his untimely death in 1911.

VARIETY/STYLE: Tennessee Whiskey

BARREL TYPE: N/A

AGE: N/A

ORIGIN: Tennessee

PROPELLERS: !!!!!

BOTTLE: 1 liter, screw cap

ALCOHOL: 40%

PROOF: 80

PRICE: mid-range

RELATED: Heaven Hill, George Dickel, Prichard's, Jailers

Brown-Forman, 850 Dixie Highway, Louisville, KY 40210, (502) 585-1100, Brown-forman@b-f.com, www.brown-forman.com **Producer:** Jack Daniel's Distillery, 280 Lynchburg Highway, Lynchburg, TN 37352, (931) 759-6357, www.jackdaniels.com

COMMENTS FROM THE BARTENDER:

ANNIE: Fruity. I'm getting stone fruit and wood, mild sweetness and a lot of tasty fun. I could drink more of this.

JEFF: Think Hot Tamales candies paired with some caramel and raisins. Quite tasty, actually.

JOHN: The song "Easy Like a Sunday Morning" comes to mind. Sweet and smooth, but I'd get bored with this quickly.

BRANDON: Well-balanced flavors of fruit and just the right amount of cinnamon. Great for summer day sipping.

GEORGE DICKEL BARREL SELECT

SUMMARY: Today, the George Dickel brand is owned by Diageo, and production is overseen by Master Distiller John R. Lunn. This premium whiskey goes through the same signature sugar maple charcoal filtering process as the other Dickel brands, and each barrel is hand-selected by Lunn, with an average age said to be around 10 to 12 years. This whiskey is often compared to Jack Daniel's Single Barrel or Gentleman Jack, and fans on both sides swear by their brand. We love putting them up against each other in blind taste tests, and the Barrel Select is often picked over the Jack, usually by people who like more fruit and oak. Either way, they're both great Tennessee whiskeys.

FUN FACT: Dickel discovered that whiskey made in the winter was smoother than whiskey made in the summer. That's why they chill it before charcoal mellowing.

VARIETY/STYLE: Tennessee Whiskey

BARREL TYPE: New White Oak

AGE: 10 to 12 years

ORIGIN: Tennessee

PROPELLERS: !!!!

BOTTLE: 750 ml, cork top

ALCOHOL: 43%

PROOF: 86

PRICE: mid-range

RELATED: Jailers, Gentleman Jack, Sam Houston, Prichard's, Jack Daniel's Single Barrel

Diageo North America, 801 Main Avenue, Norwalk, CT 06851, (646) 223-2000, www.diageo.com **Producer:** George Dickel & Company, 1950 Cascade Hollow Road, Tullahoma, TN 37380, (931) 857-4110, www.dickel.com

COMMENTS FROM THE BARTENDER:

ANNIE: Super smooth and goes down easy, but not incredibly interesting or complex.

JEFF: The first thing I think of is a Christmas fruitcake. Fig, plum and apple. There's a low burn that leaves a lingering toasted nut flavor.

JOHN: Nice aroma, very easy to drink. Not very hot, kind of sweet-vanilla tasting. No spice at all.

BRANDON: Very soft, like silk with a grass blade burn on the tongue at the end. Easy to drink but not terribly exciting.

GEORGE DICKEL CASCADE HOLLOW

SUMMARY: George Dickel increased its production in the 1990s, causing supply to exceed demand for the whiskey. To solve this problem, the distillery closed to allow for the whiskey's value to rebound. It reopened in 2003, and not a second too soon, as they were in danger of being out of supply of their No. 8 Whiskey. To fill the void, Diageo introduced Cascade Hollow, a three-year-old version intended to mimic the flavor of the original George Dickel recipe from the 1800s. This whiskey goes through the same process as its brothers and has very similar flavors. Sadly, it's very rarely picked out of the group of Dickel bottles that we have lined up, but that may soon change as production has stopped, at least for now.

FUN FACT: According to the website, Cascade Hollow is no longer being bottled. We highly suggest you try it while you can.

VARIETY/STYLE: Tennessee Whiskey

BARREL TYPE: American Oak

AGE: 3 years

ORIGIN: Tennessee

BOTTLE: 750 ml, cork top

ALCOHOL: 40%

PROOF: 80

PRICE: mid-range

RELATED: Jailers, Jack Daniel's, Jim Beam, Wild Turkey, Prichard's

PROPELLERS:

Diageo North America, 801 Main Avenue, Norwalk, CT 06851, (646) 223-2000, www.diageo.com **Producer:** George Dickel & Company, 1950 Cascade Hollow Road, Tullahoma, TN 37380, (931) 857-4110, www.dickel.com

COMMENTS FROM THE BARTENDER:

ANNIE: Very mild stuff. Too mild for my liking—just not much to write about here.

JEFF: Stiff pepper notes on the nose puts a sour pit in the throat, but not for long.

JOHN: Dang, I wanted it to be bigger. Great whiskey flavors of corn and vanilla and even light fruits that fade fast.

BRANDON: Doesn't burn up front but fades very fast. Good stuff, sweet and pepper.

GEORGE DICKEL CLASSIC NO. 8 WHISKY

SUMMARY: In the 1860s, George Dickel was an established merchant in Nashville, Tennessee. It was after a visit to Tullahoma with his wife Augusta that they decided to move there, and a few years later Cascade Hollow would become the home of the Dickel Distillery. He operated the distillery until he retired in 1888. After his death in 1894, his wife took over the operations of the facility until her death in 1916. The distillery stayed in the family but shut down altogether when Prohibition was in force. The Cascade trademark was sold to Schenley Distilling Company in 1937. Schenley shut down its Tennessee bottling operation in the 1980s, and today the brand is owned by Diageo. The most famous George Dickel whiskey is their No. 8, made from a mash bill of 84% corn, 8% rye and 8% malted barley and aged in oak barrels with a #4 char. If you haven't had a charcoal-mellowed Tennessee whiskey and are looking to try one, this is the one you want. Great Tennessee whiskey flavors and a price you can't beat.

FUN FACT: George Dickel was one of the first distillers to use the "chill filter" process.

VARIETY/STYLE: Tennessee Whiskey

BARREL TYPE: White Oak

AGE: 4 to 6 years

ORIGIN: Tennessee

BOTTLE: 750 ml, cork top

ALCOHOL: 40%

PROOF: 80

PRICE: low-range

RELATED: Jack Daniel's, Jailers, Jim Beam, Wild Turkey, Prichard's

PROPELLERS:

Diageo North America, 801 Main Avenue, Norwalk, CT 06851, (646) 223-2000, www.diageo.com **Producer:** George Dickel & Company, 1950 Cascade Hollow Road, Tullahoma, TN 37380, (931) 857-4110, www.dickel.com

COMMENTS FROM THE BARTENDER:

ANNIE: Smells like whiskey, corny and somewhat nutty with a minimal burn. Very easy going down. Good for a starter or an ender.

JEFF: I'm getting some pretty good barrel flavors, toasted nuts and honey butter—tasty.

JOHN: I taste brown sugar/caramel. Also, it has a smoky taste, like the sugar's been burned I love it.

BRANDON: Subtle notes of salted caramel. Smooth with little to no burn.

GEORGE DICKEL SUPERIOR NO. 12 WHISKY

SUMMARY: George Dickel No. 12 is our most popular of all the Dickel brands. We even use it in one of our signature drinks, the Whiskey Cadillac (see Cocktails). Dickel whiskey is charcoal mellowed, a process in which whiskey is slowly steeped through vats packed with charcoal. They make their charcoal from aged hard sugar maple trees, which are fired the old-fashioned way, in the open air. The whiskey is basically a bourbon, but cannot be called such due to the charcoal mellowing, or "Lincoln County Process." It's often referred to as the "other" Tennessee whiskey because of the dominance that Jack Daniel's has there, and everywhere for that matter. So, call it what you will, this is one of the best whiskeys you will find for the price.

FUN FACT: George Dickel felt his whiskey to be of the same quality as the finest scotches, so he chose to go with the Scottish tradition of spelling whiskey without the "e": whisky.

VARIETY/STYLE: Tennessee Whiskey

BARREL TYPE: American Oak

AGE: 8 to 10 years

ORIGIN: Tennessee

BOTTLE: 750 ml, cork top

ALCOHOL: 45%

PROOF: 90

PRICE: low-range

RELATED: Prichard's, Jack Daniel's, Jailers, Jim Beam, Wild Turkey

PROPELLERS:

Diageo North America, 801 Main Avenue, Norwalk, CT 06851, (646) 223-2000, www.diageo.com **Producer:** George Dickel & Company, 1950 Cascade Hollow Road, Tullahoma, TN 37380, (931) 857-4110, www.dickel.com

COMMENTS FROM THE BARTENDER:

ANNIE: Smells grainy and earthy. It has a good burn that warms my soul. Lemon and black pepper are hidden in there, too. I'm into it.

JEFF: Floral on the nose and palate, this has a decent body with a good amount of fruit and citrus. It's different and refreshing.

JOHN: I get strong wine on the nose. Pretty sweet. It might sound strange, but I would drink this with dinner, breakfast, or even lunch!

BRANDON: Grassy on the nose but big sweet cereal on the tongue. Great for a gray Sunday when your picnic gets rained on.

JACK DANIEL'S

SUMMARY: Jack Daniel's is our #1 selling whiskey, except for our well whiskey, which is automatically poured when someone orders a whiskey and Coke. And that says a lot, with over 900 other choices to pick from. Jasper Newton Daniel, or as most know him, "Jack," established the oldest registered distillery in the United States in 1866. It is still located in Moore County, which is dry, by the way. The whiskey is made mostly with corn, with a little rye and barley, which meets the criteria to classify it as straight bourbon. It differs, however, because they filter the whiskey through 10 feet (3 m) of sugar maple charcoal to remove impurities and mellow the whiskey. The result is a sweet, smooth sipper. Some things just seem to go together: peas and carrots, Romeo and Juliet, Smokey and the Bandit (love that car!) and, of course, Jack and Coke. Eleven million cases of Black Label were sold in 2013, proving the process works. Sip away, my friends.

FUN FACT: Legend has it that Jackie Gleason introduced Jack Daniel's Old No. 7 to Frank Sinatra in the late 1940s. It would become his signature drink.

VARIETY/STYLE: Tennessee Whiskey

BARREL TYPE: N/A

AGE: N/A

ORIGIN: Tennessee

BOTTLE: 1 liter, screw cap

ALCOHOL: 40%

PROOF: 80

PRICE: low-range

RELATED: Heaven Hill, George Dickel, Prichard's, Jailers

PROPELLERS:

Brown-Forman, 850 Dixie Highway, Louisville, KY 40210, (502) 585-1100, brown-forman@b-f.com, www.brown-forman.com **Producer:** Jack Daniel's Distillery, 280 Lynchburg Highway, Lynchburg, TN 37352, (931) 759-6357, www.jackdaniels.com

COMMENTS FROM THE BARTENDER:

ANNIE: Nice plain whiskey smell, almost bitter and botanical. Has a bit of a burn that lingers, but it's nice.

JEFF: Caramel and oak but not that flavorful. Doesn't really stand out from the crowd.

JOHN: Pretty easy-going . . . not too much burn, sweet but really mild. Reminds me of high school.

BRANDON: Smooth sipper, sweet vanilla. Very soft on the palate. Great mixer!

JACK DANIEL'S SINGLE BARREL

SUMMARY: Only one in a hundred barrels are chosen for this single barrel whiskey, and it has one of the most distinctive flavor profiles. Jack Daniel's matures the whiskey in the highest reaches of their barrel house, where they say the dramatic changes in the temperature creates a deeper color and taste. Each barrel is crafted by the Jack Daniel's Distillery, and they claim to be the only whiskey maker to do that. The elegant, short square bottle is very eye-catching, and the brown water in it isn't all that bad either. If you're a fan of the barrel flavors, this may be the pick for you from the Jack Daniel's lineup.

FUN FACT: Jeff Arnett became the master distiller of Jack Daniel's in 2008, making him only the seventh master distiller in their very long whiskey-making history.

VARIETY/STYLE: Tennessee Whiskey

BARREL TYPE: N/A

AGE: N/A

ORIGIN: Tennessee

BOTTLE: 1 liter, screw cap

ALCOHOL: 47%

PROOF: 94

PRICE: mid-range

RELATED: Heaven Hill, George Dickel, Prichard's, Jailers

PROPELLERS: !!!!

Brown-Forman, 850 Dixie Highway, Louisville, KY 40210, (502) 585-1100, Brown-forman@b-f.com, www.brown-forman.com **Producer:** Jack Daniel's Distillery, 280 Lynchburg Highway, Lynchburg, TN 37352, (931) 759-6357, www.jackdaniels.com

COMMENTS FROM THE BARTENDER:

ANNIE: Starts sweet but ends way more sweet and spicy. I taste cereal grains and corn. Maybe some burnt sugar.

JEFF: Smells sweet, but the oak with a little bit of spice helps tone it down. Pepper, caramel and a little vanilla come out halfway through.

JOHN: This whiskey is nothing special to me. Doesn't mean it's bad, just too sweet and smooth for me; I need excitement!

BRANDON: All kinds of sweet, soft flavors. A nice, easy drinker.

JAILERS PREMIUM TENNESSEE WHISKEY

SUMMARY: Jailers Tennessee Whiskey is a product from the power group of industry professionals who formed the Tennessee Spirits Company, a division of Capital Brands LLC. Even though the whiskey is sourced from a "secret stash," they claim that it follows the Lincoln County Process, and all the whiskey is cooked, fermented, distilled, charcoal filtered, barreled and aged in Tennessee. For us, whether it's sourced or not doesn't really matter if the juice is good, and it is. Folks always want to try something new, and there are only so many Tennessee whiskeys to try. This is a solid recommendation for our guests, even if they may have tried something very similar before in a bottle bearing a different label. They've recently stopped production so if you spot a bottle, grab it.

FUN FACT: The man who was in charge of overseeing production of Jailers is veteran founding master distiller for Woodford Reserve, Dave Scheurich, who received the *Whiskey Advocate* Lifetime Achievement Award in 2012.

VARIETY/STYLE: Tennessee Whiskey

BARREL TYPE: New Charred Oak

AGE: N/A

ORIGIN: N/A

BOTTLE: 750 ml, screw cap

ALCOHOL: 43%

PROOF: 86

PRICE: mid-range

RELATED: Jack Daniel's, George Dickel, Prichard's, Michter's, Bell Meade

PROPELLERS: !!!!! (9)

COMMENTS FROM THE BARTENDER:

ANNIE: I'm getting some dried fruit like apricot and peaches. Nice consistency.

JEFF: Tastes like a vanilla caramel hard candy paired with some fruit. I'll take mine neat.

JOHN: Easy drinking whiskey, enjoyable flavors that any whiskey drinker would like.

BRANDON: I could buy a round of shots and know that everybody would enjoy this one. It's a little oaky, not too sweet, with a long finish with some ripe fruit in there.

PRICHARD'S TENNESSEE WHISKEY

SUMMARY: Prichard's was founded in 1997 and has been in operation since 1999. Their Tennessee whiskey is new to the business compared to its neighbors, Jack Daniel's and George Dickel, but it offers something the others don't: a variety of other spirits, best known for their rums. It differs in the fact that it doesn't get mellowed through sugar maple charcoal, also known as the "Lincoln County Process." This whiskey is very smooth and mild with soft flavor that is enjoyed time after time by our guests.

FUN FACT: Prichard's is the only Tennessee whiskey on the market distilled in pot stills.

VARIETY/STYLE: Tennessee Whiskey

BARREL TYPE: New Charred Oak

AGE: N/A

ORIGIN: Tennessee

BOTTLE: 750 ml, cork top

ALCOHOL: 40%

PROOF: 80

PRICE: mid-range

RELATED: George Dickel, Jack Daniel's, Jim Beam, Fighting Cock, Elijah Craig, Eagle Rare

Prichard's Distillery, 11 Kelso-Smithland Rd., Kelso, TN 37348, (931) 443-5454, www.prichardsdistillery.com

PROPELLERS:

COMMENTS FROM THE BARTENDER:

ANNIE: A sweet, charred nose. Quite a bit of burn. Sweet, toasty and spicy. It's got some heat to it.

JEFF: Pretty nutty taste that hides behind a charred nose. This is one to sit back and relax with.

JOHN: Kind of hot. It has a real burn. It's a strange blend of sweet and burn with a lasting finish. All said, I like it.

BRANDON: Okay, not bad. Good, solid sipper I can wet my lips with. Flavors of ginger, spice, cola, black cherry and cinnamon sticks.

RYE

While bourbon and rye whiskeys share almost all the same legal requirements, their history is quite different. Rye whiskey had its own role in the birth of America. After the colonial supply of molasses dried up due to a British blockade, rum's reign as king had ended with the Revolution. Farmers found rye and corn easily dominating their fields, and that distilling these grains increased their value considerably over their raw state. Rye's spicy, robust character and bone-dry palate certainly help take the edge off, but it can also fuel a rebellion.

As Eastern America grew, so did rye whiskey's popularity, which led even President Washington to making whiskey at his Mount Vernon Estate. Rye whiskey has had a huge impact on the growth of America, being a product birthed from a revolution. It was "Americanized" in 1791 when Alexander Hamilton proposed a tax on this spirit. The protests in Pennsylvania soon turned violent, and a group of about 400 whiskey rebels took a stand near Pittsburgh. Washington organized a militia force of over 12,000 and when they reached the epicenter of the Whiskey Rebellion, there were no rebels to be found.

We recommend rye whiskey to anyone who loves whiskey but hasn't yet indulged in a nice rye. We also recommend getting comfortable with your chosen bottle of rye, and don't suggest going and starting America's next Whiskey Rebellion. While sipping on a deep glass of rye it's hard not to get a little nostalgic and think of its history and the huge impact it has had on the growth of this beautiful country.

We hope you enjoy our personal thoughts, because with rye comes revolution, rebellion and happiness!

BREAKOUT PREMIUM RYE WHISKEY

SUMMARY: Capital Brands was formed by a group of beverage industry experts whose goal was to build a new distillery in Pulaski, Indiana, that would beckon travelers and whiskey lovers alike to stop in for a visit. Though the whiskey is sourced from an unknown party, they have hired veteran distiller Dave Scheurich to oversee production. Dave's resume is quite impressive: he was the founding master distiller for Woodford Reserve. Most of our guests don't really care if their whiskey is sourced, and the truth is we really don't either, only that it's good and it sells. That's exactly what we hoped to capture in this guide: to help you find whiskeys you will enjoy, and Breakout Rye is very enjoyable. Even with all the stars aligned, things don't always go as planned. They've recently stopped production so grab a bottle while you can.

FUN FACT: Our bartender John picked Breakout Rye as one of his top five whiskeys for the cigar-whiskey pairing.

VARIETY/STYLE: Rye

BARREL TYPE: New American Oak

AGE: 8 years

ORIGIN: N/A

BOTTLE: 750 ml, screw cap

ALCOHOL: 43%

PROOF: 86

PRICE: mid-range

RELATED: Michter's, Masterson's, rI, Sazerac, Russell's Reserve

PROPELLERS: !!!!! !!!!

COMMENTS FROM THE BARTENDER:

ANNIE: Sweet and fruity smell. Pretty smooth. Subtle tropical sweetness with an oaky finish. Pretty solid.

JEFF: One of the sweetest ryes that I've tasted. Starts out with oak, moves to the rye and finishes with sweet fruit. Smooth and tasty.

JOHN: I love the solid burn with a sweeter fruit note and a touch of citrus. Perfect!

BRANDON: Mmmm . . . Smells like toasty oak and rye with a hint of bananas. Well, it has a big bite that dominates for a moment but leaves you tasting sweet carameled fruit.

BULLEIT RYE FRONTIER WHISKEY

SUMMARY: As rye whiskeys became more and more popular, many major brands have decided to take the plunge, and Tom Bulleit is no exception. The latest addition to the Bulleit Distilling Company lineup is the Bulleit 95 Rye. This award-winning and well-balanced rye is 95% rye and 5% malted barley. Tom is well known for putting a high content of rye in all his brands. Its taste starts off smoky with notes of tobacco and cherry, then smoothes out to finish with hints of buttery sweetness to give off a crisp and clean ending flavor. This rye is a must for the connoisseur of Manhattans and Old Fashioneds.

FUN FACT: Bulleit launched their Rye Whiskey in 2004, and literally doubled their overall sales. Smart one, Tom!

VARIETY/STYLE: Rye

BARREL TYPE: American White Oak

AGE: 4 to 7 years

ORIGIN: Kentucky

BOTTLE: 750 ml, cork top

ALCOHOL: 45%

PROOF: 90

PRICE: low-range

RELATED: Michter's Straight Rye, Knob Creek Rye, Wild Turkey Rye, Rittenhouse Rye 100

Diageo North America, 801 Main Avenue, Norwalk, CT 06851, (646) 223-2000, www.diageo.com **Producer:** MGP Ingredients, Inc., Cray Business Plaza, 100 Commercial Street, P.O. Box 130, Atchison, KS 66002, (800) 255-0302, www.mgpingredients.com

PROPELLERS: !!!! !!!

COMMENTS FROM THE BARTENDER:

ANNIE: Only alcohol, burn, burn, burn. Its only saving grace is a spicy finish that lingers.

JEFF: Has a high burn with a spicy nougat finish. Turn it into a Manhattan to scare a cold out of you.

JOHN: This is a mixing whiskey for sure. The alcohol would scare most from reordering.

BRANDON: Sweet nose but burns like hell and tastes like rye. Possible to be a well whiskey, I'm sure. Mix it up.

CORSAIR RYEMAGEDDON

SUMMARY: In early 2010 Corsair Artisan officially became a licensed brewer and distiller in the state of Tennessee. They also have a location in Nashville to help handle the demand for their varieties of craft whiskey. Their Ryemageddon is the aged version of their white whiskey Rye Moon. It's distilled from malted rye and chocolate rye. This is probably our biggest seller out of the Corsair collection that we carry. It's a great whiskey to sip and enjoy. Some sweet and spicy flavors—perfect for an after-dinner drink. We do, however, recommend it over a little ice as it has a little bite at first but quickly wins you over.

FUN FACT: The Tennessee location of the Corsair Distillery is the former home of the Yazoo Brewery.

VARIETY/STYLE: Rye

BARREL TYPE: N/A

AGE: N/A

ORIGIN: Tennessee/Kentucky

BOTTLE: 750 ml, cork top

ALCOHOL: 46%

PROOF: 92

PRICE: mid-range

RELATED: High West, Stein, Journeyman, Rough-Stock, Ballast Point

PROPELLERS:

Corsair Distillery–Nashville, 1200 Clinton Street #110, Nashville, TN 37203, (615) 200-0320, www.corsairartisan.com
Producer: Corsair Distillery–Bowling Green, 400 Main Street #110, Bowling Green, KY 42101, (270) 904-2021, www.corsairartisan.com

COMMENTS FROM THE BARTENDER:

ANNIE: Smoky and sweet with a bit of a burn. Toffee and light maple notes. Slightly spicy and corny.

JEFF: Once I get past the alcohol burn at the beginning, I found a chocolate maple flavor blended with some pepper.

JOHN: It has a nice maple sweetness combined with a sweet burn. I get sugar aftertaste.

BRANDON: This one has a real surprise ending. Malty nose, and it tastes a bit spicy at first. Then it turns very similar to a coffee stout with some chocolate-covered cordial cherries thrown in. This would be a perfect dessert whiskey.

CORSAIR WRY MOON

SUMMARY: Corsair Artisan has earned homes for their whiskeys in our first two rows of shelves, right at eye level. The reason is that they sell and they're interesting and very tasty. Guests love experimenting with all their flavor profiles. The Wry Moon is made in two copper pot stills in very small batches. The stills are hand-worked, just like in early America. The result is a sweet and spicy raw whiskey.

FUN FACT: Corsair's copper pot still is from 1920 and holds only 240 gallons (910 L).

VARIETY/STYLE: Rye

BARREL TYPE: N/A

AGE: N/A

ORIGIN: Tennessee/Kentucky

BOTTLE: 750 ml, cork top

ALCOHOL: 46%

PROOF: 92

PRICE: mid-range

RELATED: High West, Ballast Point, Stein, RoughStock, Koval

Corsair Distillery–Nashville, 1200 Clinton Street #110, Nashville, TN 37203, (615) 200-0320, www.corsairartisan.com
Producer: Corsair Distillery–Bowling Green, 400 Main Street #110, Bowling Green, KY 42101, (270) 904-2021, www.corsairartisan.com

PROPELLERS:

COMMENTS FROM THE BARTENDER:

ANNIE: Another white . . . joy. Sweet, a little smoky. Candy corn sugar finish.

JEFF: White whiskey just isn't my thing. Toasted sweet corn but a little smokier than I like.

JOHN: Sweet! I'm really getting into white whiskey. Sweet like candy. Almost no burn. Great for your weenie friends.

BRANDON: Ahhh . . . moonshine! The bourbon of America! This one is sweet and spicy. There's a little cinnamon taste and a big rye presence.

DAD'S HAT PENNSYLVANIA RYE WHISKEY

SUMMARY: Pennsylvania ryes are back, thanks to Herman C. Mihalich and John S. Cooper, founders of Dad's Hat Rye. Pennsylvania rye is truly America's regional whiskey. By the end of the 1800s, distillers were producing hundreds of thousands and some over a million gallons of whiskey per year. Business boomed with Prohibition. Bootleggers made illegal versions of rye that was poor in quality and tarnished the reputation of the reputable distillers. Pennsylvania distillers never really recovered from Prohibition, and soon a once-dominant whiskey force was gone. Dad's Hat is the first Pennsylvania-made, aged rye whiskey to be produced in over 20 years. The rye is made in small batches from locally sourced rye, grain and malt. It's aged in charred white oak quarter casks for six to nine months. Don't be discouraged by the age; this whiskey has a ton of flavors and gives your taste buds a true experience of what rye whiskey should be. We often serve flights of rye so people can experience different styles, and Dad's Hat is often picked as a favorite from the lineup.

FUN FACT: In 1791, the U.S. government imposed a whiskey tax on farmers, causing them to threaten to secede from the Union. This incident, known as the Whiskey Rebellion, was not successful.

VARIETY/STYLE: Rye

BARREL TYPE: New White Oak

AGE: 6 to 9 months

ORIGIN: Pennsylvania

BOTTLE: 750 ml, cork top

ALCOHOL: 45%

PROOF: 90

PRICE: mid-range

RELATED: High West, Koval, RoughStock, Stein, Journeyman

PROPELLERS:

Mountain Laurel Spirits, 925 Canal Street, Bristol, PA 19007, (215) 781-8300, hmihalich@dadshatrye.com, www.dadshatrye.com

COMMENTS FROM THE BARTENDER:

ANNIE: A nice warm burn with flavor of peppery cinnamon sticks and mild citrus notes. This is a spicy little number.

JEFF: A pretty tasty rye. Not overly spicy, more balanced between the rye, oak and spice.

JOHN: I like this whiskey. It has a sweet spice and just the right balance of flavors, with a nice wood finish.

BRANDON: There's an interesting maltiness mixed in with the rye. It packs a decent range of flavors that reminds me of a baker's rye. Not bad, but not my personal style.

DAD'S HAT PENNSYLVANIA RYE WHISKEY FINISHED IN VERMOUTH BARRELS

SUMMARY: The Keystone State rye produced by Mountain Laurel Spirits has a lot of tradition and heritage behind it. The distillery was launched by founder and distiller Herman C. Mihalich and cofounder John S. Cooper with the hope of recreating a rye that was once the spirit of America. We've been rooting for these guys since day one. This is their flagship rye that is double-finished in casks that once held Quady Winery's sweet vermouth. This second aging takes three months, and the end result is a spicy rye with warm flavors of sweet vermouth—almost a Manhattan in a bottle with flavors that truly complement each other.

FUN FACT: The name is to honor Herman Mihalick's father, who always wore fedora hats. The hats are a reminder of a time when quality was a tradition, and taking time to do things right was of the utmost importance.

VARIETY/STYLE: Rye/Vermouth Finish

BARREL TYPE: New American Oak/Vermouth Casks

AGE: 6 to 9 months

ORIGIN: Pennsylvania

BOTTLE: 750 ml, cork top

ALCOHOL: 47%

PROOF: 94

PRICE: mid-range

RELATED: High West, RoughStock, Koval, Journeyman, Stein

PROPELLERS:

Mountain Laurel Spirits, 925 Canal Street, Bristol, PA 19007, (215) 781-8300, hmihalich@dadshatrye.com, www.dadshatrye.com

COMMENTS FROM THE BARTENDER:

ANNIE: Dry and spicy with dominant vermouth flavors and subtle vanilla and cinnamon. This tastes like a Manhattan.

JEFF: The vermouth is overpowering. Has a little spice that comes through. Definitely an acquired taste.

JOHN: Obviously vermouth up front. My second sip was better. I think I could like this with some practice.

BRANDON: There is a dominant taste of sweet vermouth combined with a nice rye spice. Two dashes of bitters away from a Manhattan.

FEW SPIRITS RYE WHISKEY

SUMMARY: Master Distiller Paul Hletko is now distilling this whiskey in a town that was dry for a very long time, more than 100 years. It was also home to many influential advocates of Prohibition. Paul has revived rye, and we're happy about that! Distilled from the best grain, bottled in-house and aged in air-dried oak, this is a straightforward rye with a mash of 70% rye, 20% corn and 10% barley that yields some great flavors.

FUN FACT: The name FEW comes from the initials of Frances Elizabeth Willard, an anti-liquor activist.

VARIETY/STYLE: Rye

BARREL TYPE: New Oak

AGE: N/A

ORIGIN: Illinois

BOTTLE: 750 ml, cork top

ALCOHOL: 46.5%

PROOF: 93

PRICE: mid-range

RELATED: Gold Run, Templeton, Koval, Journeyman, Stein

PROPELLERS: !!!!!

FEW Spirits, LLC, 918 Chicago Avenue, Evanston, IL 60202, (847) 920-8628, info@fewspirits.com, www.fewspirits.com

COMMENTS FROM THE BARTENDER:

ANNIE: Starts sweet with a spicy bite. Burns the tongue all over but in a nice way. I taste toasted wood, too. Pretty earthy and spicy like a good rye.

JEFF: I'm getting some earthy notes and a rye grain is very present. Good, smooth burn. I would recommend this.

JOHN: Beautiful rye flavor! Really in your face and up front. Very clean aftertaste. I highly recommend this one. Rye Manhattan—let's go!

BRANDON: This one is far on the malted rye side, that gives a tingle on the tongue. Lots of flavor to enjoy here. Sip it neat!

GEORGE DICKEL RYE WHISKY

SUMMARY: In 2012, George Dickel introduced this new rye. It's made from 95% rye and 5% malted barley. The rye is produced and aged in Indiana at Lawrenceburg Distillers. It's then shipped to Illinois where it's finished the Dickel way—chilled and charcoal mellowed. Do not let the fact that it's sourced scare you away. Many great whiskey brands have been known to use (MPG's) Lawrenceburg Distillery, including Bulleit, High West, Templeton and James E. Pepper. They make great whiskey! This is a well-balanced rye, and the effects of the charcoal mellowing make a big impact. The whiskey is smooth and easy to drink.

FUN FACT: George Dickel Rye is the only product not distilled at the Cascade Hollow Distillery.

VARIETY/STYLE: Rye

BARREL TYPE: Oak

AGE: 5 years

ORIGIN: Tennessee

BOTTLE: 750 ml, cork top

ALCOHOL: 45%

PROOF: 90

PRICE: low-range

RELATED: Prichard's Rye, Wild Turkey Rye, Jim Beam Rye, Breakout Rye, Knob Creek Rye

PROPELLERS: !!!

Diageo North America, 801 Main Avenue, Norwalk, CT 06851, (646) 223-2000, www.diageo.com **Producer:** MGP Ingredients Inc., Cray Business Plaza, 100 Commercial St., P.O. Box 130, Atchison, KS 66002, (800) 225-0302

COMMENTS FROM THE BARTENDER:

ANNIE: Super vanilla extract-y nose. Not too spicy for a rye but definitely sweet. I could drink this while hanging with the family without getting angry.

JEFF: Very dry. I'm getting wood and cherries, which isn't a bad thing. The whiskey just seems a little light on the flavor side for me.

JOHN: Really well balanced. It's sweet with hints of rye. I'd enjoy this in a perfect Manhattan up with a cherry.

BRANDON: Smooth with a subtle rye bite that can easily be mixed up. Get creative with your cocktails or enjoy this straight up.

GOLDRUN RYE CALIFORNIA WHISKEY

SUMMARY: Goldrun Rye is made from 100% organic white North Dakota rye. It is fermented and distilled twice in small batches. It is a very expensive and painstakingly slow process, but the end result is a rye that is very rich with the strong floral aromas of the rye grain. Every release is a single barrel, and we appreciate their efforts. This rye is expensive and comes in 375 ml bottles with a label that complements the gorgeous golden color of the rye inside. This is a great whiskey to sip and analyze as you explore its many flavors.

FUN FACT: Goldrun's motto is "good stuff needs no special effects."

VARIETY/STYLE: Rye

BARREL TYPE: New White Oak

AGE: N/A

ORIGIN: California

BOTTLE: 375 ml, cork top

ALCOHOL: 45%

PROOF: 90

PRICE: high-range

RELATED: Masterson's, Jefferson's, Willett, RoughStock, WhistlePig

Old World Spirits LLC, 121 Industrial Road #3, #4, Belmont, CA 94002, (650) 622-9222, info@oldworldspirits.com, www.oldworldspirits.com

COMMENTS FROM THE BARTENDER:

ANNIE: Sweet and spicy, just like a rye. Delicious. Tastes like those cinnamon disk candies for grown-ups.

JEFF: Dry with earthy, sweet undertones. A well-rounded and unique feel.

JOHN: Definitely a rye! Very spicy and in your face. I love the spice, not too sweet. I will be drinking this later.

BRANDON: What else do you do in the country when you're off work? I would kick back and enjoy this rye! Reminds me of the Midwest.

HIGH WEST 16 YEAR OLD ROCKY MOUNTAIN RYE

SUMMARY: High West is known for their amazing ability to blend whiskey. This is a Kentucky straight rye with a mash bill that gives it big rye spice. It is slightly lighter than High West's Rendezvous Rye but still has plenty of spice kick and some great cherry and vanilla flavors. The price tag is high for most people to spend, especially when sitting right next to it is the Rendezvous for much less.

FUN FACT: High West Distillery and Saloon offers a truly unique experience as the world's only ski-in distillery and gastro-saloon.

VARIETY/STYLE: Rye

BARREL TYPE: New American Oak

AGE: 16 years

ORIGIN: Utah

BOTTLE: 750 ml, cork top

ALCOHOL: 46%

PROOF: 92

PRICE: high-range

RELATED: Jefferson's, WhistlePig, Masterson's, Michter's, Russell's Reserve

High West Distillery and Saloon, 703 Park Avenue, Park City, UT 84060, (435) 649-8300, david@highwest.com, www.highwest.com

COMMENTS FROM THE BARTENDER:

ANNIE: The nose is full of sweet fruit flavor like a jelly jar. After one sip, you know you've been had. Big spice kick!

JEFF: Lots of spice, very rich and full of ginger. It even has a bitterness to it that makes me want to try it again.

JOHN: Now this is whiskey! Lots of cinnamon and cherry infused with vanilla.

BRANDON: The smell is incredible, tons of warm fruit, like banana. I had to squint and shake my head after the first taste. A big spicy punch in the gut. This would be amazing with some cool water.

HIGH WEST DOUBLE RYE

SUMMARY: Although it is spicier, smoother and has a better-balanced taste profile than other ryes, this rye whiskey is a monster—if you like that swift kick, this is the one for you. Another point on this whiskey: Yes, it's a monster but a bold and smooth one at that. It will grab you with its exotic aromas of winter mint, sweet pickle, pistachio, praline, anise and pink peppercorns. But, keep in mind this could be one of the spiciest whiskeys out of America—so have at it with this one!

FUN FACT: This whiskey has a blended mash bill. It features a two-year-old that has a 95% rye, 5% barley malt mash bill and a 16-year-old that has a 53% rye, 37% corn mash bill.

VARIETY/STYLE: Rye

BARREL TYPE: New American Oak

AGE: N/A

ORIGIN: Utah

BOTTLE: 750 ml, cork top

ALCOHOL: 46%

PROOF: 92

PRICE: mid-range

RELATED: Woodford Reserve, WhistlePig, Willet, Michter's

PROPELLERS:

High West Distillery & Saloon, 703 Park Avenue, Park City, UT 84060, (435) 649-8300, david@highwest.com, www.highwest.com

COMMENTS FROM THE BARTENDER:

ANNIE: Super smooth and silky with a hint of smoke and building spicy finish that tastes like baking spices with cracked pepper. I could drink this all night during the winter.

JEFF: If you are not a fan of spice, pass this one over. This has a solid burn like Red Hot candies, but finishes solid. The longer I sit here, the more I like it.

JOHN: Crack, boom, bang! Big rye punch, followed by honey and even mint. This is a whiskey drinker's whiskey. Strap yourself in!

BRANDON: This fills the whole mouth with milk chocolate and a graham cracker crust. This is a great whiskey all on its own.

HIGH WEST RENDEZVOUS RYE

SUMMARY: This rye whiskey is best enjoyed either neat or on the rocks. It's smooth and spicy with hints of cinnamon, crisp mint and fennel. It's very much enjoyed in three of the most classic of classic cocktails: the Manhattan, Old Fashioned and Sazerac. When choosing a rye whiskey to enjoy, this one will hit your palate with a bang of spice, but it evens itself out with the cool crisp tastes of the mint.

FUN FACT: Rendezvous Rye celebrates the first recorded whiskey fest out West in Utah. The "Rendezvous" is an annual summer gathering of mountain men to exchange pelts for supplies. Although alcohol was not one of the supplies at the first Rendezvous, it was introduced with a generous supply of whiskey at the second Rendezvous in Utah's Cache Valley.

VARIETY/STYLE: Rye

BARREL TYPE: New American Oak

AGE: 6 years

ORIGIN: Utah

BOTTLE: 750 ml, cork top

ALCOHOL: 46%

PROOF: 92

PRICE: mid-range

RELATED: WhistlePig, Redemption, Journeyman Ravenswood, Corsair Ryemageddon

PROPELLERS:

High West Distillery & Saloon, 703 Park Avenue, Park City, UT 84060, (435) 649-8300, david@highwest.com, www.highwest.com

COMMENTS FROM THE BARTENDER:

ANNIE: Spicy/bready nose with a honey, vanilla taste. Burns the top of the tongue but doesn't last. Another complex and sippable rye.

JEFF: As soon as it touches the tongue, you get a spicy, peppery taste that lasts through to a sweet combination of vanilla and caramel. If you like your ryes spicy, this one's for you.

JOHN: I'd like to gulp this down on a train ride through the plains!

BRANDON: Sweet and peppery, like good beef jerky! It has a caramel aftertaste that lingers nicely, yum.

HIGH WEST SILVER WHISKEY — OMG PURE RYE

SUMMARY: The OMG Rye is a tribute to "Old Monongahela Rye." The Monongahela River runs through western Pennsylvania, an area where rye whiskey was once a booming industry in the 1800s. Monongahela whiskey was so popular it was considered the spirit of the nation. It is even mentioned in the novel *Moby Dick*, "unspeakable old Monongahela." This rye is an attempt to bring back a truly American product. Created from 80% rye and 20% malted barley, this unaged whiskey has some real raw whiskey flavors. The truth is white whiskeys are an acquired taste for sure, and you need to order it with an open mind and appreciate it for what it is. I often recommend this whiskey simply because I grew up on the Monongahela River in western Pennsylvania, and telling the story behind the whiskey always makes it taste a little better.

FUN FACT: It is said that by 1810, the Monongahela region was out producing Kentucky three to one.

VARIETY/STYLE: White Rye

BARREL TYPE: Used *Quercus Alba*

AGE: N/A

ORIGIN: Utah

BOTTLE: 750 ml, cork top

ALCOHOL: 49.3%

PROOF: 98.6

PRICE: mid-range

RELATED: Ballast Point, Koval, RoughStock, Journeyman, Dad's Hat

PROPELLERS: !!!

High West Distillery and Saloon, 703 Park Avenue, Park City, UT 84060, (435) 649-8300, david@highwest.com, www.highwest.com

COMMENTS FROM THE BARTENDER:

ANNIE: It's hard for me not to cringe when I smell this. I was surprised with pleasant citrus and even some melon, but still not for me, sorry.

JEFF: My taste buds were almost overwhelmed from the malt flavor. Has a long finish that allowed a little fruit flavor to come through, but not my cup of tea . . . I mean whiskey.

JOHN: I could sub this out for malt balls at my next movie outing. Some great flavor, half the calories!

BRANDON: Spice and citrus that's refreshing, but the burn and almost like sourness turn me off.

JAMES E. PEPPER 1776 STRAIGHT RYE WHISKEY

SUMMARY: In 2013, James E. Pepper rye earned a gold medal at the San Francisco World Spirit competition. The folks at Georgetown Trading Company spent years collecting and analyzing full reserved bottles of the original Pepper whiskey and acquired a letter written by Pepper himself describing the original recipe. The whiskey today is made from select barrels that are very close to the original, using a mash bill of over 90% rye and the rest malted barley. This is a good rye that people assume will be "peppery," go figure. The truth is it makes a great Manhattan or Sazerac, with plenty of cover spicy rye and even a little chocolate.

FUN FACT: During its tenure, Pepper Whiskey, or "old 1776 whiskey" as it was known, was the drink of choice for presidents Andrew Jackson and Ulysses S. Grant.

VARIETY/STYLE: Rye

BARREL TYPE: New American Oak

AGE: N/A

ORIGIN: Indiana

BOTTLE: 750 ml, cork top

ALCOHOL: 50%

PROOF: 100

PRICE: mid-range

RELATED: Bulleit, High West, Michter's, Wild Turkey

PROPELLERS: !!!!

Georgetown Trading Co., 4200 Cathedral Ave. NW #711, Washington, DC 20016, (301) 518-1366, www.jamesepepper.com

COMMENTS FROM THE BARTENDER:

ANNIE: Grainy at first drink. There is a corn syrup sweetness balanced with alcohol and some spice heat. The heat lingers.

JEFF: This is good. Has strong rye and clove flavors with a hint of chocolate.

JOHN: This whiskey has an enjoyable burn. Rye for sure, no mistaking that.

BRANDON: Soft nose: rye and a bit of clove. The hot rye dominates when it hits my tongue, followed by anise. This rye is Sazerac-ready!

JAMES E. PEPPER 1776 STRAIGHT RYE WHISKEY 15 YEARS

SUMMARY: Georgetown Trading Company purchased the rights to use the name James E. Pepper, and the labels on his whiskey bottles read "Old Style," a nod of respect to old grain bills (the recipe), bottling proof and production methods used by the Pepper family. With a mash bill of over 90% rye and an ABV of 45.65%, this is a big, rich whiskey. Though it may not be for everyone with a very spicy kick and a solid burn, we recommend trying the younger version first; it's much easier on the wallet.

FUN FACT: Georgetown Trading Co. was founded by Amir Peay; he also has the John L. Sullivan and Pow-Wow Botanical Rye brands.

VARIETY/STYLE: Straight Rye Whiskey

BARREL TYPE: New American Oak

AGE: 15 years

ORIGIN: Indiana

BOTTLE: 750 ml, cork top

ALCOHOL: 45.65%

PROOF: 91.3

PRICE: high-range

RELATED: Masterson's, Russell's Reserve 6 Year, Redemption, RoughStock Montana, Templeton

Georgetown Trading Co., 4200 Cathedral Ave. NW #711, Washington, DC 20016, (301) 518-1366, www.jamesepepper.com

PROPELLERS:

COMMENTS FROM THE BARTENDER:

ANNIE: Syrupy smell, super alcohol forward. Lots of spice on the tip of my tongue. Peppery for sure.

JEFF: Between the alcohol and the peppery spices, this burn doesn't let up. The sweet maple nose was rather misleading.

JOHN: Wowsers, this stuff slaps you in the face. After a few minutes you get some spicy flavors, but not enough to enjoy.

BRANDON: Smells sweet! Tastes grainy. Powerful rye!

JEFFERSON'S STRAIGHT RYE 10 YEAR

SUMMARY: If you're looking for a big spicy 100% rye, you just found it. This rye is sourced from Canada, which often raises the eyebrows of loyal American whiskey drinkers, but it tested well and makes a great high-end mixer. The rye is often compared to WhistlePig, and for good reason: they're both Canadian. The Jefferson's is less sweet with more of a rye presence, which we love.

FUN FACT: Jefferson's offers an ocean-aged bourbon that has been rocked in the bow of a research vessel in the tropics for four years.

VARIETY/STYLE: Rye

BARREL TYPE: New American Oak

AGE: 10 years

ORIGIN: Canada

BOTTLE: 750 ml, cork top

ALCOHOL: 47%

PROOF: 94

PRICE: mid-range

RELATED: Knob Creek, Michter's, WhistlePig 10 Year, Masterson's, Pendleton

Castle Brands Inc., 122 East 42nd Street, Suite 4700, New York, NY 10168, (646) 356-0200, info@castlebrands.com, www.castlebrands.com

PROPELLERS:

COMMENTS FROM THE BARTENDER:

ANNIE: Sweet and spicy. Lots of black pepper and maybe nutmeg. I taste grains and maybe some bread flavors. Toast, yum!

JEFF: Ginger and spice and everything nice. Is well balanced, from the rye nose to the ginger vanilla taste.

JOHN: Gooood burn. I would recommend this to a drinking buddy who's outgrown his usual.

BRANDON: Definitely a rye. Flavors of the barrel are present and appreciated.

JIM BEAM STRAIGHT RYE WHISKEY

SUMMARY: Jim Beam Straight Rye tastes pretty much like it smells. Like so many ryes in its price and age group, you will find spice, pepper, wood and some sweet fruit notes. It's good drinkable whiskey that unfortunately doesn't get poured very often, as the name tends to scare people off. Yes, believe it or not, it's true. Almost everyone knows the Jim Beam name, and they like to try something they haven't had, so Bulleit Rye is almost always ordered over it when people are looking for a lower price rye whiskey.

FUN FACT: Jim Beam Rye just meets the legal requirement to be called a rye whiskey, with its mash bill consisting of just 51% rye.

VARIETY/STYLE: Rye

BARREL TYPE: Charred White Oak

AGE: 4 years

ORIGIN: Kentucky

BOTTLE: 750 ml, screw cap

ALCOHOL: 40%

PROOF: 80

PRICE: low-range

RELATED: Bulleit, Old Overhold, Knob Creek, Wild Turkey, George Dickel

Beam Suntory Inc., 222 W Merchandise Mart Plaza, Chicago, IL 60654, (312) 964-6999, www.jimbeam.com

PROPELLERS:

COMMENTS FROM THE BARTENDER:

ANNIE: Sweet and spicy. Nothing incredibly outstanding, but definitely something to drink all day.

JEFF: Hot and spicy the whole way through. Would probably be better with a couple of ice cubes. If you like a spicy Manhattan or Old Fashioned, give it a try.

JOHN: This has got to be rye? Toasty and earthy, but light.

BRANDON: The nose is malty, taste infused with some spice. I don't know, recommend for someone who likes artisan whiskeys.

JOHN JACOB HANDMADE RYE WHISKEY

SUMMARY: Mike Sherlock is the owner and master distiller of Fremont Mischief, a "full circle" distillery that uses the finest organic, heirloom and small-farm conventional grains and botanicals along with artisan waters. The ingredients are crafted into spirits, then the spent grain is reused as organic compost for farms and gardens, and that's pretty cool in our book. This 100% rye is loaded with sweet breakfast flavors that make it an easy recommendation for the guest who has just finished up a big dinner and is looking to unbutton that top button of their pants, yawn, stretch out and sip on some whiskey.

FUN FACT: John Jacob is named after the master distiller's grandfather.

VARIETY/STYLE: Rye

BARREL TYPE: New American Oak

AGE: 3 years

ORIGIN: Washington

BOTTLE: 750 ml, cork top

ALCOHOL: 40%

PROOF: 80

PRICE: mid-range

RELATED: RoughStock, Stein, Journeyman, Templeton, James E. Pepper

Fremont Mischief, 132 N. Canal Street, Seattle, WA 98103, (206) 632-7286, www.fremontmischief.com

PROPELLERS:

COMMENTS FROM THE BARTENDER:

ANNIE: Maple and butter—this is basically pancakes with a proof. I'm getting bananas crème brûlée, too. This is incredibly smooth with zero burn. Maybe almost too easy to drink.

JEFF: Definitely makes me think of a home-cooked breakfast, but the maple makes the sweetness go overboard.

JOHN: Dang, too sweet for me, but I just found my new go-to for someone looking for a dessert whiskey after dinner.

BRANDON: Before tasting this, I jokingly asked to make sure I wasn't given nail polish remover. It's buttery and sweet, but I don't like it at all!

JOURNEYMAN RAVENSWOOD ORGANIC RYE WHISKEY

SUMMARY: Master Distiller and owner Bill Welter learned a lot of his trade while training at Koval Distillery in Chicago before opening Journeyman Distillery. Ravenswood is an organic whiskey with grain sourced from Michigan and Minnesota. The mash bill consists of equal amounts of rye and wheat. This craft whiskey is matured in 15-gallon new white oak barrels that give it a beautiful russet color. It gives you a lot of flavors to figure out, including fruit, citrus and spice. We often recommend this to someone who likes to sip and analyze their drink.

FUN FACT: The first batch of rye was made in the Chicago neighborhood of Ravenswood. The whiskey is now produced at the Journeyman Distillery in the old Featherbone Building in Three Oaks, Michigan, and the Ravenswood name lives on.

VARIETY/STYLE: Rye

BARREL TYPE: New American Oak

AGE: 15 years

ORIGIN: Michigan

BOTTLE: 750 ml, cork top

ALCOHOL: 45%

PROOF: 90

PRICE: high-range

RELATED: Redemption, RoughStock Montana, Templeton, High West, Koval Rye

PROPELLERS:

Journeyman Distillery, Historic Featherbone Factory, 109 Generations Drive, Three Oaks, MI 49128, (269) 820-2050, info@journeymandistillery.com, www.journeymandistillery.com

COMMENTS FROM THE BARTENDER:

ANNIE: This I would need to try again: too much going on to figure out in one taste. This is a fun whiskey!

JEFF: On the nose it's bittersweet, but where does it go? Nowhere. I was left dry but not high.

JOHN: Very interesting . . . It is sweet but also a bit hot. Can't put my finger on it—caramel?

BRANDON: This one's a little sweet, but it's mellow and dry.

KNOB CREEK KENTUCKY STRAIGHT RYE WHISKEY

SUMMARY: Knob Creek is made in small batches and aged in deeply charred oak barrels that age in their nine-story rick house. Barrel placement plays a big factor in the aging process. The top racks are warmer and experience more evaporation, creating a higher proof. The cooler, damper bottom rack will actually take in moisture, resulting in a lower proof. Knob Creek blends barrels from fixed locations to create consistent flavors. It seems to work well for this rye. It's perfect for the bourbon drinker looking to venture into ryes.

FUN FACT: Voted Best Rye and won Double Gold at the 2012 San Francisco World Spirits Competition.

VARIETY/STYLE: Rye

BARREL TYPE: New American Oak

AGE: 9 years

ORIGIN: Kentucky

BOTTLE: 750 ml, screw cap

ALCOHOL: 50%

PROOF: 100

PRICE: mid-range

RELATED: Russell's Reserve, Masterson's, Redemption, Sazerac, Breakout

PROPELLERS:

Beam Suntory Inc., 222 W Merchandise Mart Plaza, Chicago, IL 60654, (312) 964-6999, www.beamglobal.com
Producer: Jim Beam American Stillhouse, 526 Happy Hollow Road, Claremont, KY 40110, (502) 543-9877

COMMENTS FROM THE BARTENDER:

ANNIE: Smells floral and perfume-y, tastes like alcohol and grains. Whiskey for farm life.

JEFF: Very alcohol forward and grassy. Give me a few cubes, please!

JOHN: Gotta say, I like this one, too! This is getting hard. A little hard at first, mellows on the finish.

BRANDON: Teases the nostrils. Very interesting flavors of grain and citrus. Finishes fast with small spice. I bet it's a rye.

KOVAL WHITE RYE WHISKEY

SUMMARY: Koval was established in 2008 by Robert and Sonat Birnecker, who vowed to make organic spirits from scratch. They set out to bring the distilling traditions of Robert's Austrian family to America. The Koval White Rye comes in a tall, sleek bottle and is made from 100% organic rye from the Midwest. It's very much your standard unaged whiskey with flavors that are enjoyable at the low ABV. It's pretty cut and dry: If you're a fan of white whiskeys and especially the rye grain, then you will be happy with this selection. If your palate is unsure, you may want to steer clear.

FUN FACT: Koval has been producing spirits in Chicago's first distillery since the mid-1800s.

VARIETY/STYLE: White Rye

BARREL TYPE: N/A

AGE: N/A

ORIGIN: Illinois

BOTTLE: 750 ml, cork top

ALCOHOL: 40%

PROOF: 80

PRICE: mid-range

RELATED: Journeyman, Stein, RoughStock, Lion's Pride, Dry Fly

Koval Distillery, 5121 North Ravenswood Avenue, Chicago, IL 60640, (312) 878-7988, www.koval-distillery.com

PROPELLERS:

COMMENTS FROM THE BARTENDER:

ANNIE: Nutty smell, incredibly smooth and sweet going down. Almost tastes like almond extract. Pairs well with cookies!

JEFF: Smooth and creamy mouthfeel. A well-rounded spirit, solid but not overwhelming.

JOHN: I've said it before and I will say it again: These are slowly winning my heart. I was a skeptic but now this whiskey gets my vote.

BRANDON: This would be a great mixer. Maybe add a dash of almond liqueur, stir and serve up. Then dry shake banana liqueur with some egg white until frothy and gently layer on top—delicious!

LEGS DIAMOND WHISKEY

SUMMARY: Nahmias ET Fils Distillery was founded by Dorit Nahmias and Master Distiller David Nahmias; both are world travelers who became inspired to distill after sampling a variety of spirits throughout their international travels. Legs Diamond is made from organic rye from Upstate New York. This white whiskey is not for everyone; it has a very distinct tequila aroma and flavor that will instantly make you squint if you're not a fan of agave stuff. There are smoother, easier unaged whiskeys out there to try. This one is a very acquired taste.

FUN FACT: Legs Diamond is the name of a bootlegger who made quite a name for himself in New York during Prohibition.

VARIETY/STYLE: White Rye

BARREL TYPE: N/A

AGE: N/A

ORIGIN: New York

BOTTLE: 750 ml, cork top

ALCOHOL: 40%

PROOF: 80

PRICE: mid-range

RELATED: Dad's Hat, Stein, Kamal, Journeyman, High West

PROPELLERS:

Nahmias ET FILS Distillery, 201 Saw Mill River, Yonkers, NY 10701, (646) 644-4256, info@nahmiasetfils.com, www.baronnahmias.com

COMMENTS FROM THE BARTENDER:

ANNIE: After smelling this, I didn't even want to taste it. It smells exactly like tequila and guess what? I was right.

JEFF: A bitter, alcohol-forward whiskey that has some rye spice I'm not a fan of it.

JOHN: Maybe I'm crazy, but I kind of like this one. It's the kind of stuff you can slam down your throat as you pound your fist down on the bar.

BRANDON: If a kamikaze pilot crashed into the desert and had to use his fuel line to syphon water from a cactus, this is what his breath would taste like.

LION'S PRIDE ORGANIC SINGLE BARREL RYE

SUMMARY: Koval Distillery has been producing quality organic products since it was founded in 2008. They source their supplies from the surrounding Midwest region and use charcoal-purified water sourced from Lake Michigan. This single barrel whiskey is made from 100% rye and aged for about two years in lightly toasted barrels. They also choose not to chill-filter their whiskey to preserve the character of the grain. This whiskey is rye in all its glory and a great way to really taste the difference between large production and craft distilling.

FUN FACT: This whiskey is named for their son, Lion.

VARIETY/STYLE: Rye

BARREL TYPE: Oak

AGE: About 2 years

ORIGIN: Illinois

BOTTLE: 750 ml, cork top

ALCOHOL: 40%

PROOF: 80

PRICE: mid-range

RELATED: Goldrun Rye, Journeyman, Corsair, High West, Koval

PROPELLERS:

Koval Distillery, 5121 North Ravenswood Avenue, Chicago, IL 60640, (312) 878-7988, www.kovaldistillery.com

COMMENTS FROM THE BARTENDER:

ANNIE: Smells like rubber cement. Tastes like sweetened rubber cement.

JEFF: I swear I ate this this morning. Bananas, oats and honey all jumped out at me. The finish was more wooded with vanilla.

JOHN: Fruity (maybe coconut?) with a hint of pepper on the nose. Complex, it smells good! Quick, intense alcohol burn that quickly mellows out into a sweet, toasty cereal flavor.

BRANDON: Honey Nut Cheerios with bananas may be this whiskey's mash bill ingredients. But it really tastes peppery and woody and has a medium finish that's quite enjoyable.

MASTERSON'S STRAIGHT RYE WHISKEY

SUMMARY: Masterson's Rye is made from 100% rye. It's distilled in a pot still and aged 10 years in new white oak barrels. The whiskey is named after and is a tribute to the man whose picture is on the label, William "Bat" Masterson, a larger-than-life figure who was said to help tame the Wild West. This rye is much tamer than Bat's gun-slinging, buffalo-hunting image. It's a smooth sipper that any rye drinker would enjoy. It sells well here, even with a higher price tag than some really good competitors sitting next to it. The 10 years it spends in the oak doesn't hurt as a selling point either. It has a wonderful profile of flavors that you won't mind spending a couple of extra dollars for.

FUN FACT: Don't be surprised if this whiskey tastes similar to WhistlePig or Jefferson's Rye. They're all sourced from Canada.

VARIETY/STYLE: Rye

BARREL TYPE: New White Oak

AGE: 10 years

ORIGIN: Canada

BOTTLE: 750 ml, cork top

ALCOHOL: 45%

PROOF: 90

PRICE: high-range

RELATED: Michter's, WhistlePig, Redemption, Jefferson's, Bulleit Rye 10 Year

PROPELLERS:

35 Maple Street Spirits, 35 Maple Street, Sonoma, CA 95476, (707) 996-8463, info@togwines.com, www.mastersonsrye.com

COMMENTS FROM THE BARTENDER:

ANNIE: Sweet! Toasty sugar. Sweet at first and a smooth finish with enjoyable spice that lingers.

JEFF: With its notes of rye, spice and orange, this is one that any rye drinker should keep their eye out for. I think I might even put it in my Old Fashioned tonight.

JOHN: Very mild whiskey. Light spice. No finish. Sunday morning flask whiskey.

BRANDON: This one's great! A full-flavored, spicy rye whiskey with a grainy finish. This defines rye whiskey!

MICHTER'S SINGLE BARREL RYE

SUMMARY: This Michter's whiskey has only the name in common with its roots at the historic Michter's Distillery in Pennsylvania. The whiskey is sourced from the powerhouse whiskey makers, Kentucky Bourbon Distillers, for now. There's no doubt the whiskey made today is a little different than the one back in Pennsylvania, but one thing is for sure—it's good. This single barrel rye is one of our bestsellers and we recommend it often. If you're looking for barrel flavors and spicy rye notes from start to finish, this may be what you're looking for.

FUN FACT: Once named Bomberger's Distillery before it became Michter's, the still house, warehouse and jug house date back to 1840, and the site is now declared a national historic landmark.

VARIETY/STYLE: Rye

BARREL TYPE: New White Oak

AGE: 3 plus years

ORIGIN: Kentucky

BOTTLE: 750 ml, cork top

ALCOHOL: 42.4%

PROOF: 84.8

PRICE: mid-range

RELATED: Masterson's, Breakout, Willett 4 Year, (R1)[1], Knob Creek

PROPELLERS: ! ! ! ! !

Chatham Imports, 245 Fifth Avenue, New York, NY 10016, (212) 473-1100, info@michters.com, www.michters.com
Producer: Kentucky Bourbon Distillers, 1869 Loretto Road, Bardstown, KY 40004, (502)-561-1001, kentuckybourbon@bardstown.com, www.kentuckybourbonwhiskey.com

COMMENTS FROM THE BARTENDER:

ANNIE: This one is like eating peppered turkey jerky and drinking a caramel Frappuccino. Very tasty.

JEFF: Not a very complex taste. The rye covers up most of the caramel and vanilla that you pick up from the nose. Would make a great Manhattan.

JOHN: It smelled much milder than it is. Nice rye spice with a bit of corn sweetness. It's sweet and spicy. Nice finish.

BRANDON: Very sweet aroma full of vanilla and caramel. It's peppery and oaky, but some dark fruit is present. Not too much rye, and it's a little sour.

OLD OVERHOLT STRAIGHT RYE WHISKEY

SUMMARY: Known as your grandpa's rye, Old Overholt started back in the 1800s and was originally made in the state of Pennsylvania. This dated rye whiskey is currently made in Kentucky under the Beam Distillery and is favored as one of the best bargain brown spirits. Old Overholt Rye has had its hardships over the years with the struggle of Prohibition. It also struggled when rye was no longer the American whiskey of choice. But this rye has made a strong comeback and Old Overholt Rye is available in most liquor stores across the country. This true American rye whiskey has strong notes of oak and a mildness of sweet corn. Its aroma is pleasant to the nose, with smoky and spicy hints of sweet wheat. Its moderate dry finish makes for a moderate rye whiskey.

FUN FACT: It was the so-called "medicinal" alcohol of the United States Navy during World War II.

VARIETY/STYLE: Rye

BARREL TYPE: Charred White Oak

AGE: 3 years

ORIGIN: Kentucky

BOTTLE: 750 ml, screw cap

ALCOHOL: 40%

PROOF: 80

PRICE: low-range

RELATED: Bulleit, Michter's, Sazerac, Breakout, Knob Creek

PROPELLERS: ! ! ! !

James B. Distilling Company, 526 Happy Hollow Road, Clermont, KY 40110, (502) 543-9877, www.americanstillhouse.com

COMMENTS FROM THE BARTENDER:

ANNIE: Very light nose ... slightly herbal or grassy. Bold and intense at first. Spicy, just enough burn, cinnamon on the finish.

JEFF: Pepper and wood up front, but fades into a little more of a grassy taste. Overall, pretty well balanced.

JOHN: Kind of in your face at first. I get spice and vapor on the front. Sugary finish. I would make a Manhattan with this.

BRANDON: Peppery and grassy. Any rye fan would love this whiskey.

OLD POTRERO STRAIGHT RYE WHISKEY

SUMMARY: This rye is single malt, meaning it's made of 100% malted rye and distilled at the same location. This release is made in a small copper still in San Francisco. Bruce Joseph and his crew started distilling whiskey in 1996. They have come a long way from a bunch of beer brewers who wanted to make whiskey. Some have called it Christmas in a bottle with aromas and tastes of molasses, vanilla, sugar cookies, toffee and of course spice. The rye sells well here, partly because we are so close to San Francisco but mainly because it's good.

FUN FACT: Old Potrero also offers a single malt eighteenth-century-style whiskey. It has a very acquired taste you may enjoy if you like Islay Scotches.

VARIETY/STYLE: Rye

BARREL TYPE: New American Oak

AGE: N/A

ORIGIN: San Francisco

BOTTLE: 750 ml, cork top

ALCOHOL: 45%

PROOF: 90

PRICE: high-range

RELATED: Masterson's, (R1)[1], Journeyman, Copper Fox, Ballast Point

PROPELLERS: !!!!

Anchor Distilling Co., 1705 Mariposa Street, San Francisco, CA 94107, (415) 863-8350, info@anchorsf.com, www.anchordistilling.com

COMMENTS FROM THE BARTENDER:

ANNIE: Hot, very hot at first, followed by a sweet molasses flavor.

JEFF: All kinds of stuff going on: sugar and spice and everything nice. Not one to mix, too much fun flavor.

JOHN: Potent concentrated whiskey, not the one you want to start the night with.

BRANDON: Gotta be a rye. Quick blast of ginger and Granny Smith apples. Yum!

POW-WOW BOTANICAL RYE

SUMMARY: We decided to include Pow-Wow Botanical Rye for one simple reason: it sells and has begun to get a following. It's a rye that is lightly infused with saffron, orange peel and other whole botanicals. It's kind of like an Old Fashioned in a bottle. Don't get us wrong, we love peeling, zesting and muddling as much as the next guy or gal and we take a lot pride in our craft, but sometimes when you're five guests deep, all looking to get your undivided attention, Pow-Wow on the rocks is a welcome order.

FUN FACT: The origins of rye date back to colonial Pennsylvania where early European settlers farmed and distilled rye.

VARIETY/STYLE: Botanical Rye

BARREL TYPE: New Charred Oak

AGE: N/A

ORIGIN: N/A

BOTTLE: 750 ml, cork top

ALCOHOL: 45%

PROOF: 90

PRICE: mid-range

RELATED: Templeton, Stein, High West, RoughStock, Journeyman

PROPELLERS: !!!

Georgetown Trading Company, 4200 Cathedral Avenue NW, #711, Washington, DC 20016, (301) 518-1366, info@georgetowntrading.com, www.botanicalrye.com

COMMENTS FROM THE BARTENDER:

ANNIE: Smells sweet and botanical and like cotton candy. Spicy and sweet but super low-key. I taste faint licorice.

JEFF: I get plum with a zesty herbal, tobacco flavor and cedar chips. Interesting.

JOHN: Nice, sweet, mildly spicy whiskey. I get the licorice finish. Not sure if I would drink this neat. Probably mixed.

BRANDON: Initially this smelled like a fresh pack of bubble gum. It quickly turned sweet and packed with rye. Let's mix this one up!

PRICHARD'S RYE WHISKEY

SUMMARY: Phil Prichard founded his distillery in 1997 in Kelso, Tennessee, just a few miles south of where his great-great-great-grandfather distilled whiskey nearly two centuries ago. The rye produced today has a mash bill of 95% rye and 5% malted barley and is aged for three to five years. The result is a well-balanced rye that we often recommend. Most guests haven't heard of it and are excited to try it. The feedback has been great.

FUN FACT: Prichard's has been turning out award-winning rums for more than 10 years.

VARIETY/STYLE: Rye

BARREL TYPE: New American Oak

AGE: 3 to 5 years

ORIGIN: Tennessee

BOTTLE: 750 ml, screw cap

ALCOHOL: 43%

PROOF: 86

PRICE: mid-range

RELATED: Bulleit, Breakout, Willet's, Old Overholt, Sazerac

Prichard's Distillery, 11 Kelso Smithland Rd., Kelso, TN 37348, (931) 443-5454, www.prichardsdistillery.com

PROPELLERS:

COMMENTS FROM THE BARTENDER:

ANNIE: Sweet nose with hints of apple and spice. Oak, vanilla, faint apple flavor and a touch of lingering burn.

JEFF: A really well-done rye. It has a great balance of rye, vanilla and apples. It's smooth with just enough burn to warm you up.

JOHN: It's actually really good. To me, it is perfectly balanced. I get spice but also a deeper flavor. I can't describe it. Like "love"?

BRANDON: Smells like candy apples and it tastes like it too. Just with a huge spicy rye flavor. Bomb!

REDEMPTION STRAIGHT RYE WHISKEY

SUMMARY: Redemption Rye has a mash bill consisting of 95% rye and is produced and aged in Lawrenceburg, Indiana, at the old Lawrenceburg Distillery. This young rye has all the classic flavors that a rye should have (golden color, medium body with dusty, earthy notes) but no real wow factor. Guests will occasionally order it just to try something new but second orders are rare. It's worth a try to decide for yourself.

FUN FACT: Lawrenceburg Distillers product is a 95% rye whiskey that is used under various brand names, including Bulleit, Dickel and Templeton.

VARIETY/STYLE: Rye

BARREL TYPE: New American Oak

AGE: 2 plus years

ORIGIN: Indiana

BOTTLE: 750 ml, screw cap

ALCOHOL: 46%

PROOF: 92

PRICE: mid-range

RELATED: Russell's Reserve, Bulleit, Templeton, Michter's, Masterson's

Bardstown Barrel Selection, 1050 Withrow Court, Bardstown, KY 40004, (203) 226-4181, ds@redemptionrye.com, www.redemptionrye.com **Producer:** MGP Ingredients, Inc., Cray Business Plaza, 100 Commercial Street, P.O. Box 130, Atchison, KS 66002, (800) 255-0302, www.mgpingredients.com

PROPELLERS:

COMMENTS FROM THE BARTENDER:

ANNIE: Cinnamon, cloves, kind of dry. Not sweet at all, but smooth and tasty.

JEFF: A nice earthy, woody nose with a dry, quick finish. Not my favorite.

JOHN: It has a nice spice, not overpowering at all.

BRANDON: Light nose, warm spicy taste of gingerbread. Reminds me of Grandma's kitchen and Grandpa's breath.

(R1)¹ STRAIGHT RYE WHISKEY

SUMMARY: Rye was once king of the hill when it came to American whiskey. It was used in all the classic cocktails, and was enjoyed by the masses. Then came Prohibition and other whiskeys emerged, like sweet corn–based moonshines and softer Canadian spirits. Rye whiskey sat on the shelf as American palates craved the milder bourbons and scotches. Today, however, rye is on the rise, rapidly becoming the whiskey of choice. Jim Beam launched this rye in 2008 with an edgy new look and label in an attempt to market to a new generation of rye drinkers. The rye sells well mostly because people see the label and want to try something new. They are often surprised when we tell them it is a Beam product, and it's too late to take back that they said they like it.

FUN FACT: Beam also produces Old Overholt.

VARIETY/STYLE: Rye

BARREL TYPE: New American Oak

AGE: 4½ years

ORIGIN: Kentucky

BOTTLE: 750 ml, cork top

ALCOHOL: 46%

PROOF: 92

PRICE: mid-range

RELATED: Knob Creek, Michter's, Old Overholt, Sazerac, Bulleit

PROPELLERS: !!!! !!!!

Beam Suntory Inc., 222 W Merchandise Mart Plaza, Chicago, IL 60654, (312) 964-6999, www.beamglobal.com
Producer: Jim Beam American Stillhouse, 526 Happy Hollow Road, Claremont, KY 40110, (502) 543-9877

COMMENTS FROM THE BARTENDER:

ANNIE: One I could drink with the girls; a sure thing at a nice house party.

JEFF: With its soft spice flavors, this is really easy to drink neat or in a cocktail. I could see it making a delicious Whiskey Sour.

JOHN: Very mild, nice and easy. It has a nice rye flavor. Not spicy—definitely a sweeter rye.

BRANDON: Canned fruits and sweet, spicy flavors with soft spices. Very mild.

RIVERBOAT RYE

SUMMARY: This is a sleeper rye that not much is known about other than it's produced by MPG at its Lawrenceburg, Indiana, distillery and that it uses the same high-rye mash bill as Redemption Rye 95%. We haven't had too much success selling this whiskey, as its flavor just can't compete with others in its price range. A mixer for sure. Don't, however, let this deter you from trying the Redemption Rye. The two are nothing alike; the Redemption is good!

FUN FACT: 2012 Beverage Testing Institute posted, "It's very nice on its own." Our guests beg to differ.

VARIETY/STYLE: Small Batch Rye

BARREL TYPE: New American Oak

AGE: N/A

ORIGIN: Indiana

BOTTLE: 750 ml, screw cap

ALCOHOL: 40%

PROOF: 80

PRICE: low-range

RELATED: Bulleit, Old Overhold, Jim Beam, Wild Turkey, George Dickel

Dynamic Beverages, 1010 Withrow Court, Bardstown, KY 40004, (203) 226-4181, DS@redemptionrye.com, www.redemptionrye.com **Producer:** MPG Ingredients, Inc., Cray Business Plaza, 100 Commercial St., P.O. Box 130, Atchison, KS 66002, (800) 255-0302, www.mpgingredients.com

PROPELLERS: !

COMMENTS FROM THE BARTENDER:

ANNIE: This doesn't tickle my fancy. Boring and flat, no fun!

JEFF: A strong rye flavor covers up any other flavor. This will end up lost in the wall of whiskey.

JOHN: No real flavor on the nose, strong rye burn and not too much else. Its only hope is to be mixed.

BRANDON: Dude, once again. A clean, no-finish whiskey. Don't get me wrong, I like it. I would most likely mix this.

ROUGHSTOCK MONTANA STRAIGHT RYE

SUMMARY: According to RoughStock, this rye whiskey is a throwback of American distilling culture that takes us back to its origins by using a grain that was dismissed after Prohibition. There's no doubt rye has made a huge comeback. Though we still pour more bourbon, many of our mixed whiskey cocktails are rye based. It's a robust and spicy grain that complements the sweet flavors it draws from lightly charred American oak. RoughStock uses 100% whole grain rye mash to achieve a big rye flavor. We recommend trying it straight first so you can experience the flavor, and if it's not for you, no worries—a good bartender can transform it into a classic cocktail you will enjoy.

FUN FACT: RoughStock is the first legal distillery in Montana since Prohibition.

VARIETY/STYLE: Rye

BARREL TYPE: New American Oak

ORIGIN: Montana

BOTTLE: 750 ml, cork top

ALCOHOL: 45%

PROOF: 90

PRICE: mid-range

RELATED: High West, WhistlePig, Prichard's, Dad's Hat, Templeton

PROPELLERS: !!!

RoughStock Distillery, 81211 Gallaten Road Suite A, Bozemen, MT 59718, (406) 551-6409, www.montanawhiskey.com

COMMENTS FROM THE BARTENDER:

ANNIE: Smells syrupy. Sweet without being sugary and spicy without too much burn. Super mellow and drinkable

JEFF: I prefer a little more richness in my dinner; this is good but I'm not going to fill up on it.

JOHN: This is a delicate little number that I'd like to dance with nice and easy, soft and slow. Like the end of an '80s movie where I realize I loved the average girl all along.

BRANDON: Very, very mild. Clean finish with no nose to speak of. It was good, but sure didn't hang around long.

RUSSELL'S RESERVE SMALL BATCH 6 YEAR OLD KENTUCKY STRAIGHT RYE WHISKEY

SUMMARY: With over 90 years of combined experience, Master American Distiller Jimmy Russell joined Wild Turkey in 1954 and his son Eddie is fourth in a line of distillers. Wild Turkey is pretty much a household name, which makes people think they are corporate and not great, but we think the line of Russell's Reserve whiskeys are great. There's no mistaking this six-year whiskey is a rye; it shows off the grain wonderfully. If you want to know what a good rye tastes like, try this whiskey.

FUN FACT: Jim Russell was inducted into the Bourbon Hall of Fame in 2000, and his son was inducted in 2010.

VARIETY/STYLE: Small Batch Rye

BARREL TYPE: New American Oak

AGE: 6 years

ORIGIN: Kentucky

BOTTLE: 750 ml, cork top

ALCOHOL: 45%

PROOF: 90

PRICE: mid-range

RELATED: Knob Creek, Michter's, Masterson's, James E. Pepper 1776

PROPELLERS: !!!!!

Beam Suntory Inc., 222 W Merchandise Mart Plaza, Chicago, IL 60654, (312) 964-6999, www.jimbeam.com

COMMENTS FROM THE BARTENDER:

ANNIE: It definitely has a rye bread flavor at first. Good mid-burn and solid finish.

JEFF: This doesn't have much of a nose, but I was surprised with the allspice flavor and sweet burn.

JOHN: Ahh, fetch my pipe and slippers and warm up my rocking chair; it's time to drink whiskey.

BRANDON: Solid whiskey, all the usual flavors that are supposed to be there

SAZERAC STRAIGHT RYE WHISKEY

SUMMARY: Opening up a bottle of Sazerac is like opening up a bottle of whiskey that you expect to make into a cocktail (a Sazerac perhaps?), or at least that is what I assumed before I actually sipped this whiskey. I expected something young and big and burly. What I got was something a bit more refined than that, much to my delight! Prepared for an overpowered high-proof rye, I was gently cradled by a quality distillate that reminded me of something more toward the bourbon scale than anything else. Well, there is a reason for that. Sazerac Rye is made from the bare minimum requirement for a rye whiskey—51% rye, 39% corn, and 11% malted barley. After further investigation I also realized that this is close to one of the better mixing ryes that I have tried to date. Fantastic rye Manhattan, delicious Old Fashioned and of course… the Sazerac is a historical walk down cocktail lane.

FUN FACT: In 1859 the Sazerac cocktail was the first "branded" cocktail in existence. Originally calling for a French brandy called Sazerac-de-Forge & Fils, Peychaud's bitters and Herb Sainte, it wasn't until 2000 that The Official Sazerac Cocktail called for Sazerac Kentucky Straight Rye Whiskey.

VARIETY/STYLE: Rye

BARREL TYPE: 6 years

ORIGIN: Kentucky

BOTTLE: N/A

ALCOHOL: 45%

PROOF: 90

PRICE: mid-range

RELATED: Willet Single Barrel, Old Overholt Rye, Bulleit Rye

PROPELLERS: 🌀🌀🌀🌀🌀

Sazerac Company, Inc., 3850 N Causeway Blvd., Suite 1695, Metairie, LA 70002, (866) 729-3722, info@sazerac.com, www.sazerac.com

COMMENTS FROM THE BARTENDER:

ANNIE: The nose on this is beautiful. Vanilla, spice (cloves, I think) and maybe a hint of orange blossom. There's some burn to it but you'll still get the vanilla and spice. This is a good one.

JEFF: Flat sort of smell but in a good, balanced way. Like a stale spice cabinet. The taste really opens up on the palate.

JOHN: Really pretty spice. It has a great spice finish. This would be perfect for my Manhattan, so many options!

BRANDON: Smells good, tastes good and makes me feel good!

STEIN STRAIGHT RYE SMALL BATCH WHISKEY

SUMMARY: Oregon-based Stein Distillery takes a lot of pride in their whiskey. All are made in small batches and aged in new American white oak barrels. Each label is applied by hand and has the barrel and bottle number on it. There has been a resurgence of rye whiskey in the past few years that has bartenders making more classic cocktails than ever. Manhattans, Old Fashioneds and Sazeracs are being muddled more than ever. The Stein Rye is two years old with a mash bill of 75% rye, 25% corn and a price tag around $40, which makes it hard to sell, as its too expensive for most people to order in a mixed drink and too young for most to order on the rocks.

FUN FACT: Stein also produces a variety of spirits, including rum, vodka and cordials.

VARIETY/STYLE: Rye

BARREL TYPE: New American Oak

AGE: 2 years

ORIGIN: Oregon

BOTTLE: 750 ml, cork top

ALCOHOL: 40%

PROOF: 80

PRICE: mid-range

RELATED: Dad's Hat, Lion's Pride, Legs Diamond, High West, Wiser's

Stein Distillery, P.O. Box 200, 604 N Main St., Joseph, OR 97846, (541) 432-2009, whiskey@steindistillery.com, www.steindistillery.com

PROPELLERS: 🌀🌀

COMMENTS FROM THE BARTENDER:

ANNIE: Almost smells like cigarette ashes; tastes like it too. This is smoky for an American whiskey, but I'm starting to like it the more I let it linger.

JEFF: Strong rye flavors, almost too much for me. I'm betting this is very young.

JOHN: Up-front spice and medium neat. The spice is the strongest flavor with a sweet, clean finish.

BRANDON: Not my favorite. Just kind of a quick spice hit with not many other flavors to play with.

TEMPLETON SMALL BATCH RYE WHISKEY

SUMMARY: We have a great relationship with the folks at Templeton, but we can see how they have some naysayers who like to take shots at them about the credibility of their marketing. The whiskey is sourced and produced in Lawrenceburg, Indiana, by MPG Distillery, not in Templeton, Iowa, and whether or not Al Capone drank Templeton Whiskey or a version of it and considered it "the good stuff" is a little questionable. But we're here to discuss how it tastes and if you should recommend it as a bartender. The answer is yes; the whiskey is good—a little mild, but good. People head out to their local whiskey bar to relax and have a good time, and if they choose to believe they're drinking the same juice as Mr. Capone, then who are we to rain on their parade? We're sure many legends and tall tales have developed over a few glasses of whiskey. Enjoy.

FUN FACT: The Aero Club has a mural painted on the south side of the building featuring Al Capone and Templeton Rye.

VARIETY/STYLE: Rye

BARREL TYPE: New American Oak

AGE: N/A

ORIGIN: Indiana

BOTTLE: 750 ml, cork top

ALCOHOL: 40%

PROOF: 80

PRICE: mid-range

RELATED: High West, Michter's, Bulleit, Corsair, Willett

PROPELLERS: ! ! ! !

Templeton Rye Spirits LLC, 209 East 3rd Street, Templeton, IA 51463, (712) 669-8793, info@templetonrye.com, www.templetonrye.com **Producer:** MGP Ingredients Inc., Cray Business Plaza, 100 Commercial Street, P.O. Box 130, Atchison, KS 66002, (800) 255-0302, www.mgpingredients.com

COMMENTS FROM THE BARTENDER:

ANNIE: Smells malty and sweet. Oh dang, there's spice! Not incredibly remarkable, but I do dig the spice.

JEFF: The word mild is what defines this from beginning to end. Soft, sweet notes on the nose, with some fruit, cinnamon and spice on the finish. I wish the taste was stronger.

JOHN: Nothing big about this. Up front very mild with some mild spice on the finish. I like it for a cocktail.

BRANDON: This would be a good go-to whiskey if the price were right. It'll temporarily scratch your itch.

WASMUND'S RYE SPIRIT

SUMMARY: Rick Wasmund is the founder of the Copper Fox Distillery set in the village of Sperryville in the Virginia countryside. It's here that he lives the dream of doing something that he loves, and that's making whiskey—innovative new whiskey using cherry and apple woods to smoke the barley. Wasmund's Rye is made with a generous amount of smoked malt, the mash bill consisting of two-thirds Virginia rye and one-third apple- and cherry-wood-smoked barley. What really adds the flavor is the aging process; Rick adds new and used apple wood and oak chips into the barrel. This unique aging process produces tons of fruit, wood and smoke flavors. It's also why it has to be called a "spirit" instead of whiskey, as is doesn't meet the legal requirements.

FUN FACT: Rick worked as an intern at the Bowmore Distillery in Scotland.

VARIETY/STYLE: Rye Spirit

BARREL TYPE: Used Bourbon

AGE: N/A

ORIGIN: Virginia

BOTTLE: 750 ml, screw cap

ALCOHOL: 62%

PROOF: 124

PRICE: mid-range

RELATED: Koval, High West, RoughStock, Journeyman, Lion's Pride

PROPELLERS: ! ! !

The Copper Fox Distillery, 9 River Lane, Sperryville, VA 22740, (540) 987-8554, rick@copperfox.biz, www.copperfox.biz

COMMENTS FROM THE BARTENDER:

ANNIE: Initial burn with herbal and fruit flavors. I almost taste juniper.

JEFF: These white whiskeys just don't do it for me. A spicy burn up front with notes of apple and nutmeg.

JOHN: Quaker oats! That gave me the shakes. First smell and taste was hot. But after getting it down, I said, "Whoa, hit me again."

BRANDON: Very oily and strong coating on my mouth immediately. A lot of warmth. Minutes after my tasting there was still some delicious malty and fruit notes present.

WHISTLEPIG STRAIGHT RYE WHISKEY

SUMMARY: WhistlePig produces a 100-proof, straight rye whiskey that has turned the heads of many mixologists and critics alike. Dave Pickerell, former master distiller from the renowned Maker's Mark Distillery, was introduced to this wonderful expression of Canadian rye. Pickerell searched far and long to find the finest extraction of rye whiskeys, until one day he stumbled upon what he thought was the form of a new Canadian version of superlative quality. Teaming up with founder Raj Bhakta, a former contestant on *The Apprentice*, they purchased a farm in Shoreham, Vermont, which is where WhistlePig is bottled. The farm has a dated history going back to the 1700s as it was cleared by Revolutionary War veterans for the purpose of farming on this fertile and beautiful stretch of land. The 230 acres of land grow hay—and of course, winter rye grain. Aged for 10 years, they claim it hits the sweet spot in all three categories. At first smell it gives a strong but clean hint of floral tones with sweet spice of nutmeg and clove. A hint of rye grass and old leather comes to mind as it remains open to the air, allowing time for the bottle to breathe. As you continue to savor this fine rye, it expresses a subtle spice with caramel and vanilla tastes that has a very low burn. WhistlePig 100/100 has a refined smokiness with a spice and clove finish that complements the dry oak, leaving a very pleasant taste on the palate. This rye whiskey is a winner and ranks high on our list of reviews. Great for mixing with cocktails but certainly a delightful snort for one to kick back and enjoy neat.

PROPELLERS:

FUN FACT: Raj Bhakta ran for the United States House of Representatives in 2006.

VARIETY/STYLE: Rye

BARREL TYPE: American Oak

AGE: 10 years

ORIGIN: Vermont and Canada

BOTTLE: 750 ml, cork top

ALCOHOL: 50%

PROOF: 100

PRICE: mid-range

RELATED: Jefferson's, Masterson's, Dad's Hat, High West, Koval

WhistlePig LLC, 2139 Quiet Valley Rd., Shoreham, VT 05770, (802) 897-7700, www.whistlepigwhiskey.com

COMMENTS FROM THE BARTENDER:

ANNIE: Smells like a farm in a good way. Great rye flavors with toasted almonds and fig, with a pinch of spice

JEFF: If the cereal Honey Toasted Oats and a rye whiskey had a baby, this would be it. Honey and oat nose with a strong rye flavor.

JOHN: Very strong rye flavors. It kind of had a bourbon feel but more rye I like this a lot. Make me a Sazerac with this one

BRANDON: The nose is sweet; enjoyable notes of honey, spice and some charred oak. Nothing special about this one, but I would sip it neat.

WHISTLEPIG "THE BOSS HOG"

SUMMARY: Master Distiller Dave Pickerell has created a one-of-a-kind rye that displays a bold, complex aroma of orange peel, ginger, nutmeg, clove and other baking spices that are complemented by notes of charred oak, caramel and a hint of gingerbread. Full bodied and rich on the palate, sweet, warming notes of caramel and vanilla are followed by rye, spice and mint flavors, which blend seamlessly into butterscotch and dark chocolate on the long, crisp finish. Consider yourself lucky if you are able to find a bottle, especially if you're a fan of rye whiskey; we have trouble keeping this stuff on our shelf even with a rather high price tag.

FUN FACT: On the farm in Vermont where they bottle this fine rye whiskey, they also raise pigs. Yes, they have pigs, and not just any pigs. They raise Mangalitsas—a rare breed from the Carpathian Mountains originally bred by the Hungarian royalty to weather the harsh winters and yield delicious (and surprisingly healthy) marbled fat.

VARIETY/STYLE: Rye

BARREL TYPE: American Oak

AGE: 12½ years

ORIGIN: Vermont

BOTTLE: 750 ml, cork top

ALCOHOL: 67%

PROOF: 134

PRICE: high-range

RELATED: Templeton, Masterson's, Michter's, Dad's Hat, High West

PROPELLERS: !!!!!!

WhistlePig LLC, 2139 Quiet Valley Rd., Shoreham, VT 05770, (802) 897-7700, www.whistlepigwhiskey.com

COMMENTS FROM THE BARTENDER:

ANNIE: A delicate balance of flavor that work well together. Spicy rye kick and wonderful vanillas from the oak.

JEFF: Very good deep burn, nice and chewy, spicy wood chips and a great finish.

JOHN: Well dog my cats, we got something here, boys! No need for lengthy descriptions here, just order it.

BRANDON: This has a rich oily flavor and a big burn that screams quality product. This little taster is not enough, more, please.

WHISTLE PIG TRIPLE ONE

SUMMARY: WhistlePig "Triple One" takes the standard rye release and adds a year to the age along with 11 proof more to the mix. The bigger, bolder, and older companion to 100/100, it was also selected as one of the best whiskeys in the world for 2013. Aged 11 years and bottled at 111 proof, it is a powerful spirit in extremely limited quantities. With such scarcity, this truly is a collector's item. The taste has a strong sense of spice at first but eases off with ginger backed by intense wood notes. Triple One has a complex nose of oak, caramel, smoke and vanilla that leads to a bold, spicy palate boasting layers of clove, mint, allspice and ginger. Notes of caramel, butterscotch and vanilla linger through the lasting finish. High rye, high proof and high price. Go out and splurge, as this rye is worth every penny.

FUN FACT: The Triple One (as the 11 year is called) is the first limited release by the distillery.

VARIETY/STYLE: Rye

BARREL TYPE: American Oak

AGE: 11 years

ORIGIN: Vermont

BOTTLE: 750 ml, cork top

ALCOHOL: 55.5%

PROOF: 111

PRICE: high-range

RELATED: Templeton, Michter's, Jefferson's, High West, Masterson's, Dad's Hat

PROPELLERS: !!!!

WhistlePig LLC, 2139 Quiet Valley Rd., Shoreham, VT 05770, (802) 897-7700, www.whistlepigwhiskey.com

COMMENTS FROM THE BARTENDER:

ANNIE: Sweet fruit. This tastes like grape juice with a fire behind it.

JEFF: Very complex, none of fruit. Flavors of fruit, cane, plum and grape. Bit of a burn that may be too much for some.

JOHN: Nice burn, kind of fruity with a spicy finish. Dark fruit flavors.

BRANDON: I really get a lot of sugar cane on the nose, like rum. It's definitely a high-proof, spicy rye that numbed my tongue. Look for a warning label.

WILD TURKEY 101 KENTUCKY STRAIGHT RYE WHISKEY

SUMMARY: Rye is becoming very popular these days with people falling in love with stories of early American whiskey made when rye was the grain of choice. Wild Turkey Rye is often overlooked by this new breed of adventurous rye drinkers simply because it is Wild Turkey, and everyone has tried the bourbon and assumes its rye can't be much different. Well, they are not far off. Wild Turkey uses a good amount of rye in their bourbon mix. That being said, their rye makes for a great mixer, at a great price. Try it in a Mule.

FUN FACT: In 1940, Wild Turkey got its name from a distillery executive who was inspired while hunting turkey.

VARIETY/STYLE: Rye

BARREL TYPE: New American Oak

AGE: 4 to 5 years

ORIGIN: Kentucky

BOTTLE: 1 liter, cork

ALCOHOL: 50.5%

PROOF: 101

PRICE: low-range

RELATED: Bulleit, Old Overholt, James E. Pepper 1776, Russell's Reserve, Journeyman Ravenswood

PROPELLERS: !!!!

Austin, Nichols Distilling Co., 1535 Tyrone Road, Lawrenceburg, KY 40342, wildturkey@qulitycustomercare.com, www.wildturkey.com

COMMENTS FROM THE BARTENDER:

ANNIE: Almost nonexistent nose. Tropical fruits! Weird! Super complex and tasty: slightly sweet, pretty smooth. I'm sold!

JEFF: Easy drinking whiskey. Nothing you need to run out and try.

JOHN: It's so hot. I get heat and spice from this. It also coats your tongue. Very clean finish with a sweet aftertaste.

BRANDON: Complex sweetness on the nose; sweet, smooth burn that I could drink all day—well, maybe with a splash.

WILLETT FAMILY ESTATE BOTTLED RYE

SUMMARY: The Willett Distillery released its first batch of production in 1937. It yielded 30 barrels and was produced using a charged beer still. Times have certainly changed since then, but one thing is for sure: rye was the whiskey of choice for many then, and it's rapidly becoming that way again. This is a rye-drinker's rye. When our guests sit down, stretch their arms, crack their knuckles and say (as they smile from ear to ear, glancing over the selection of 900 whiskeys), "Tonight I'd like a good rye," the Willett 4 Year is often the bottle we suggest.

FUN FACT: At one time A. L. "Thompson" Willett was the president of the Kentucky Distillers Association.

VARIETY/STYLE: Rye

BARREL TYPE: New American Oak

AGE: 4 years

ORIGIN: Kentucky

BOTTLE: 750 ml, cork top

ALCOHOL: 55%

PROOF: 110

PRICE: high-range

RELATED: Masterson's, Sazerac, Michter's, Redemption, High West

PROPELLERS: !!!!!

Kentucky Bourbon Distillers, 1869 Loretto Road, Bardstown, KY 40004, (502) 348-0899, kentuckybourbon@bardstown.com, www.kentuckybourbonwhiskey.com

COMMENTS FROM THE BARTENDER:

ANNIE: Sweet grains, also peaches and cinnamon. This one is layered and delicious. Doesn't burn too much and isn't too sweet.

JEFF: A blast of heat and rye spice made me squint, but the finish was awesome.

JOHN: For me this is kind of too hot. It is sweet and spicy. The longer the aftertaste, the better.

BRANDON: I was not expecting something so full-bodied. This one is a little malty but finishes long and tastes like fresh rye bread.

CANADIAN

Sweet and smooth, crisp and clean, refreshing like velvet on the palate. These are the most common remarks made by our guests after their first few sips of Canadian whiskey. Yes, Canadian whiskeys are typically very easy to drink.

Canadian whiskeys are blended whiskeys that don't have the same strict mash bill requirements as those in the States do. It's a common misconception that Canadian whiskey is made primarily from rye, but in reality, most use a large percentage of corn spirits in their blend. The whiskey must be made in Canada, and aged for at least three years in wooden barrels. The final product must contain at least 40% alcohol by volume. Where things get a little loose compared to the States is that the barrels can be new or used, and flavorings, such as caramel, can be added.

Canadian whiskey skyrocketed in popularity during Prohibition. It was smuggled across the border into the speakeasies, and today, consumption of Canadian whiskey is stronger than ever. Have you ever seen a bar without a bottle of Crown Royal sitting around somewhere? Many of our whiskeys from the north share similar flavor profiles, and it was easy for the bartenders to pick them out. However, there are a few that are really raising the bar through quality and craftsmanship, and we enjoy offering them to our guests as an alternative to their usual elixir.

In general, Canadian whiskeys are perfect for mixing your favorite cocktails, and we certainly found a few that easily stand on their own. We hope this chapter entices you to indulge in some wonderful whiskey from our neighbors to the north.

8 SECONDS BLACK 8 YEAR OLD

SUMMARY: Eight seconds on a bull is very hard to take; eight seconds with this eight-year blended Canadian whiskey is easy. With a cowboy, rodeo, hard-working, rough-and-tough image very similar to Hood River's Pendleton brand, you may be expecting a whiskey that has those kinds of flavors. The reality is 8 Seconds 8 Year is very mild. We did prefer it over the younger version bearing the same name from Frank-Lin Distillers. The extra time in the barrel adds some much-needed flavor notes, but it's hard to convince anyone to try any other Canadian whiskey than Crown, at least here in Southern California so far from the Canadian border. In the world of Canadian whiskey, 8 Seconds 8 Year can hang. It's worth a shot, especially for the price.

FUN FACT: Eight seconds is the amount of time a cowboy needs to ride the bull or bronco before the bell rings, signaling the end of the ride.

VARIETY/STYLE: Canadian

BARREL TYPE: Oak

AGE: 8 years

ORIGIN: Canada

BOTTLE: 750 ml, cork top

ALCOHOL: 40%

PROOF: 80

PRICE: mid-range

RELATED: Black Velvet, Crown Reserve, Forty Creek, Caribou Crossing, Canadian Mist

PROPELLERS: !!!

Frank-Lin Distillers, 2455 Huntington Drive, Fairfield, CA 94533, (707) 437-1264, www.8secondswhisky.com

COMMENTS FROM THE BARTENDER:

ANNIE: Lots of vanilla on the nose with some very light toffee and caramel. Subtle pepper finish. Another good sip and bake (cookies) whiskey.

JEFF: Great color, but the sweet and spicy nose is misleading. I'd be hesitant to recommend this.

JOHN: John no like this. It tastes like water.

BRANDON: This one is really rich and sweet. It finishes peppery, but it tastes better as it fades out. Honestly, not my style.

8 SECONDS PREMIUM BLENDED CANADIAN WHISKY

SUMMARY: 8 Seconds is a blended Canadian whiskey. It's a new whiskey from Frank-Lin Distillers, which has been a bottler and producer of distilled spirits since 1966 and is currently operating out of their new facility in Fairfield, California. The whiskey comes from an unknown source in Canada. The brand is marketed with slogans and images of cowboys and cowgirls (browse their website for images of a bikini bull-riding event), which may lead you to believe it's a real ass-kicker. This Canadian juice, however, is very mild, which makes it very hard for us to sell it here in Mission Hills, San Diego. For one thing, there's not much of a rodeo scene here, and there are just too many other well-known Canadian brands that are picked over it.

FUN FACT: The slogan for the 8 Seconds brands is "Ride 'em hard and drink 'em smooth."

VARIETY/STYLE: Canadian

BARREL TYPE: N/A

AGE: N/A

ORIGIN: Canada

BOTTLE: 750 ml, cork top

ALCOHOL: 40%

PROOF: 80

PRICE: low-range

RELATED: Caribou Crossing, Canadian Mist, Seagram's VO, Crown Royal, Black Velvet

PROPELLERS: !!

Frank-Lin Distillers, 2455 Huntington Drive, Fairfield, CA 94533, (707) 437-1264, www.8secondswhisky.com

COMMENTS FROM THE BARTENDER:

ANNIE: Sweet nose. Very mild fruit and spice, but very tame, too tame. Let me guess—Canadian blended?

JEFF: Nose has some spicy peppery aromas, but the flavor profile is very mild. Subtle raisin and nut flavors.

JOHN: Okay, here it is . . . I like it but come on, why so mild? Great first-time whiskey. Enough said.

BRANDON: This whiskey has a sweet nose. It smells like maple and oatmeal cookies, but the taste is quite different. It's smooth but not anything special.

BLACK VELVET

SUMMARY: Black Velvet was originally called Black Label—the name was changed in the 1940s on a suggestion by Master Distiller Jack Napier. Jack thought the whiskey's velvety smoothness warranted the change. The Black Velvet label has changed hands a few times over the years and has used some great marketing campaigns, most notably its Black Velvet girls, who over the years have include such names as Christy Brinkley, Cybill Shepherd, Kim Alexis, Cheryl Tiegs and currently, Tami Donaldson. The whiskey is indeed like velvet, maybe even a little too smooth for the new wave of whiskey drinkers who seem to be looking for the big spice of American ryes and high-rye bourbons. I can tell you this, however: If someone orders it, I usually smile and strike up a conversation because people who drink it usually have some pretty good stories to tell.

FUN FACT: The brand is #2 in the Canadian market behind #1 Crown Royal.

VARIETY/STYLE: Canadian

BARREL TYPE: Oak

AGE: 3 years

ORIGIN: Canada

BOTTLE: 1 liter, screw cap

ALCOHOL: 40%

PROOF: 80

PRICE: low-range

RELATED: 8 Seconds, Canadian Mist, Pendleton, Canadian Club, Seagram's VO

PROPELLERS: ! !

Constellation Brands, 207 High Point Drive, Building 100, Victor, NY 14564, (585) 218-3600, www.blackvelvetwhiskey.com

COMMENTS FROM THE BARTENDER:

ANNIE: Sweet and watery. Boo water!

JEFF: Very sweet taste of honey, with only a slight scent on the nose I'll be staying away from this one

JOHN: I got some malty sweetness here It's a nice switch. It's got to be a strange blend I like it for the sweetness and no finish.

BRANDON: Ahh, sweet summer rain, almost like a flavored whiskey.

CAMPBELL & COOPER CANADIAN WHISKY

SUMMARY: Canadian whiskey appeals to the masses because it is smooth and easy to drink and, well . . . it's usually pretty inexpensive. Even premium Canadian whiskeys are affordable compared to a lot of American brands, especially ones with some time in the barrel. Most Canadian whiskey ends up in a mixed cocktail, and this one is no exception.

FUN FACT: Canadians choose to adopt the spelling of "whisky" (without the "e"), like it is in Scotland, whereas most American distillers choose the Irish spelling with the "e."

VARIETY/STYLE: Canadian

BARREL TYPE: N/A

AGE: N/A

ORIGIN: Canada

BOTTLE: 750 ml, cork top

ALCOHOL: 43.4%

PROOF: 86.8

PRICE: mid-range

RELATED: Black Velvet, Crown Royal, Canadian Club, Caribou Crossing, Canadian Mist

PROPELLERS: !

Frank-Lin Distillers, 2455 Hunting Drive, Fairfield, CA 94533, (707) 437-1264, www.frank-lin.com

COMMENTS FROM THE BARTENDER:

ANNIE: Some vanilla and corn notes, but overall light and crisp. Seems very young.

JEFF: Very light and easy to drink Not a lot of flavor, even kind of sour. Strange blend

JOHN: This is like watered-down whiskey. Not trying to be mean, it's just super light.

BRANDON: With bourbon, rye and high-rye bourbons in such demand today, I find it hard to recommend this style. There may be a time and place for this, but it lacks the characteristics of my favorite whiskeys.

CANADIAN CLUB

SUMMARY: Canadian Club, or "CC," is our second most popular selling Canadian whiskey behind Crown Royal. The brand has been around since 1858. The first Canadian Club distillery was founded in Walkerville, Ontario, by Hiram Walker. The brand gained its popularity in the States due to the fact that it was sold exclusively in the finer gentlemen's clubs and became known as "club whiskey." Its popularity grew so big that it started to affect American bourbon sales, so the U.S. government forced all Canadian distillers to put the country of origin on the label. And so the whiskey became Canadian Club. CC has stood the test of time, and today is produced by Beam Suntory Inc. We rarely get a call for this on the rocks or straight, nor would we recommend it. But if you're looking for a light night out, the stuff is excellent with ginger ale and a lime.

FUN FACT: Al Capone was said to have smuggled thousands of cases of CC from Canada into the States during Prohibition.

VARIETY/STYLE: Canadian

BARREL TYPE: N/A

AGE: N/A

ORIGIN: Canada

BOTTLE: 750 ml, screw cap

ALCOHOL: 40%

PROOF: 80

PRICE: low-range

RELATED: Seagram's VO, Forty Creek, Crown Royal, Black Velvet, Caribou Crossing

PROPELLERS: ! !

Beam Suntory Inc., 222 W Merchandise Mart Plaza, Chicago, IL 60654, (312) 964-6999, info@jimbeam.com, www.jimbeam.com

COMMENTS FROM THE BARTENDER:

ANNIE: No nose on this one. No burn. This is almost like sugar-water. I need a little more substance to my whiskey. But it kind of tasted like toasted marshmallows, and I like that.

JEFF: Not for me. I need more than just brown sugar in my whiskey.

JOHN: Sweet sipping juice. Kind of flat, but would mix a refreshing cocktail for sure.

BRANDON: Here's a real sweet whiskey all around. It really just tastes like walking through a canyon in the rain. Too much fennel and anise for me.

CANADIAN MIST

SUMMARY: It's hard to recommend this whiskey because all I can picture when I hear the name is a cruise ship full of seniors all wearing white, playing shuffleboard and sipping whiskey. Why I have this image I don't know, but I know that I'm not alone. This whiskey is distilled in Ontario under the watchful eye of Master Distiller Harold Ferguson and contains a mash bill of corn, rye and malted barley. The juice is triple distilled, which most certainly accounts for its ultra-smoothness. It spends some time in charred oak barrels, but unfortunately the barrel flavors are hardly noticeable. However, this, like a lot of other Canadian whiskeys, would make a great Sunday brunch cocktail mixer: light, fresh and clean.

FUN FACT: Canadian Mist is among the 10 highest-rated Canadian whiskeys on the market and won Double Gold in 2009 at the San Francisco World Spirits Competition.

VARIETY/STYLE: Canadian

BARREL TYPE: Charred White Oak

AGE: N/A

ORIGIN: Canada

BOTTLE: 1 liter, screw cap

ALCOHOL: 40%

PROOF: 80

PRICE: low-range

RELATED: Crown, 8 Seconds, Black Velvet, Rich and Rare, Seagram's VO

PROPELLERS: !

Brown-Forman, 850 Dixie Highway, Louisville, KY 40210, (502) 585-1100, brown-forman@b-f.com, www.brown-forman.com

COMMENTS FROM THE BARTENDER:

ANNIE: Sweet and super clean. Almost tasteless. Whiskey water, anyone?

JEFF: Almost nothing on the nose. Very mild flavors. Brunch mixer for sure.

JOHN: Very plain and mild. I thought for a minute I was getting some spice, but it is pretty clean.

BRANDON: Sweet, mild whiskey that doesn't really have anything fancy going on. I suspect this came from the well.

CARIBOU CROSSING SINGLE BARREL CANADIAN WHISKY

SUMMARY: Caribou Crossing is a solid Canadian whiskey that comes in an attractive bottle with a solid metal maple leaf cork. The price is a little higher than some of its competitors sitting just down the shelf doing their best to get picked. The fact that it's a single barrel seems to help justify the price somewhat. Most guests who know Canadian whiskey always say, "Oh, ya, that's good," when we offer it up as one of our premium Canadian whiskeys. So it may come down to: Do you like Canadian whiskey in general? If you do, then we recommend Caribou Crossing.

FUN FACT: Caribou Crossing is the first single barrel Canadian whiskey produced by a major whiskey company since the nineteenth century.

VARIETY/STYLE: Canadian

BARREL TYPE: N/A

AGE: N/A

ORIGIN: Canada

BOTTLE: 750 ml, cork top

ALCOHOL: 40%

PROOF: 80

PRICE: mid-range

RELATED: Forty Creek, Crown Reserve, 8 Seconds 8 Year, Pendleton, Wiser's

PROPELLERS: ⚙⚙

Sazerac Company, 3850 N. Causeway Boulevard, Suite 1695, Metairie, LA 70002, (504) 831-9450, info@sazeraz.com, www.sazerac.com

COMMENTS FROM THE BARTENDER:

ANNIE: Some toasted marshmallows and cream flavors that are nice but overall very light.

JEFF: Very smooth with a little rye spice. Some fruit flavors like tangerine and vanilla waffles, but I dug deep for those.

JOHN: Nothing to report here. I honestly have nothing to write. There is no whiskey in my whiskey.

BRANDON: Looks like whiskey, smells like alcohol and it tastes like alcohol.

CROWN ROYAL

SUMMARY: Crown Royal was introduced in 1939 by Samuel Bronfman, president of Seagram. It was a tribute to the royal visit of King George VI and his wife Queen Elizabeth. This is one of the most beloved whiskeys in the world and a must-have for any bar. It truly is the essence of Canadian whiskey. It's sweet, rich and buttery. If any of those adjectives sound good to you and you haven't tried Crown yet, you may have just found your favorite whiskey. If your brand new to whiskey and maybe want to start with a cocktail, look no further than a Crown and Coke. We're giving Crown a solid rating because it's simply one of our bestselling brands.

FUN FACT: Crown Royal is the top-selling Canadian whiskey in the U.S.

VARIETY/STYLE: Canadian

BARREL TYPE: Oak

AGE: N/A

ORIGIN: Canada

BOTTLE: 1 liter, screw cap

ALCOHOL: 40%

PROOF: 80

PRICE: mid-range

RELATED: Caribou Crossing, Canadian Mist, Forty Creek, Canadian Club

PROPELLERS: ⚙⚙⚙⚙

Diagio North America, 801 Main Ave., Norwalk, CT 06851, (646) 223-2000, www.diageo.com

COMMENTS FROM THE BARTENDER:

ANNIE: Almost slightly gingery. No stand-out qualities.

JEFF: Another sweet whiskey. This one uses vanilla and maple notes. Still a bit too sweet though. Mix it if you're going to drink it.

JOHN: I like how buttery this is. No burn at all, just buttery sweetness. Great aftertaste.

BRANDON: This is your average sweet whiskey. Reminiscent of cake batter; it isn't the whiskey you wanted but the whiskey you settled for.

CROWN ROYAL BLACK

SUMMARY: Crown Black is the whiskey we recommend out of the line of the Crown products. There's no arguing the popularity of the standard Crown Royal, but to us the Black is just a little more exiting. The main reason, and what makes it different than the original, is the higher alcohol and deeper, darker color. It has all the things you like about Crown but with slightly sharper teeth.

FUN FACT: Crown Royal comes in a signature velvet-like bag that you often see bartenders carrying their belongings in. Next time you go to your local watering hole, ask your bartender for one. If their bar is anything like ours, there should be dozens of them lying around.

VARIETY/STYLE: Canadian

BARREL TYPE: Oak

AGE: N/A

ORIGIN: Canada

BOTTLE: 1 liter, screw cap

ALCOHOL: 45%

PROOF: 90

PRICE: mid-range

RELATED: Canadian Club, 8 Seconds, Pendleton, Seagram's VO, Back Velvet

PROPELLERS: !!! !!! !!!

Diageo North America, 801 Main Ave., Norwalk, CT 06851, (646) 223-2000, www.diageo.com

COMMENTS FROM THE BARTENDER:

ANNIE: Mild flavors of caramel and cereal, like cornflakes, sort of plain but easy to drink.

JEFF: Full of maple and caramel flavors. Almost like a Sugar Daddy, but without the sweetness.

JOHN: Nice and sweet with a slight bite. I would like this in an Old Fashioned. It's got that zest that I like.

BRANDON: Sweet and grainy with a slight kick. Pretty simple other than that.

CROWN ROYAL SPECIAL RESERVE

SUMMARY: Crown Royal Special Reserve was introduced in 1992. The Reserve refers to the longer aging time than standard Crown. Other than that the whiskeys are very similar. If you already like Crown, you will love the maple sweetness that this one offers. The bartenders seem to think it's not worth the price increase and that there are some better Canadian whiskeys to sip on for your hard-earned dollars.

FUN FACT: Crown Royal was only available in Canada until 1964.

VARIETY/STYLE: Canadian

BARREL TYPE: Oak

AGE: N/A

ORIGIN: Canada

BOTTLE: 750 ml, screw cap

ALCOHOL: 40%

PROOF: 80

PRICE: mid-range

RELATED: Seagram's VO, Canadian Mist, Caribou Crossing, Canadian Club

Diageo North America, 801 Main Ave., Norwalk, CT 06851, (646) 223-2000, www.diageo.com

PROPELLERS: !! !!

COMMENTS FROM THE BARTENDER:

ANNIE: I always appreciate a little spice and cinnamon; I've had worse.

JEFF: It has a balance of spice and sweetness, just not a lot of either. Not bad, but it needs more flavor.

JOHN: Very mild burn with light sugars. I could drink this—if I had no other whiskey.

BRANDON: Ginger and cinnamon sticks with some wood chips. If the flavor were bigger this would be great, seems young.

CROWN ROYAL XO

SUMMARY: Crown Royal is a brand that is owned by Diageo and is produced at their plant on the shores of Lake Winnipeg in Manitoba, Canada. The juice produced here is stored in two million barrels, in 46 warehouses, spread out over five acres of land. The Crown Royal XO was introduced in January 2014 in an effort to break into a more premium category of whiskeys. The whiskey is finished in Cognac casks said to be from the French Limousin Forest. We were excited to try this new product as soon as it hit our shelves, but after the gang saw what they had blind tasted, they were let down. The whiskey really didn't pick up much flavor from the extra finishing; maybe the barrels were too old or overused. Maybe the Crown needed a little more time in them. Either way, we were expecting more.

FUN FACT: According to Impact Data Bank, Crown Royal distributed 4.3 million cases of whiskey in 2013.

VARIETY/STYLE: Canadian

BARREL TYPE: Oak

AGE: N/A

ORIGIN: Canada

BOTTLE: 750 ml, screw cap

ALCOHOL: 40%

PROOF: 80

PRICE: mid-range

RELATED: Caribou Crossing, Forty Creek, Wister's, Pendleton

Diageo North America, 801 Main Ave., Norwalk, CT 06851, (646) 223-2000, www.diageo.com

PROPELLERS:

COMMENTS FROM THE BARTENDER:

ANNIE: Smells mild and it tastes mild too. Fairly sweet and no bite. Pretty wimpy—bust this out for your weenie friends.

JEFF: There is nothing that really stands out in this whiskey. Both the nose and the taste are very mild. Got a little dried fruit, but not enough to distinguish which fruits.

JOHN: Very mild and blah. It has a funky smell and no bite.

BRANDON: This tastes like your average whiskey, nothing really stands out. It's very dry on the palate. It's like it wants to play but isn't allowed out of the house.

FORTY CREEK BARREL SELECT

SUMMARY: John Hall started making Forty Creek whiskey in 1992. No stranger to the spirits world, John is the owner of Kittling Ridge Wine and Spirits and has over 20 years' experience as a winemaker. His Forty Creek Barrel Select is a premium Canadian whiskey made from a blend of rye, barley and corn. To highlight the best characteristics of each grain, they are distilled separately in a copper pot still and then aged in new American oak barrels with different degrees of char. Forty Creek Barrel Select takes the aging process one step further by aging the whiskey another six months in sherry cask barrels to achieve a silky smooth finish. The extra aging really shows with some very unique flavors. It's nice to see a Canadian whiskey maker with such passion. Forty Creek is a must-have in your Canadian whiskey collection.

FUN FACT: John Hall was awarded Pioneer of the Year in 2007 for his innovative ideas for producing whiskey.

VARIETY/STYLE: Canadian

BARREL TYPE: New American Oak / Sherry Casks

AGE: N/A

ORIGIN: Canada

BOTTLE: 750 ml, screw cap

ALCOHOL: 40%

PROOF: 80

PRICE: mid-range

RELATED: Canadian Club, Seagram's VO, Crown Royal, Black Velvet, 8 Seconds

Forty Creek Distillery, 297 South Service Road, Grimsby, Ontario, Canada L3M 1Y6, (800) 694-6798, comments@fortycreekcreekwhiskey.com, www.fortycreekwhiskey.com

PROPELLERS:

COMMENTS FROM THE BARTENDER:

ANNIE: Vanilla and nutmeg, kind of oaky and sweet. Smooth with a slow, lasting burn. Yum!

JEFF: A buttery vanilla flavor that coats the tongue with a sweet taste.

JOHN: Man, this is awesome! Nice burn. Sweet! The total package!

BRANDON: Here's one that's a little different! It smells sweet and woody, but that's not exactly how it tastes. It's very winey and sort of oily. You can feel it coat your tongue. Take this neat for a unique taste.

FORTY CREEK DOUBLE BARREL RESERVE

SUMMARY: In 1992, John Hall set out to enhance the heritage of Canadian whiskey. The Canadian crafts-manship seems to have suffered over the years with distillery closings and consolidations. Forty Creek aims to change that, first by aging each individual grain in its own special charred barrel. They are then blended and put into "seasoned," or used, Kentucky bourbon barrels to hang out together for a while and take on the subtle qualities offered by the bourbon barrels. John Hall's craftsmanship shines through in his whiskeys, and the guest appreciates it when we explain the process by which the stuff is made. If you're looking to try a Canadian brand, we recommend this one, especially their Barrel Select.

FUN FACT: John Hall is the only independent whiskey maker in Ontario.

VARIETY/STYLE: Canadian

BARREL TYPE: New American White Oak

AGE: N/A

ORIGIN: Canada

BOTTLE: 750 ml, screw cap

ALCOHOL: 40%

PROOF: 80

PRICE: high-range

RELATED: Crown Reserve, Canadian Mist, Caribou Crossing, Wiser's Deluxe, Pendleton

PROPELLERS: ♨♨♨♨

Forty Creek Distillery, 297 South Service Road, Grimsby, Ontario, Canada L3M 1Y6, (800) 694-6798, comments@fortycreekwhiskey.com, www.fortycreekwhiskey.com

COMMENTS FROM THE BARTENDER:

ANNIE: Sweet and gingery. This would make a delicious Manhattan or Old Fashioned. It goes down super easy with a pleasant, warming burn.

JEFF: Vanilla and nutty with almost a little butterscotch. Smooth and sweet, but feels thin. I'd mix it before letting it slide down my throat.

JOHN: Not a fan. This whiskey leaves a bad taste in my mouth, like dirt and leaves.

BRANDON: It smells so tasty with just a touch of crème and old wood. It kind of tastes like an old attic, too . . .

HIRSCH BLENDED CANADIAN RYE

SUMMARY: Canadian whiskeys are typically smoother and lighter than their cousins below the border, and sometimes that can be a good thing, such as in the case for this Canadian rye by Hirsch. The whiskey is sourced from the Glendora distillery on Cape Breton Island, Nova Scotia. The rye is double distilled to smooth things out, and the second time around it's through a pot still. Even though it spends only three years in the oak barrel, the flavors are present. This is a great whiskey to order if you're thinking about taking your taste buds on a trip up to Canada.

FUN FACT: Hirsch Canadian Rye is made from 100% rye.

VARIETY/STYLE: Canadian Rye

BARREL TYPE: Oak

AGE: 3 years

ORIGIN: Canada

BOTTLE: 750 ml, cork top

ALCOHOL: 43%

PROOF: 86

PRICE: mid-range

RELATED: Pendleton, Canadian Club, Crown Royal, Seagram's VO, Caribou Crossing

PROPELLERS: ♨♨♨♨

Priess Imports/Anchor Brewers and Distillers, 1705 Mariposa Street, San Francisco, CA 94107, (415) 863-8350, Info@anchorsf.com, www.anchordistillery.com

COMMENTS FROM THE BARTENDER:

ANNIE: Tastes like cereal with a kick! I'd rather have this for breakfast.

JEFF: Sweet and soft on the nose. Sweet honey coating on the tongue, no bite. Simple and pleasant.

JOHN: This reminds me of watered-down Honey Combs cereal. This is too light for me to recommend with a straight face.

BRANDON: I know it's Canadian and it smells sweet and roast-y, but I like it, eh!

J. P. WISER'S 18 YEAR OLD

SUMMARY: Okay, now we're talking: some Canadian comfort whiskey. This takes you back to a simpler time, coming in from working the farm to find fresh-baked apple pie cooling on the windowsill. Roll all that up and put it in a bottle, and you have Wiser's 18 Year blended Canadian whiskey. They say that blending whiskey is an art, and we appreciate the artists behind the scenes at Wiser's for this 18 Year whiskey. When guests are inquiring about Canadian juice, this is one of the few we recommend.

FUN FACT: Hiram Walker is the only "grain to glass" operation in Canada and boasts the largest distillery capacity in North America.

VARIETY/STYLE: Canadian

BARREL TYPE: Oak

AGE: 18 years

ORIGIN: Canada

BOTTLE: 750 ml, cork top

ALCOHOL: 40%

PROOF: 80

PRICE: high-range

RELATED: Crown Royal Reserve, Royal Canadian, Caribou Crossing, Forty Creek, Pendleton

PROPELLERS: !!!!

Pernod Ricard, 250 Park Avenue, New York, NY 10177, (212) 372-5400, www.pernodricardusa.com **Producer:** Hiram Walker and Sons Limited, 2072 Riverside East, Windsor, Ontario N8Y 4S5, Canada, (519) 254-5171, www.corby.ca

COMMENTS FROM THE BARTENDER:

ANNIE: There is some weird taste that I can't put my finger on. Slightly smoky and a little maple, but that weird taste is indefinable for me.

JEFF: Sawdust, tobacco and fruit notes make for an interesting taste. Also found a little butterscotch on the nose. I'd need to give this a second chance to figure out if I like it.

JOHN: Okay, now we're talking. Apples and wood, light but enough going on to keep my interest. Shake this ice cold in a martini.

BRANDON: How 'bout some sweet honey-baked apples!? I've come to be able to recognize Canadian whiskey, and this is among the best. Try adding some water for a velvety finish.

J. P. WISER'S RYE

SUMMARY: J. P. Wiser started his whiskey company in the 1800s. He was known as a man who would not be rushed. He was quoted as saying, "Quality is something you just can't rush. Horses should hurry; whiskey should take its time." Today the whiskey is produced the same way Mr. Wiser had envisioned, handmade using traditional methods. Wiser's is one of our favorite Canadian whiskeys, especially the 18 Year. This rye, however, is a tough sell. There are just too many good American ryes to spend your hard-earned dollar on. The usual flavor suspects are here—caramel, toffee and a spicy rye kick—but they're just not strong enough for us to recommend it over its shelf mates.

FUN FACT: Wiser's ambition was simply to produce whiskey "that pleases the nose, tongue, and eye."

VARIETY/STYLE: Canadian Rye

BARREL TYPE: Oak

AGE: N/A

ORIGIN: Canada

BOTTLE: 1 liter, screw cap

ALCOHOL: 40%

PROOF: 80

PRICE: mid-range

RELATED: Pendleton, Jefferson's, Forty Creek, Masterson's, Bulleit

PROPELLERS: !!

Pernod Ricard, 250 Park Avenue, New York, NY 10177, (212) 372-5400, www.pernodricardusa.com **Producer:** Hiram Walker and Sons Limited, 2072 Riverside East, Windsor, Ontario N8Y 4S5, Canada, (519) 254-5171, www.corby.ca

COMMENTS FROM THE BARTENDER:

ANNIE: Some toffee flavors and light molasses. Quick spice finish gone in a flash. Wish the spice could have lingered.

JEFF: Not too much is given away on the nose. Some toasted oats and a pinch of spice, but not much is going on.

JOHN: This is another whiskey that tastes like Christmas. Man, I used to like Christmas.

BRANDON: With so many good whiskeys to pick from, I'm afraid this bottle neck will never have my fingers wrapped around it. It's just too light.

PENDLETON 1910 CANADIAN RYE WHISKY

SUMMARY: Hood River Distillers was founded in 1934 and is the Pacific Northwest's largest and oldest importer, producer, bottler and marketer of distilled spirits. Staying true to its rough and tough cowboy image, this 12-year Canadian rye comes in a beautiful bottle with unique and intricately embossed detailing reminiscent of tooling on a saddle. The 100% rye will take you on a wild ride of sweet, then quickly buck your palate to spice. Give this one eight seconds, and I'll bet you'll get back in the saddle again.

FUN FACT: The 1910 name pays homage to the first ever Pendleton Roundup, one of the most prestigious rodeos in the world.

VARIETY/STYLE: Canadian Rye

BARREL TYPE: Oak

AGE: 12 years

ORIGIN: Canada

BOTTLE: 750 ml, cork top

ALCOHOL: 40%

PROOF: 80

PRICE: mid-range

RELATED: WhistlePig, Jefferson's, Masterson's, Forty Creek, Crown Royal Reserve

Hood River Distillers, 116 3rd Street, Suite 300, Hood River, OR 97031, (541) 386-1588, www.hrdspirits.com

PROPELLERS:

COMMENTS FROM THE BARTENDER:

ANNIE: Smells like maple and vanilla, tastes like a smoked pancake—maybe not as sweet as a pancake. Smoked cornbread with a hint of maple sweetness and cinnamon. Long afterburn.

JEFF: A sweeter rye. The spice doesn't kick in till the finish. Was expecting a little more vanilla since it is extremely noticeable on the nose.

JOHN: Sooooo good! Nice rye spice with a total vanilla expression. Nice burn! Love this.

BRANDON: Rye for sure. Everything a good rye should have. If you Google rye, this is what you should find.

PENDLETON BLENDED CANADIAN WHISKY

SUMMARY: The Pendleton brand was created in 2003 and was born of the rich tradition of the Pendleton Roundup, one of the most prestigious rodeos in the world. The question is whether you need to be as tough as a cowboy to drink it. The bartenders were split with their reviews, but our sales don't lie. It's our third bestselling Canadian whiskey. Not too bad.

FUN FACT: Pendleton whiskey was created to honor the American cowboy and cowgirl and is widely known as "the cowboy whiskey."

VARIETY/STYLE: Canadian

BARREL TYPE: Oak

AGE: N/A

ORIGIN: Canada

BOTTLE: 1 liter, cork top

ALCOHOL: 40%

PROOF: 80

PRICE: mid-range

RELATED: Crown Royal, Caribou Crossing, Alberta Premium, 8 Seconds, Forty Creek

Hood River Distillers, 116 3rd Street, Suite 300, Hood River, OR 97031, (541) 386-1588, www.hrdspirits.com

PROPELLERS:

COMMENTS FROM THE BARTENDER:

ANNIE: Whoa, vanilla! This tastes like cake with a throat burn. Digging it. Maybe some light stone fruit along with the vanilla and maybe some burnt sugar. Mmmm.

JEFF: Lots of burn that fades fast into some pretty solid vanilla and almond.

JOHN: A mixer for sure. May I interest you in a Mule?

BRANDON: What the?! How do they get away with labeling rubbing alcohol as whiskey?!

RICH & RARE

SUMMARY: Rich & Rare is a Canadian whiskey that's distilled, matured and blended in Canada, then shipped to Kentucky where it is bottled by its owner, the Sazerac Company. This is pretty much your basic Canadian whiskey. If you were to try five different whiskeys in a blind taste test, there's no doubt you'd pick this as the Canadian. It's sweet, rich and creamy. Great for a mixer, but we recommend going with their Rich & Rare Reserve offering.

FUN FACT: One thing this whiskey has going for it is the name; guests often order it simply because of that.

VARIETY/STYLE: Canadian

BARREL TYPE: Oak

AGE: N/A

ORIGIN: Canada

BOTTLE: 750 ml, screw cap

ALCOHOL: 40%

PROOF: 80

PRICE: low-range

RELATED: Black Velvet, Campbell & Cooper, Canadian Mist, 8 Seconds, Canadian Club

PROPELLERS:

Sazerac Company, 3850 N. Causeway Boulevard, Suite 1695, Metairie, LA 70002, (504) 831-9450, info@sazeraz.com, www.sazerac.com

COMMENTS FROM THE BARTENDER:

ANNIE: I get a lot of alcohol on the nose, with some hints of maple. It's pretty light and sweet with a mild syrupy flavor. It tastes better than it smells.

JEFF: I was not expecting this smooth sweetness from such an alcohol-y nose. I wish they would tone down the sugar. Then it might actually taste good.

JOHN: I'm a bit surprised that the nose was crazy harsh, but it is so mild. Like, "Canadian" mild. So easy to drink.

BRANDON: Caramel and candy all up in my nose. But to me, it's another whiskey that tastes like nail varnish.

RICH & RARE RESERVE SMALL BATCH

SUMMARY: The Rich & Rare brand has been around a very long time. It was originally produced by the firm Gooderham and Worts, but really became an established brand under the ownership of Hiram Walker. Over the years the whiskey label has had a few different homes—today it's owned by the Sazerac Company. Rich & Rare Reserve is aged in hand-picked oak barrels and bottled at 40% alcohol by volume. The brand was specifically produced for the U.S. market as part of a movement to change the image of Canadian whiskey. The Rich & Rare Reserve has a little more depth than the standard offering, with much-needed rye and oak flavors.

FUN FACT: The bottle is short and square with a gold cap that resembles Canada's #1 selling whiskey, Crown Royal.

STYLE/VARIETY: Canadian

BARREL TYPE: Oak

AGE: N/A

ORIGIN: Canada

BOTTLE: 750 ml, screw cap

ALCOHOL: 40%

PROOF: 80

PRICE: mid-range

RELATED: Caribou Crossing, Crown Royal, Forty Creek, Canadian Club, Royal Canadian

PROPELLERS:

Sazerac Company, 3850 N. Causeway Boulevard, Suite 1695, Metairie, LA 70002, (504) 831-9450, info@sazeraz.com, www.sazerac.com

COMMENTS FROM THE BARTENDER:

ANNIE: Light fruits and no burn. Good for vodka drinkers.

JEFF: Mellow notes of caramel, pepper and a few other spices make this whiskey completely sippable. The drinkability makes it best for introducing your friends to the world of whiskey.

JOHN: It's got that Sunday morning, pancake breakfast thing going on. I had no problem drinking it; it's a bit sweet and tangy.

BRANDON: Honestly, I only really like the aftertaste of some whiskeys. I just want to shoot it and be done.

ROYAL CANADIAN SMALL BATCH CANADIAN WHISKY

SUMMARY: Sazerac Master Blender Drew Mayville came to Buffalo Trace after 23 years with the Seagram's organization. Mayville believes Canadian whiskey is a misunderstood spirit and that single barrel whiskeys like this one will bring Canadian whiskey to a whole new level. Sazerac has a diverse inventory of whiskeys for Drew to choose from, roughly 200,000 barrels. This whiskey is very rich and sweet, like good barbecue, and works well as a mixer

FUN FACT: All the barrels were hand-picked under the watchful eye of Master Blender Drew Mayville.

STYLE/VARIETY: Canadian

BARREL TYPE: Oak

AGE: N/A

ORIGIN: Canada

BOTTLE: 750 ml, cork top

ALCOHOL: 40%

PROOF: 80

PRICE: mid-range

RELATED: Crow Reserve, Forty Creek, Rich & Rare, Caribou Crossing, Black Velvet

Sazerac Co., 3850 N. Causeway Boulevard, Suite 1695, Metaire, LA 70002, (504) 831-9450, www.sazerac.com

PROPELLERS:

COMMENTS FROM THE BARTENDER:

ANNIE: Super light and almost refreshing. It has light, woodsy flavors. It would be good with ginger beer.

JEFF: It's too sweet for me. Thin and light, the sweet tastes overpower other flavors that try to come through.

JOHN: I really enjoy citrus in whiskey and this has just enough for me to okay it. For best results, Dr. John recommends this in a mixer. It's too sweet on its own.

BRANDON: It has a really sweet, citrusy and tangy nose that I really enjoy. It is a bit wine-y and sugary, which makes it stand out among some similar styled whiskeys.

SEAGRAM'S VO CANADIAN WHISKY

SUMMARY: Joseph E. Seagram became a partner in a distillery that was founded in Ontario, Canada, in 1857. He would become sole owner in 1883, with the company becoming Joseph E. Seagram & Sons. After his death, the distillery was acquired by Samuel Bronfman and his company Distillers Corporation Limited. The company was passed through the family to Edgar Bronfman Jr. in the 1980s. Seagram was a true powerhouse company that would sadly be dismantled and sold due to poor business decisions and investments. Today the brand is owned by Diageo and produced at their distillery in Valleyfield, Quebec. The whiskey has a flavor profile that covers everything from pepper and heat to sweet and creamy and can be enjoyed straight if you're in a Canadian whiskey mood. But this whiskey really works its best with a good ginger ale and pinch of lime.

FUN FACT: The dismantling of the Seagram empire resulted in one of the biggest financial losses sustained by a single family.

VARIETY/STYLE: Canadian

BARREL TYPE: N/A

AGE: N/A

ORIGIN: Canada

BOTTLE: 1 liter, screw cap

ALCOHOL: 40%

PROOF: 80

PRICE: low-range

RELATED: Black Velvet, Canadian Club, Crown Royal, Pendleton, Canadian Mist

Diageo North America, 801 Main Avenue, Norwalk, CT 06851, (646) 223-2000, www.diageo.com

PROPELLERS:

COMMENTS FROM THE BARTENDER:

ANNIE: Astringent but it mellows. It reminds me of when I first started bartending. Shout-out to the old men!

JEFF: This is a very mellow whiskey that is very easy to drink. The bad news is this is a very mellow whiskey that is easy to drink.

JOHN: No nose to speak of. A little bit of a bite but mostly sweet, like toffee. It's cool, I'd drink it.

BRANDON: Soft nose, but it tastes a bit like nail polish remover. I'm sure it's a bit smoother, though.

WISER'S DELUXE

SUMMARY: Wiser's Deluxe is their signature brand of Canadian whiskey that was produced at a distillery in Ontario in 1857. In the 1990s, it was the third largest distillery in Canada. Following the death of company leader J. P. Wiser, the brand struggled and was sold. Today, it's produced and bottled at Hiram Walker and Sons in Windsor, Ontario. There are several brands in the Wiser's portfolio, and the Deluxe is probably the one voted most likely to end up in a mixed drink. Spend a couple of bucks more and get their 18 Year offering.

FUN FACT: At one time Wiser's whiskeys were produced under strict Canadian supervision. However, current bottles of Deluxe no longer display the age nor carry the Canadian government supervision note.

VARIETY/STYLE: Canadian

BARREL TYPE: Oak

AGE: 10 years

ORIGIN: Canada

BOTTLE: 750 ml, screw cap

ALCOHOL: 40%

PROOF: 80

PRICE: low-range

RELATED: Black Velvet, Canadian Club, Crown Royal, Campbell & Cooper, Seagram's VO

PROPELLERS:

Pernod Ricard, 250 Park Avenue, New York, NY 10177, (212) 372-5400, www.pernodricardusa.com **Producer:** Hiram Walker and Sons Limited, 2072 Riverside Drive East, Windsor, Ontario, Canada N84 4S5, (519) 254-5171, www.corby.ca

COMMENTS FROM THE BARTENDER:

ANNIE: No nose. Super sweet but not a syrupy sweet. Getting malt and corn. No real burn.

JEFF: Barely any nose, just sweetness. The taste had notes of apricot and peach. Too sweet the whole way through for me, though.

JOHN: Almost Christmas-like flavors. My grandma would love this stuff.

BRANDON: Another whiskey that only gives off the odor of acetone. Do I have to drink it? . . . okay! It tastes like acetone, too. Bleh!

BLENDED/OTHER

Order a whiskey and Coke at the bar down the street and chances are their house whiskey sitting in the well is a blend. Blended whiskeys are much cheaper and easier to produce for the masses. Bar owners love them because the profit margin is very high (you can usually make your money back in about three cocktails). This does not mean that all blended whiskeys are rot gut and should be served up in a paper bag. The truth is, there are some excellent blends out there that are not only great in any classic cocktail but also have incredible flavors due to the fact they don't have to follow the strict rules for production that bourbon and rye do. Many craft distillers are using exciting new techniques for distilling their whiskeys—multigrain combinations combined with aging in various wine and other type barrels, and using old family recipes that have been handed down through the generations. If a distiller wants to produce a blended whiskey with a particular grain type such as rye, wheat or corn, and label it as such, at least 51% of the blend must be of that grain type. As for the other 49%, they have some freedom to play around with ingredients, like unaged grain distillates, neutral spirits and even a pinch of flavoring or a dash of coloring.

We've assembled our crack team of whiskey-drinking bartenders to dig deep and sample their way through this diverse category to help guide you through these good, bad and ugly whiskeys that call this category home. We hope you have as much fun exploring them as we did!

ALASKA OUTLAW WHISKEY

SUMMARY: Alaska Distillery is located in the fertile plain of Alaska's Matanuska Valley in the shadow of Mt. McKinley. They use some of the purest water on earth, water that is collected from glaciers and icebergs harvested in Prince William Sound. They use Alaskan grain, and the whiskey is aged in alder and birch. The flavors from the wood really come through in this blended whiskey. There is no doubt this stuff will warm you up, and that was the goal. Tons of spices and burn, but hang in there, the finish is great! Try this in a "buck" or Moscow Mule.

FUN FACT: Alaska's most notorious outlaw, Soapy Smith, is featured on the label.

VARIETY/STYLE: Blended

BARREL TYPE: Alder and Birch

AGE: 3 years

ORIGIN: Alaska

BOTTLE: 750 ml, cork top

ALCOHOL: 40%

PROOF: 80

PRICE: mid-range

RELATED: Kessler, Clyde May's, Early Times, Sam Houston, Jailers

PROPELLERS:

Alaska Distillery, 1540 Shoreline Drive, Wasilla, AK 99654, (907) 382-6250, toby@alaskadistillery.com, www.alaskadistillery.com

COMMENTS FROM THE BARTENDER:

ANNIE: Smells like bread and maple syrup. French toast anyone? Slightly bitter beginning with a sweet and pretty spicy finish. Black pepper spicy.

JEFF: A lot of pepper and spice on the back end, along with a slight note of smoke. A little too heavy on the spices in my opinion.

JOHN: Wow, this is a real nipple twister! Great mixer for drinks with a spice kick.

BRANDON: The spice and pepper really dominate my palate. Really robust with quite the burn, but the finish and aftertaste are pleasant.

ALIBI AMERICAN WHISKEY

SUMMARY: Alibi is a new blended whiskey that has a very cutting-edge image. Their website makes you want to take a couple shots, grab your glow sticks and hit the clubs. Alibi is meant to be an everyman's whiskey. Drink and be merry, and if you don't like it . . . we don't really care. There's a fine line you walk when you operate a whiskey bar. On the one hand you have the whiskey snobs who want a quiet atmosphere with some Sinatra playing on the juke box, while some of the younger generation want to slam shots and dance the night away with no real concern about how many years the whiskey was in a barrel, just the cost and effect (which is why we refuse to sell a certain cinnamon whiskey). So if Alibi can help bridge that generation gap, then we're all for it. So, shoot, mix or sip away . . . recommended for ages 21 and up.

FUN FACT: In August 2013, Panache Beverages, Inc., acquired a preexisting distillery as a means to manage its own supply chain for its brands.

VARIETY/STYLE: Blended

BARREL TYPE: N/A

AGE: 3 years

ORIGIN: New York

BOTTLE: 750 ml, cork top

ALCOHOL: 45%

PROOF: 90

PRICE: mid-range

RELATED: Sam Houston, Hirsch, Alaska Outlaw, Corsair, Bowen's

PROPELLERS:

Panache Beverage, Inc., 150 Fifth Avenue, 3rd Floor, New York, NY 10011, (646) 480-7479, www.panachespirits.com

COMMENTS FROM THE BARTENDER:

ANNIE: Rich flavors of canned fruits and malt balls, almost like a flavored whiskey.

JEFF: Don't let the soft nose mislead you. This whiskey comes with a lot of flavor: a fairly complex combination of fruit and malt.

JOHN: Big corn and nut flavor with a molasses richness. Can't quite put my finger on this, so I say just shoot it!

BRANDON: This whiskey got my attention. Not with the nose but with the unique taste. It's malty, fruity, corny and smooth. This one deserves another taste!

BEAM'S 8 STAR KENTUCKY WHISKEY

SUMMARY: Beam's 8 Star is a mass-produced natural-grain spirit made from 75% natural spirits and 25% rye. It's cheaper to produce and doesn't have to be aged like a straight bourbon or rye. This makes it very affordable. So if you're planning a party for a group that doesn't really drink too much whiskey and just want a few bottles there just in case, this may work. It sells simply because Beam is on the label, but we highly recommend paying the extra buck or two and getting the standard Jim Beam white label.

FUN FACT: Rectified spirit, also known as natural spirits, is a highly concentrated ethanol that has been purified by means of repeated distillation. This process is called "rectification."

VARIETY/STYLE: Blended

BARREL TYPE: N/A

AGE: N/A

ORIGIN: Kentucky

BOTTLE: 750 ml, screw cap

ALCOHOL: 40%

PROOF: 80

PRICE: low-range

RELATED: Kessler, Kentucky Gentleman, Old Grand-Dad, Early Times, Fleischmann's

PROPELLERS: ⁐

Beam Suntory Inc., 222 W Merchandise Mart Plaza, Chicago, IL 60654, (312) 964-6999, info@jimbeam.com, www.jimbeam.com

COMMENTS FROM THE BARTENDER:

ANNIE: No nose at all. Almost no taste. I would drink this if I hated whiskey and fun.

JEFF: Not worth a second chance. A little grain and caramel but weak.

JOHN: Flat juice with nothing to waste time with. Only chance is a well mixer.

BRANDON: Uhh, okay. This tastes like sour apples. It may need a mash bill revision or to go back in the barrel for a while. I might pour this for you if you aren't tipping at all.

BOWEN'S WHISKEY

SUMMARY: According to the website, proprietor and CEO Wade Bowen met "Old Bud," a fifth-generation moonshiner with a lineage dating back to the American Whiskey Rebellion. The two worked together, and Bowen learned the Bud family craft. Wade continued experimenting with the recipes for years after Bud's passing, and the result is the smoky smooth whiskey he produces today. They start with a 100% corn base and then cut it with proprietarily structured water. But most of the flavor comes from its being aged in reclaimed fire-ravaged oak from the forests of central California. This is a great whiskey to recommend anytime a guest has the word smoke in the description when explaining to you what they like. It has found a welcome home here at the Aero Club.

FUN FACT: Bowen's has a great selection of whiskey cocktails on their website. Try the Smoked Peach: 1½ ounces (45 ml) Bowen's, ½ ounce (15 ml) peach schnapps.

VARIETY/STYLE: Blended

BARREL TYPE: Fire-Ravaged Oak

AGE: N/A

ORIGIN: California

BOTTLE: 1 liter, cork top

ALCOHOL: 45%

PROOF: 90

PRICE: mid-range

RELATED: Hirsch, Heaven Hill, Jailers, Corsair, High West

PROPELLERS: ⁐⁐⁐⁐⁐

Bowen's Spirits Inc., 1901 Mineral Court, Bakersfield, CA 93308, (661) 343-2041, www.bowenswhiskey.com

COMMENTS FROM THE BARTENDER:

ANNIE: I'm getting a good smoky, maple wood flavor. Great recommendation for someone looking for smoky whiskey.

JEFF: The smoke, wood and maple notes bring me back to making breakfast over a campfire while camping.

JOHN: Ah yes, this is another one to add to my list of smoky recommendations. It has some sweeter flavors of maple that peek through as well. This would make an interesting Bloody Mary.

BRANDON: What a unique whiskey! The nose is sweet and smoky. The taste is smooth, but the campfire flavor really takes over. It really feels like sitting around a campfire smoking cigarettes and getting drunk in the desert.

BULLY BOY STRAIGHT AMERICAN WHISKEY

SUMMARY: We had to review this whiskey, Jeremy being from Boston and myself growing up on a farm in Pennsylvania. The story behind this whiskey is an interesting one. Brothers Dave and Will Willis were inspired to make whiskey by their childhood home and fourth generation working family farm. The story goes that the farm had a vault in its basement that was used to store local artisan spirits during Prohibition. Roughly 70 years passed till the vault was rediscovered. Talk about inspiration! The wheels were set in motion and Bully Boy Distillery was born. Their plan for success is pretty simple: hand-produced small batches using high-caliber ingredients. Corn, rye and malted barley come together to create this wicked good straight American whiskey.

FUN FACT: The name is a tribute to "Bully Boy," a favorite farm work horse of Will and Dave's great-grandfather. The word "bully" means superb or wonderful.

VARIETY/STYLE: Blended

BARREL TYPE: New Charred Oak

AGE: N/A

ORIGIN: Massachusetts

BOTTLE: 750 ml, cork

ALCOHOL: 42%

PROOF: 84

PRICE: mid-range

RELATED: Sam Houston, Michter's, Stein, High West, RoughStock

PROPELLERS: !!!!

Bully Boy, 44 Cedric Street, Roxbury, MA 02119, (617) 442-6000, info@bullyboydistillers.com, www.bullyboydistillers.com

COMMENTS FROM THE BARTENDER:

ANNIE: Welcoming sweetness on the nose, cherry, cinnamon and vanilla. Upon a second whiff I even got some citrus. The nose is very close to the flavors on this one, spiced nuts and maple. Good whiskey but it's short-lived, fast finish.

JEFF: The complex nose grabbed my attention but I was kind of let down when the oak flavor covered up just about everything but a bit of rye.

JOHN: This seems like a whiskey that is so close to being great, it's just missing something. Like there's a short in your car stereo and you're one speaker short of rocking out. Maybe some more barrel time.

BRANDON: Nice! I love all the wood and spice! Just the right amount if you ask this guy. I would love this in a Manhattan.

CALVERT EXTRA 100% BLENDED AMERICAN WHISKEY

SUMMARY: This is a great whiskey for mixing cocktails, especially ones that have citrus and fruit flavors. Often overshadowed by Seagram's 7, Calvert is maybe the best mixing whiskey you've never tried. The flavors are very crisp and clean. Ask your bartender to whip you up a Ricky or a Buck. The juice can be enjoyed straight, but if you're used to bourbon or rye, you're gonna feel let down. So let's just call it what it is . . . cocktail whiskey.

FUN FACT: Calvert Extra is a blend of grain-neutral spirits and bourbon.

VARIETY/STYLE: Blended

BARREL TYPE: N/A

AGE: N/A

ORIGIN: Kentucky

BOTTLE: 1 liter, screw cap

ALCOHOL: 40%

PROOF: 80

PRICE: low-range

RELATED: Beam's 8 Star, Kentucky Gentleman, Kessler, Seagram's 7, Sally Times

Luxco Inc., 1000 Clark Avenue, St. Louis, MO 63102, (314) 772-2626, contactus@luxco.com, www.luxco.com

PROPELLERS: !!

COMMENTS FROM THE BARTENDER:

ANNIE: This is a mixing whiskey for sure. Clean, crisp flavors of fruit and candies, but not strong enough to stand on its own.

JEFF: The notes of light fruit, like apple and maybe pear, help smooth out a slightly alcohol taste. There are some spice notes in the front but not long lasting.

JOHN: Very, very mild. Nothing stands out. Hints of vanilla and cherry.

BRANDON: Some sweet and some spice, even an odd sour note. Not for me.

CLYDE MAY'S CONECUH RIDGE ALABAMA STYLE

SUMMARY: The stories behind some of the whiskeys are fascinating: moonshiners up in the mountains and down in the hollers producing illegal whiskey from illegal stills. One of the most famous was notorious Alabama moonshiner Clyde May. Clyde's Alabama-style whiskey was revered by customers as well as local law enforcement. The whiskey is made from corn, barley and rye and is aged in oak barrels. This is a sweet, young sipping whiskey. Sipping whiskey that reminds you of Grandma's kitchen on Thanksgiving. So throw on an old Bill Monroe record, sit back in a rocking chair and enjoy.

FUN FACT: In 2004, it was designated the official state spirit of Alabama by legislative resolution.

VARIETY/STYLE: Blended

BARREL TYPE: Oak

AGE: N/A

ORIGIN: Kentucky

BOTTLE: 750 ml, screw cap

ALCOHOL: 45%

PROOF: 90

PRICE: mid-range

RELATED: Sam Houston, Wasmund's, Jailers, George Dickel, Sam Houston

Conecuh Brands, LLC., 1050 Franklin Avenue, Suite 304, Garden City, NY 11530, www.cmwhiskey.com

PROPELLERS: !!!! !!!!

COMMENTS FROM THE BARTENDER:

ANNIE: This reminds me of Thanksgiving with the family. All the smells and tastes—ahh yes, Thanksgiving with the family. God, I need a drink!

JEFF: Has a sweet cinnamon nose, almost like snickerdoodle cookies. This made the spicy grain taste a surprise. This could grow on me after a few.

JOHN: Nice caramel finish—that's the stand out for this. On the front it's mild spice but then sweet candy.

BRANDON: Smells sweet; reminds me of pecan pie. It's got good spice and a little kick. Just a drop of water made this as smooth as can be.

CORSAIR QUINOA WHISKEY

SUMMARY: Corsair is great about providing tons of information on their labels, and since people often raise an eyebrow when we recommend this, we're glad they do. So here's a quick description from the label: "Quinoa is a South American grain crop grown for its seeds. Quinoa adds an earthy, nutty flavor to the whiskey. Quinoa seeds come in red, white and black varieties. This whiskey uses red and white quinoa grains. It can often be easily malted, as it germinates quickly." Well, that sounds good to us, and definitely good enough to drink on the rocks.

FUN FACT: Quinoa dates back 3,000 years to the Incas. They believed consumption of it increased the stamina of their warriors.

VARIETY/STYLE: Blended

BARREL TYPE: N/A

AGE: N/A

ORIGIN: Tennessee/Kentucky

BOTTLE: 750 ml, cork top

ALCOHOL: 46%

PROOF: 92

PRICE: mid-range

RELATED: RoughStock, Ballast Point, Stein, Koval, High West

Corsair Distillery–Nashville, 1200 Clinton Street #110, Nashville, TN 37203, (615) 200-0320, www.corsairartisan.com
Producer: Corsair Distillery–Bowling Green, 400 Main Street #110, Bowling Green, KY 42101, (270) 904-2021, www.corsairartisan.com

PROPELLERS: !!! !!

COMMENTS FROM THE BARTENDER:

ANNIE: Super smoky and malty sweet. Getting cereal grains but mostly just campfire.

JEFF: I'm getting some barley, clove and spice. Not a big fan of clove, so I'll pass on this one.

JOHN: I'm a fan. There, I said it. It has just enough spice and sweetness, with grains and mild, mild smoke.

BRANDON: Very malty and a bit sweet, like sherry. What a peppery finish, though! It must be a very unique mash bill.

EARLY TIMES KENTUCKY WHISKEY

SUMMARY: Early Times Whiskey dates back to the 1800s, and from 1923 to 1953 it was close to if not the bestselling whiskey in the United States. The label reads "Kentucky Whiskey" instead of straight bourbon because it's aged in used barrels, leaving it a little short of the legal requirements to be a bourbon. In 2010, a new variation became available that does meet the requirements; its label reads "Early Times 354." This whiskey is super easy to drink and often ends up as the house whiskey in a lot of bars. It's frequently used as a mixer, but it can stand on its own straight, especially if you're looking for a cheap, sweet sipper.

FUN FACT: Early Times Mint Julep is the official drink of the Kentucky Derby.

VARIETY/STYLE: Blended

BARREL TYPE: New American Oak

AGE: N/A

ORIGIN: Kentucky

BOTTLE: 1 liter, screw cap

ALCOHOL: 40%

PROOF: 80

PRICE: low-range

RELATED: Jim Beam, Wild Turkey, Fighting Cock, Old Crow, Old Grand-Dad

PROPELLERS:

Brown-Forman, 850 Dixie Highway, Louisville, KY 40210, (502) 858-1100, www.brown-forman.com

COMMENTS FROM THE BARTENDER:

ANNIE: Sweet, malty and no burn. Kind of boring but overall tasty and super smooth and easy to drink.

JEFF: This went down super easy. Sweet with a bit of malt but almost no burn.

JOHN: Easy drinker. Recommend this to someone who is low maintenance, just looking to have a good time.

BRANDON: A little sweet for me, but it's pretty smooth. There's a hint of dry fruit, but the taste doesn't last long. This one might be a shooter.

FLEISCHMANN'S PREFERRED BLENDED WHISKEY

SUMMARY: Fleischmann's Blended Whiskey is a product of Barton Brands, which became part of the Sazerac Company in 2009. This whiskey is your basic house mixer, and that's about the extent of it. It has found a nice, cozy spot on our top shelf, eleven rows high, or, as we refer to it, "the home for lost or unwanted spirits." You see we have to get a ladder to get them down from there, and on a busy Friday, that's just no fun. This is the whiskey you want to recommend to the guy who has to be the center of attention in the bar, shouting over people to get his drink first, but then stiffs you on the tip!

FUN FACT: This whiskey has a mash bill of 75% natural-grain spirits (i.e., vodka).

VARIETY/STYLE: Blended

BARREL TYPE: Oak

AGE: 4 years

ORIGIN: Kentucky

BOTTLE: 750 ml, screw cap

ALCOHOL: 40%

PROOF: 80

PRICE: low-range

RELATED: Seagram's 7, Calvert, Beam's 8 Star, Early Times, Sam Houston

PROPELLERS:

Sazerac Company, 3850 N. Causeway Boulevard, Suite 1695, Metairie, LA 70002, (504) 831-9450, info@sazerac.com, www.sazerac.com

COMMENTS FROM THE BARTENDER:

ANNIE: Earthy and toasty with a slight burnt-molasses flavor. Smooth and pretty tasty but it's a little boring.

JEFF: The caramel comes through from the very first sip. A little bit of spice, but no complexity. Nice taste, but not very interesting.

JOHN: It has a nice spice to it. Definitely a light to medium body. Best for a mixed drink.

BRANDON: My first thought was that I was about to pop a caramel candy cube in my mouth. It just happened to taste like it dropped into rubbing alcohol. But it is smooth.

HEAVEN HILL KENTUCKY BLENDED WHISKEY

SUMMARY: We're big fans of Heaven Hill Distilleries. They produce many great whiskeys, including Elijah Craig, Evan Williams and Rittenhouse. They also make a lot of whiskey for private labels, but those names are under lock and key. Throughout its history the master distillers have been descendants of the "Jim" Beam family. Heaven Hill's Blended Whiskey is one of our most popular. It's often ordered in a mixed cocktail but can be recommended on the rocks with total confidence. Just be aware, it's sweeter than most bourbons or ryes. The label states it's 36 months old with a mash bill of natural-grain spirits and Kentucky straight whiskey. This is a great, inexpensive go-to whiskey.

FUN FACT: Heaven Hill Distilleries is America's largest independent, family-owned and -operated producer and marketer of distilled spirits.

VARIETY/STYLE: Blended

BARREL TYPE: Oak

AGE: 36 months

ORIGIN: Kentucky

BOTTLE: 1 liter, screw cap

ALCOHOL: 40%

PROOF: 80

PRICE: low-range

RELATED: Sam Houston, Early Times, Seagram's 7, Kentucky Gentleman, Beam's 8 Star

PROPELLERS: !!!

Heaven Hill Distilleries, P.O. Box 729, Bardstown, KY 40004, (502) 348-3921, www.heavenhill.com

COMMENTS FROM THE BARTENDER:

ANNIE: So smooth I didn't know it was whiskey.

JEFF: I swear it smells like banana pudding. The flavor is very sweet and smooth, even with hints of cola. Super easy drinker.

JOHN: So mellow! It is so easy to drink! I think I would recommend this to a beginner for sure. At the same time, I like it.

BRANDON: Banana nose but really well balanced. Caramel and nuts, very soft to the touch. This is a fun and easy whiskey.

HIGH WEST BOURYE

SUMMARY: This whiskey is very intriguing due to the fact that it's married with a 10-year-old bourbon with a mash bill of 75% corn, 20% rye and 5% barley malt and a 12-year-old straight rye whiskey that's 95% rye and 5% barley malt and finally a 16-year-old straight rye with 53% rye, 37% corn and 10% malt. Even with the rye note very noticeable, it's quite vibrant, clean and crisp. This whiskey is best enjoyed around the campfire looking up at the Milky Way, but only neat—it's not recommended on ice.

FUN FACT: Bourye is named after the mythical creature the jackalope. It is said to be a creature out of the West that was part rabbit and part antelope. This creature is part of lore tales: cowboys would sing by the fire and the "jackalope" would sing back. They say the best way to catch one is by luring it with whiskey.

VARIETY/STYLE: Blended

BARREL TYPE: New American Oak

AGE: N/A

ORIGIN: Utah

BOTTLE: 750 ml, cork top

ALCOHOL: 46%

PROOF: 92

PRICE: mid-range

RELATED: Hirsch, Wasmund's, Lion's Pride, Big Bottom, Alaska Outlaw

PROPELLERS: !!!!

High West Distillery & Saloon, 703 Park Avenue, Park City, UT 84060, (435) 649-8300, david@highwest.com, www.highwest.com

COMMENTS FROM THE BARTENDER:

ANNIE: This nose is vibrant. Upon tasting, you're greeted with some warm sweet flavors of molasses and sweet corn and it finishes with a boatload of spice.

JEFF: This is a very complex whiskey that I would recommend to my whiskey snobs. It's like a flavor playground for your taste buds to play in.

JOHN: This is a whiskey that I can enjoy. Good burn with some funky vanilla and even mint. This warmed me up in a good way.

BRANDON: Great whiskey with flavors you can really take your time and go through. Don't rush this one; it changes like crazy as time passes.

HIGH WEST SILVER WHISKEY – WESTERN OAT

SUMMARY: Silver Oat is another great expression from the master blenders at High West. Oat whiskeys are tricky and more expensive to make. The mash bill of this white whiskey consists of 85% oats and 15% barley malt and spends a brief time in French Limousin casks. This whiskey is very mild with a velvet feel on the palate, almost like a good vodka. It seems to fall into a tough category for us to sell because it's too mild for a seasoned whiskey drinker to appreciate and too expensive to recommend as a mixer. It is perfect for someone looking to stick a toe into the whiskey river to test if it's good for swimming. The flavors are sweet and subtle.

FUN FACT: High West is Utah's first distillery since the 1870s.

VARIETY/STYLE: Blended

BARREL TYPE: French Limousin Oak

AGE: N/A

ORIGIN: Utah

BOTTLE: 750 ml, cork top

ALCOHOL: 40%

PROOF: 80

PRICE: mid-range

RELATED: Ballast Point, Koval, Dad's Hat, RoughStock, Journeyman

PROPELLERS: !!!!!

High West Distillery and Saloon, 703 Park Avenue, Park City, UT 84060, (435) 649-8300, david@highwest.com, www.highwest.com

COMMENTS FROM THE BARTENDER:

ANNIE: I'm not usually a fan of fresh whiskey but this has some fruit notes that are enjoyable. Banana and mild coconut with vanilla flavors.

JEFF: Very sweet on the nose. I think a first-timer or an old whiskey sage would both enjoy this. Smooth and slightly complex—I really enjoyed it.

JOHN: Hey! I have a beverage here, man! So good—sweet vanilla, the nose is exactly how it fades.

BRANDON: In between the fruity, corn nose, it's highly dominated by an acetone flavor. The finish is the best part and really nice.

HIGH WEST WHISKEY CAMPFIRE

SUMMARY: High West Whiskey Campfire is the world's only and possibly first blend of Scotch, bourbon and rye whiskeys. Its nose is floral, fruity, bright and spicy with some caramel, butterscotch and a light smoke and smoldering wood. The best way to describe this bourbon is like sitting around a campfire, and when it's ready to put it out you do so with a pail of water, and after you take the wood and squeeze it into a bottle. Very smoky and peaty but just as smooth as your typical Scotch. We recommend this for the adventurous drinker who also has a palate for scotch.

FUN FACT: Source of the whiskeys? The bourbon and rye are from the old Seagram's plant in Indiana.

VARIETY/STYLE: Blended

BARREL TYPE: New American Oak

AGE: 5 plus years

ORIGIN: Utah

BOTTLE: 750 ml, cork top

ALCOHOL: 46%

PROOF: 92

PRICE: mid-range

RELATED: Prichard's, Wasmund's, Westward, Rogue, RoughStock

PROPELLERS: !!!!

High West Distillery & Saloon, 703 Park Avenue, Park City, UT 84060, (435) 649-8300, david@highwest.com, www.highwest.com

COMMENTS FROM THE BARTENDER:

ANNIE: I hate the smell of campfires. Enough said.

JEFF: Ton of malt flavor with a solid smoke hit that will raise your brow. After a few seconds you're rewarded with a very pleasant sweetness.

JOHN: A lot going on here, I'm not sure I like it. It tastes a lot like scotch but with sweet, smoky flavors. A great whiskey to sip and analyze.

BRANDON: Smokey nose, numbs up the throat like a highland scotch on the swallow but left a toffee rye-ness on the tongue. I'm smiling and intrigued.

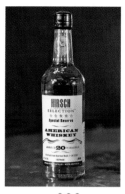

HIRSCH SELECTION SPECIAL RESERVE 20 YEAR OLD AMERICAN WHISKEY

SUMMARY: This 20-year-old whiskey was distilled from bourbon mash, but cannot be labeled as a bourbon because it was aged in used barrels. It's pricey but very few people complain after tasting it. It has complementing flavors of soft vanilla from the time in the barrel and solid spices from the rye. There is a little burn that leaves you with a dry palate so a couple cubes helps.

FUN FACT: This whiskey was awarded 4 stars by F. Paul Pacult's *Spirit Journal*.

VARIETY/STYLE: Blended

BARREL TYPE: Used Charred Oak

AGE: 20 years

ORIGIN: N/A

BOTTLE: 750 ml, cork top

ALCOHOL: 48%

PROOF: 96

PRICE: high–range

RELATED: Prichard's, Heaven Hill, Sam Houston, High West, Michter's

Priess Imports / Anchor Brewers and Distillers, 1705 Mariposa Street, San Francisco, CA 94107, (415) 863-8350, info@anchorsf.com, www.anchordistillery.com

PROPELLERS: !!!

COMMENTS FROM THE BARTENDER:

ANNIE: Outdoorsy at first taste, with an oatmeal finish. Tasty and smooth but nothing extraordinary.

JEFF: The burn is just too strong for the butterscotch to hold up. After a little water, a vanilla finish poked its head, but wasn't anything remarkable as a whole.

JOHN: Bit of a tiger in a bottle. Pretty deep burn that's not very enjoyable. This needs water for any chance of me recommending it.

BRANDON: On first bite there is a hint of maple but that immediately disappears with a cereal burn.

JEFFERSON'S CHEF'S COLLABORATION BLENDED STRAIGHT WHISKEYS

SUMMARY: In 1997, Jefferson's was founded by Trey Zoeller and his father Chet. The guys are always experimenting with new blends of whiskey and changing conventional thinking of what bourbon and rye can be. The Chef's Collaboration is the brainchild of Trey and Chef Edward Lee. They set forth to create a whiskey that would pair well with the bold flavors in Lee's cookbook as well as other cuisine. Well congratulations, fellas, you nailed it! This whiskey garnered some of the best blind-tasting notes from the bartenders. We can't keep it on our shelves.

FUN FACT: Founder Trey Zoeller's eighteenth-century grandmother was arrested in 1799 for the "production and sales of spirituous liquors."

VARIETY/STYLE: Blended

BARREL TYPE: New American Oak

AGE: N/A

ORIGIN: Kentucky

BOTTLE: 750 ml, cork top

ALCOHOL: 46%

PROOF: 92

PRICE: mid-range

RELATED: Sam Houston, Heaven Hill, Hirsch, High West, Michter's

Castle Brands Inc., 122 East 42nd Street, Suite 4700, New York, NY 10168, (646) 356-0200, info@castlebrands.com, www.castlebrands.com

PROPELLERS: !!!!!

COMMENTS FROM THE BARTENDER:

ANNIE: Wonderful mix of spices and vanilla oak. Wouldn't be afraid to recommend this to a fellow bartender.

JEFF: Tastes like a bakery in my mouth. Has a very nice balance of sweetness and spice.

JOHN: This is just the right amount of spice for me. I love it. This would be perfect in an Old Fashioned.

BRANDON: It smells like candy corn. There are huge notes of spices like nutmeg and cinnamon that just hang out in the back of my tongue.

JOURNEYMAN SILVER CROSS WHISKEY

SUMMARY: Master Distiller and owner Bill Welter has a love for the game of golf, and Silver Cross Whiskey is named after a medal given in the early days of the British Open, making the whiskey a tribute to the game. Silver Cross has something in it for everyone, with a mash bill consisting of equal parts of rye, wheat, corn and barley. We often recommend it to people looking for something outside the box, and they don't seem to mind paying a little more for the experience. We recommend trying it straight at first, but it also mixes well.

FUN FACT: One percent of sales of this whiskey in Michigan will be dedicated to the First Tee Program; learn about it at www.fourgrainsforegolf.com.

VARIETY/STYLE: Blended

BARREL TYPE: New American Oak, 5 Gallon

AGE: N/A

ORIGIN: Michigan

BOTTLE: 750 ml, cork top

ALCOHOL: 45%

PROOF: 90

PRICE: mid-range

RELATED: Hirsch, Leopold Brothers Small Batch, Sam Houston, RoughStock Montana, Michter's Small Batch

PROPELLERS: !!!!

Journeyman Distillery, Historic Featherbone Factory, 109 Generations Drive, Three Oaks, MI 49128, (269) 820-2050, info@journeymandistillery.com, www.journeymandistillery.com

COMMENTS FROM THE BARTENDER:

ANNIE: Can't quite guess what this is; it tastes a little like an Irish whiskey. This would make a great Bloody Mary.

JEFF: Picking up notes of barley and rye. Tastes a little too much like a Scotch for my palate.

JOHN: Dude! I like the rough character of this whiskey. I kind of want to guess; I think I know! Blended whiskey with high malted barley?

BRANDON: At first I thought this was gasoline! After the initial burn, the flavors start to arrive, and there are a lot. Give this one a second chance.

KESSLER AMERICAN BLENDED WHISKEY

SUMMARY: In 1888, a man by the name of Julius Kessler began selling whiskey door to door—saloon doors, that is. His whiskey was a success in Leadville, Colorado, and Kessler would run a profitable business until he retired in 1921. The Kessler brand is now owned by Beam Suntory Global, and their website claims it's the number two selling American blended whiskey and that it's distilled according to the exact standards of its founder. This is just whiskey, plain and simple. You can almost picture a prospector standing in the 1800s propped up against the bar with a shot glass and a bottle.

FUN FACT: Julius Kessler's slogan for the whiskey was and still is "smooth as silk."

VARIETY/STYLE: Blended

BARREL TYPE: N/A

AGE: N/A

ORIGIN: Kentucky

BOTTLE: 750 ml, screw cap

ALCOHOL: 40%

PROOF: 80

PRICE: low-range

RELATED: Old Williamsburg, Kentucky Gentleman, Beam's 8 Star, Early Times, Heaven Hill

Beam Suntory Inc., 222 W Merchandise Mart Plaza, Chicago, IL 60654, (312) 964-6999, www.beamglobal.com

PROPELLERS: !

COMMENTS FROM THE BARTENDER:

ANNIE: The nose doesn't give you any idea of what the flavor profile is. Whiskey burn and wet oak.

JEFF: Not the easiest whiskey to figure out. The notes kind of contradict each other. The one thing I do know is this won't be a name I throw out to people.

JOHN: Whiskey! Pass the bottle and take a swig, no need for a glass.

BRANDON: Not much of a nose present on this one. Then when I taste it, it reminds me of dish soap. I honestly won't ever drink this whiskey again.

KOVAL WHITE OAT WHISKEY

SUMMARY: Koval Distillery was founded by the husband and wife team of Robert and Sonat Birnecker, who claim the whole family is involved in the production of their products. Koval is a very fast growing micro-distillery that proudly maintains organic ingredients and produces their spirits from scratch. Koval White Oat Whiskey is distilled from organic American oats. That's right; oats are not just for breakfast anymore, unless you start your day with oatmeal stout. But we don't recommend that. This is a very unique whiskey that may remind you of Grandma's oatmeal, especially if Grandpa had a still out back.

FUN FACT: The name Koval means "black sheep," or someone who forges ahead and does something out of the ordinary.

VARIETY/STYLE: Blended

BARREL TYPE: N/A

AGE: N/A

ORIGIN: Illinois

BOTTLE: 750 ml, cork top

ALCOHOL: 40%

PROOF: 80

PRICE: mid-range

RELATED: Stein, Lion's Pride, Dry Fly, RoughStock, Journeyman

PROPELLERS: ▮▮

Koval Distillery, 5121 North Ravenswood Avenue, Chicago, IL 60640, (312) 878-7988, www.koval-distillery.com

COMMENTS FROM THE BARTENDER:

ANNIE: Sweet, botanical and grassy. Tastes fresh and astringent.

JEFF: The oat flavor helps tone down the sweetness, but it leaves me wanted something more.

JOHN: I'm hooked on fresh whiskey. I love the raw flavors of the grain. This one, however, may not be for everyone, as no real flavors pop.

BRANDON: Mellow nose on this, kind of a moonshine feel with toasted almonds. Coats like kerosene on the aftertaste.

LEOPOLD BROTHERS AMERICAN SMALL BATCH WHISKEY

SUMMARY: Leopold Brothers produces whiskey that is a reminder of a time before industrialization and mass-marketing changed the crafting of American whiskey, a time when farmers and miners made whiskey from their surplus grains. They ferment at colder temperatures without the aid of refrigeration, a process that takes a little longer but results in stronger flavors of vanilla and fruits. The whiskey is copper-pot distilled and barreled at 98 instead of the more common 125 proof, a method that is supposed to enable more whiskey to come into contact with the barrel and assert more sugar and molasses notes. This whiskey emphasizes raw materials and the fermentation process. Each barrel produces about 240 hand-bottled, old-school whiskeys. There's no doubt about the quality and craftsmanship being top notch, so order up and see if it's for you.

FUN FACT: Leopold Brothers distills at least 17 hand-numbered, batch-made products.

VARIETY/STYLE: Blended

BARREL TYPE: Oak

AGE: N/A

ORIGIN: Colorado

BOTTLE: 750 ml, cork top

ALCOHOL: 43%

PROOF: 86

PRICE: mid-range

RELATED: Jailers, High West, Ballast Point, Koval, RoughStock

PROPELLERS: ▮▮▮▮

Leopold Brothers, 5285 Jollet Street, Denver, CO 80239, (303) 307-1515, www.leopoldbros.com

COMMENTS FROM THE BARTENDER:

ANNIE: This smells like spiced apple cider. And it's strong and spicy enough to make a lovely whiskey apple cider.

JEFF: Light and fruity with hints of spice. Kind of like pancakes with a strawberry syrup.

JOHN: As a punk rocker turned hippie, this whiskey is green like a forest. I am definitely a fan. Sweet and green.

BRANDON: Hold on, I recognize this smell! Oh yeah, it reminds me of laundry day. I think someone may have filtered this whiskey through a damp kitchen towel. The taste is an improvement with some notes of sweet fruit and vanilla.

LION'S PRIDE ORGANIC 47TH WARD SINGLE BARREL WHISKEY

SUMMARY: Lion's Pride is a series of aged whiskeys provided by husband and wife team Robert and Sonet Birnecker at their Koval Distillery in Chicago. The 47th Ward is made from a blend of 35% oat, 35% barley, 15% rye and 15% wheat. This crazy combination makes it a must-try for the adventurous whiskey drinker out there. The relatively short time it spends in the barrel is very present, offering a rich vanilla flavor.

FUN FACT: Every Koval product is kosher and certified organic.

VARIETY/STYLE: Blended

BARREL TYPE: Oak

AGE: Approximately 1 year

ORIGIN: Illinois

BOTTLE: 750 ml, cork top

ALCOHOL: 47%

PROOF: 94

PRICE: mid-range

RELATED: Journeyman, Stein, Ballast Point, Dry Fly, RoughStock

Koval Distillery, 5121 North Ravenswood Avenue, Chicago, IL 60640, (312) 878-7988, www.kovaldistillery.com

PROPELLERS: !!! !!

COMMENTS FROM THE BARTENDER:

ANNIE: This tastes like cough syrup.

JEFF: A shortbread cookie that won't leave your mouth dry.

JOHN: Sweet nose with a hint of banana bread. A bit of a burn, yet smooth and creamy at the same time. Hints of vanilla, too.

BRANDON: Instantly, the smell makes me think of saltwater taffy and banana. It is just as delicious and creamy.

MICHTER'S SOUR MASH WHISKEY

SUMMARY: "The Whiskey that warmed the American Revolution," or at least so the saying goes. You can trace Michter's roots to 1753 when John Shenk established the first commercial distilling company. The label is now owned by Chatham Imports. Joseph Magliocco and Dick Newman have resurrected the brand along with Master Distiller Willie Pratt, a.k.a. Dr. No. Though their whiskey has been sourced, they are distilling at their new location in Louisville, Kentucky. The sour mash comes in a distant third in sales compared to their bourbon and rye that we carry, but I'm guessing that's going to change after reading the blind tasting from the bartenders. This is a great blended whiskey.

FUN FACT: Michter's very limited edition bottles of Celebration Sour Mash Whiskey sell for nearly $4,000 a bottle.

VARIETY/STYLE: Blended

BARREL TYPE: N/A

AGE: N/A

ORIGIN: Kentucky

BOTTLE: 750 ml, cork top

ALCOHOL: 43%

PROOF: 86

PRICE: mid-range

RELATED: Sam Houston, Prichard's, Bowen, Heaven Hill, Alibi

Chatham Imports, 245 Fifth Avenue, New York, NY 10016, (212) 473-1100, info@michters.com, www.michters.com
Producer: Kentucky Bourbon Distillers, 1869 Loretto Rd., Bardstown, KY 40004, (502)-561-1001, kentuckybourbon@bardstown.com, www.kentuckybourbonwhiskey.com

PROPELLERS: !!!!! !!!!

COMMENTS FROM THE BARTENDER:

ANNIE: Soft fruits and candy with a pleasant burn, nothing too crazy. Perfect for my herds of thirsty drinkers after a hard day's work.

JEFF: No need to mix this one. Really pleasant flavor combination of vanilla, corn and wood.

JOHN: Mild at first, but then it had a nice burn. Quality whiskey. I would probably give this a splash of water.

BRANDON: This one here is full of flavor. Lots of dry fruit like oranges. It finishes smooth, piney and oaky. I wouldn't mess with this one too much. Maybe a few cubes.

ROGUE DEAD GUY WHISKEY

SUMMARY: Rogue is known for producing amazing craft beers, and they are starting to collect a pretty nice trophy collection for their spirits as well. The Dead Guy Whiskey is created on the Pacific Ocean and Yaquina Bay by crafting four different types of malt combined with coastal water. It's double-distilled in a 150-gallon Vendome copper pot still, then briefly aged in charred American white oak. This whiskey has gotten some pretty harsh reviews by critics saying that it's made cheaply and quickly with loose quality control. We're not sure if all that's true, but we do know what hundreds of people who taste it are saying. The whiskey sells fairly well because of the loyalty of the Rogue beer drinkers, but very few order a second round. The word "interesting" is often used, but very rarely "good" and never "great." An acquired taste for sure.

FUN FACT: The website proudly displays its Distillery of the Year award from the World Beverage Competition in Geneva, Switzerland.

VARIETY/STYLE: Blended Malt

BARREL TYPE: Oak

AGE: 1 month

ORIGIN: Oregon

BOTTLE: 750 ml, cork top

ALCOHOL: 40%

PROOF: 80

PRICE: mid-range

RELATED: Ballast Point, RoughStock, Stein, Corsair, High West

PROPELLERS: ♠

Rogue Spirits, 2320 Southeast OSU Drive, Newport, OR 97365, (541) 867-3660, john@rogue.com, www.rogue.com

COMMENTS FROM THE BARTENDER:

ANNIE: I get burnt sugar on the nose. It starts with a burn, then mellows out to a peppery sweetness.

JEFF: Lots of malt leads to a pepper-filled finish. A bit too malty for me.

JOHN: Cinnamon all the way for me. It's a little too zesty.

BRANDON: I really get the small of burnt chocolate and the malty peppery palate offsets it nicely. This could be aged a little longer for more oak.

SAM HOUSTON AMERICAN STRAIGHT WHISKEY

SUMMARY: Sam Houston is a relatively new whiskey on the market. It is a bourbon-based whiskey produced in Kentucky. There's not really a ton of info out there on this whiskey yet, so let's stick to what we do know—how it tastes and how it sells. The tall sleek bottle does a great job of catching the eye of our thirsty guests even sitting among 900 competitors, so it is often ordered. When we ask the question "Are you happy with your purchase?" the answer is "yes, it's good." Never great, mind you, just good. It's a little too sweet for most to classify it as great.

FUN FACT: There is also a Sam Houston Bourbon, a 10-year straight bourbon in a short, squatty bottle with a black label.

VARIETY/STYLE: Blended

BARREL TYPE: Oak

AGE: N/A

ORIGIN: Kentucky

BOTTLE: 750 ml, cork top

ALCOHOL: 43%

PROOF: 86

PRICE: mid-range

RELATED: Jack Daniel's, Hirsch, Heaven Hill, Old Crow, Kentucky Gentleman

PROPELLERS: ♠♠♠

Western Spirits Beverage Company, 2200 Lapsley Lane, Bowling Green, KY 42103, (270) 796-5851, info@westernspirits.com, www.westernspirits.com

COMMENTS FROM THE BARTENDER:

ANNIE: Sweet and sugary, no burn, no real smell. I'm getting apricots and crème brûlée.

JEFF: You can smell the sugar in this one, a little caramel too. The fresh fruit helps the flavor, but still a bit too sweet.

JOHN: This is the whiskey for your little sister; hide the good stuff for yourself.

BRANDON: Nose is light and so is the booze. Easy drinker if the price is right.

SEAGRAM'S 7 CROWN

SUMMARY: Who hasn't had or at least heard of a 7 and 7? Seagram's 7 is often confused as a Canadian whiskey, but it's not. It's a blended American whiskey owned and produced by spirits giant Diageo. The whiskey had its heyday in the seventies, reaching iconic status. Today, it's still a must-have in any whiskey bar, but the younger generation considers it the whiskey their grandpa drinks. Image aside, it's a great mixer that proudly sits in our second-tier speed rack. Crisp, clean and refreshing, try it with a couple of muddled limes, a splash of Saint-Germain and some soda water on the rocks.

FUN FACT: Seagram's 7 is our most requested blended American whiskey.

VARIETY/STYLE: Blended

BARREL TYPE: N/A

AGE: N/A

ORIGIN: Connecticut

BOTTLE: 750 ml, screw cap

ALCOHOL: 40%

PROOF: 80

PRICE: low-range

RELATED: Heaven Hill, Sam Houston, Beam's 8 Star, Kessler, Seagram's VO

PROPELLERS: !!!

Diageo North America, 801 Main Avenue, Norwalk, CT 06851, (646) 223-2000, www.diageo.com

COMMENTS FROM THE BARTENDER:

ANNIE: Light whiskey with soft caramel crème brûlée flavors. Also some peach and apricot. Wine cooler whiskey.

JEFF: Enjoyable with its sweet buttery taste with hints of apricot.

JOHN: This tastes like something I would sneak out of the liquor cabinet as a kid.

BRANDON: I felt a little let down by this one. The nose is sweet and buttery, but it tastes very boozy and young.

STEIN STRAIGHT SMALL BATCH BLENDED WHISKEY

SUMMARY: Stein Distillery is a family-owned and-operated distillery in Joseph, Oregon, that grows rye, wheat and barley. They rely as much as possible on their own harvest for distilling their products. The Stein Big Buck is a blend of three different barreled whiskeys: corn, rye and barley. It's aged two years in new American oak. The whiskey is good but is hard to sell to the masses due to its high price tag for a two-year-old blended whiskey.

FUN FACT: Blended American whiskey must contain a minimum of 20% straight whiskey that is made from a distillate of 160 proof. The mash bill must be greater than 51% of its respective grain and aged two years in newly charred barrels.

VARIETY/STYLE: Blended

BARREL TYPE: New American Oak

AGE: 2 years

ORIGIN: Oregon

BOTTLE: 750 ml, cork top

ALCOHOL: 40%

PROOF: 80

PRICE: mid-range

RELATED: Kessler, Michter's, Alibi, Calvert

PROPELLERS: !!

Stein Distillery, P.O. Box 200, Joseph, OR 97846, (541) 432-2009, whiskey@steindistillery.com, www.steindistillery.com

COMMENTS FROM THE BARTENDER:

ANNIE: Smells like a face-scruncher. It tastes smoother than the smell, with light fruit and maybe citrus. An alcohol burn that hugs your chest tight.

JEFF: Not the most welcoming of smells, but the flavor wasn't bad. Definitely a mixer.

JOHN: Very mild and sweet. I like it. This is one of those horse-leather whiskeys.

BRANDON: Surprisingly lighter and easier than I thought it would be to drink. Good earthy notes of saddle and fresh oak.

WHIPPERSNAPPER OREGON SPIRIT WHISKEY

SUMMARY: This is for sure one of the most unique whiskeys in our collection. It's the creation of Tad Seestedt, who initially started making grappa, brandy and fine wines. In 2008, they purchased a farm outside Sheridan, Oregon, where they planted barley and grapevines, and the rest is history. They use a hand-hammered pot still and make several cuts by taste and smell. True craftsmen, no computers or robots are used here. Ransom makes their WhipperSnapper Whiskey from a grain profile similar to a bourbon but with a barley content as well. After distillation, it spends a little time in oak as well as pinot noir barrels. "Whippersnapper" is a term used to describe a youngster who is mischievous or disrespectful. We'll let you decide if the label describes the whiskey.

FUN FACT: The name of the distillery was chosen to represent the debt incurred to start the business. Tad was paying his own ransom to realize his dream.

VARIETY/STYLE: Blended

BARREL TYPE: Oak

AGE: N/A

ORIGIN: Oregon

BOTTLE: 750 ml, screw cap

ALCOHOL: 42%

PROOF: 84

PRICE: mid-range

RELATED: Journeyman, Stein, RoughStock, Dry Fly, Ballast Point

PROPELLERS: !!!! !!!!

Ransom Wine & Spirits, 525 NE Third Street, McMinnville, OR 97128, (503) 472-2493, www.ransomspirits.com

COMMENTS FROM THE BARTENDER:

ANNIE: Ginger, burnt sugar and tree bark. I would dedicate this to an all whiskey drinking night. It is so complex; I think I could always get something new from it. It kind of numbed my tongue though.

JEFF: A sugary vanilla that has a little spice that kicks in late. Smooth with no burn, you could make an evening out of this bottle.

JOHN: Made my nose hair tingle. This reminds me of a white whiskey, but sweeter.

BRANDON: It's difficult to pinpoint what type of whiskey this is. But it's a mouthful. There's a curious spiciness to it—I like it!

WHEAT

As the famous writer Mark Twain once said, "Too much of anything is bad, but too much good whiskey is barely enough." This is certainly true in the case of wheat whiskey. It has been flying off our shelves.

These tasty whiskeys generally have a softer palate, providing sweetness with little to no bitterness. The sweetness doesn't come from the wheat itself, but since wheat isn't as rich as other grains, it allows more of the sweet notes from the barrels to shine through. This often translates into sweet caramel and vanilla notes with a bit of spice on the back of the tongue.

Wheat whiskeys have recently been thrown into the spotlight due to the craze over the Van Winkle brand. While this cult following has not been able to get its fix due to the elusiveness of their bottles, we have been able to recommend several other wheat whiskeys that have turned into our new favorite brands.

While this section focuses on whiskeys that use wheat as the primary ingredient, if not the only grain involved, there are many wheat bourbons. These delectable concoctions still comply with the rules for making bourbon. This means that they are still comprised of at least 51% corn, with the secondary grain being wheat. Be sure to check them out in the Bourbon chapter.

Wheat whiskeys are perfect for mixing into your favorite cocktails, or simply enjoying on the rocks. These are some of the staff's favorite go-to whiskeys, as the soft, smooth flavors always leave our guests smiling.

DRY FLY WASHINGTON WHEAT WHISKEY

SUMMARY: Dry Fly Wheat is a very unique whiskey full of interesting flavors. Located in Spokane, Washington, Dry Fly is a true craft distillery. Their pot stills are custom designed and built in Germany. They feature multiple rectification columns and 450-liter capacities. Dry Fly embraces the farm-to-bottle approach, producing every drop of liquor from locally grown materials. We appreciate their efforts and often recommend this wheat whiskey. It's almost like a mixed cocktail in a glass. Every time we serve the stuff, the reaction from the guests is the same: They say, "Wow, that's interesting," and have a very confused look on their face as they set out on a scavenger hunt for the flavors. This is great conversation whiskey.

FUN FACT: Dry Fly won the Gold Medal for Wheated Whiskey at the World Spirit Awards in Germany in 2014.

VARIETY/STYLE: Wheat

BARREL TYPE: N/A

AGE: N/A

ORIGIN: Washington

BOTTLE: 750 ml, cork top

ALCOHOL: 40%

PROOF: 80

PRICE: mid-range

RELATED: Stein, RoughStock, Journeyman, Corsair, Koval

PROPELLERS: !!!!!

Dry Fly Distilling Company, 1003 East Trent, #200, Spokane, WA 99202, (509) 489-2112, www.dryflydistilling.com

COMMENTS FROM THE BARTENDER:

ANNIE: Warm and minty. Anyone who likes Mint Juleps will probably dig this.

JEFF: The nose made me think I was getting a whiskey, full of caramel and butterscotch, but I was pleasantly surprised with tastes of cinnamon and peppermint, with a hint of citrus.

JOHN: Total mint explosion! This has got to be herbal. It's surprisingly good. Drink this if you want to explore new whiskeys.

BRANDON: The way the mint pops out at you in between the nose and the finish is very unique! Pick this whiskey for the next round of shots to really surprise your friends.

JOURNEYMAN BUGGY WHIP ORGANIC WHEAT WHISKEY

SUMMARY: Visionary, distiller and owner Bill Welter opened the doors of his Journeyman Distillery in October 2011, and it's been growing ever since. With a slew of products on the market, including six whiskeys, the Michigan-based distillery is quickly making a name for itself. We currently carry three of their brands: Ravenswood Rye, Featherbone Bourbon and this one. Made from a base of 100% wheat, the whiskey tends to be a little softer and sweeter than bourbons and ryes. We only carry a handful of wheat whiskeys but often recommend this one. It's a mid-range price spirit and has what you'd expect in flavors. Soft, toasty, buttery—we recommend it with a little water.

FUN FACT: Buggy Whip Wheat is named after the location of the distillery, an old corset and buggy whip factory.

VARIETY/STYLE: Wheat

BARREL TYPE: New American Oak

AGE: N/A

ORIGIN: Michigan

BOTTLE: 750 ml, cork top

ALCOHOL: 45%

PROOF: 90

PRICE: mid-range

RELATED: Dry Fly Wheat, Koval White Wheat, RoughStock Montana Spring Wheat, Larceny, Old Weller Antique

PROPELLERS: !!!!

Journeyman Distillery, 109 Generations Drive, Three Oaks, MI 49128, (269) 820-2050, info@journeyman.com, www.journeymandistillery.com

COMMENTS FROM THE BARTENDER:

ANNIE: Grainy with some herbal notes. Light, sour fruits and heavy spice. This is some interesting stuff.

JEFF: With the first sip, the burn was immediately noticeable. Added a little water and it opened up to a sweet, nutty taste with a bit of caramel. Definitely preferred it after the water.

JOHN: Crunchy, like a Butterfinger. I'm curious what grain this is. It feels like chewing on wheat. It has plenty of bite with no burn.

BRANDON: This is different; I like it. Smooth cereal flavors that you can drink all night while listening to my band, Danny and the Tramp. Am I allowed to plug my band? Anyway, this one's worth a try.

KOVAL WHITE WHEAT

SUMMARY: Koval embraces the grain-to-bottle mentality. Each step is carefully monitored, from working with farmers to on-site milling and mashing as well as distilling and bottling. Koval has one of the most technologically advanced custom copper pot stills in the world. The distillery is growing fast: just five years ago they were using a 300-liter still; now their still is a 5,000-liter beast! They provide a wide range of spirits, whiskeys and liqueurs. Distilled from 100% Midwest wheat, it has some very enjoyable soft and sweet wheat flavors. This can be mixed in a cocktail almost like vodka. It's a perfect whiskey or "American spirit," if you're looking for something smooth and easy to drink.

FUN FACT: Koval uses only the "heart" cut of distillate—affording a brighter, cleaner take on whiskey.

VARIETY/STYLE: Wheat

BARREL TYPE: N/A

AGE: N/A

ORIGIN: Illinois

BOTTLE: 750 ml, cork top

ALCOHOL: 40%

PROOF: 80

PRICE: mid-range

RELATED: Stein Shine, Ballast Point, Journeyman, Dry Fly

PROPELLERS: ❢❢❢❢

Koval Distillery, 5121 North Ravenswood Avenue, Chicago, IL 60640, (312) 878-7988, www.kovaldistillery.com

COMMENTS FROM THE BARTENDER:

ANNIE: Oh man, smells like rubbing alcohol, tastes like rubbing alcohol with Cheerios cereal.

JEFF: I could drink this, but it's not something I would order regularly. It does have an interesting combination of banana, pear and breakfast grains.

JOHN: I was really hoping for more after smelling this. Just kinda plain Jane. Let's mix'er up in a Whiskey Mind Eraser.

BRANDON: Getting vanilla on the nose, mild burn up front that settles into earthy cereal flavors and some faint dried fruits. Not going to be for everyone.

ROUGHSTOCK MONTANA SPRING WHEAT WHISKEY

SUMMARY: Some of the best advice I ever got as a bartender was to read the labels on the bottles. You can learn a lot about what you are selling. The folks at RoughStock pack all the info they can on their labels and it's appreciated. The hard white spring wheat used to distill this whiskey is harvested just up the road from the distillery. This Western-style whiskey is made from 100% wheat using pure mountain stream water. It's distilled twice and then aged in freshly emptied malt casks. If you're looking for a wheat whiskey for your cabinet, you may have found it. Grab this while you can—RoughStock has recently closed.

FUN FACT: Each bottle of RoughStock is hand signed with the batch number and the individual who bottled it.

VARIETY/STYLE: Wheat

BARREL TYPE: Oak Malt Casks

AGE: N/A

ORIGIN: Montana

BOTTLE: 750 ml, cork top

ALCOHOL: 45%

PROOF: 90

PRICE: mid-range

RELATED: Wiser's, High West, Prichard's, Corsair, Journeyman

PROPELLERS: ❢❢❢❢❢

COMMENTS FROM THE BARTENDER:

ANNIE: Smells like flowers and pretty girls. Tastes like herbs and grains with a touch of sugar and spice.

JEFF: The sweet floral nose adds to a nice soft taste like a butterscotch candy.

JOHN: Right off the bat I like the aroma. Really nice flavor. Sweet and floral. A nice change of pace.

BRANDON: This one's a little citrusy and a lot of grain is present, but it's still sweet with a big burn. It really tastes home-made and from the countryside.

CORN/WHITE

There are many names used to describe the whiskey in this category: corn liquor, white lightning, mule kick, moonshine and many others. This chapter contains some different but similar types of whiskey that are produced in the same way, but probably don't want to be associated with each other. Legal moonshines are very different now compared to when our country was just a baby. Pennsylvania farmers made shine from their leftover crops and sold it to their friends straight from the still. This high-octane stuff was basically just fermented sugar water with some grain mixed in.

Most fresh or unaged whiskeys today are of high quality and consist of corn, rye, wheat or oat. The most popular by far are the corn whiskeys. They must consist of at least 80% corn in the mash and are often aged for short periods of time to give them extra flavors and a little color. If the label reads "straight" corn whiskey, it has spent at least a couple of years in a barrel aging. Many distillers will have you taste their fresh whiskeys at the beginning of their distillery tour to show the quality of the product before aging. Trying a whiskey raw will give you a great appreciation for the flavor of the primary grain and we highly recommend it.

So whether you're looking to slam a couple shots outta a mason jar or sit back and sip on some super smoky corn whiskey that has been crafted with the utmost care, this section has something for the adventurous whiskey drinker in all of us. Order one up with an open mind and really try and enjoy the fresh whiskey flavors; you'll be glad you did!

BALCONES BABY BLUE CORN WHISKEY

SUMMARY: Baby Blue is a Texas whiskey made from 100% corn, actually atole, a roasted blue cornmeal. Each batch is a mixing of barrels that are personally tasted by Chip Tate, Balcones head distiller. In the past five years, Chip has gone from building his own stills to producing and releasing seven unique spirits and collecting 40 national and international awards. Balcones is known for its smoky whiskey, and Baby Blue delivers. Don't be fooled by the sweet nose; this whiskey has a smoky bite that will raise your eyebrows. If you're a fan of Islay Scotches, you may like this Texas whiskey.

FUN FACT: Baby Blue was the first Texas whiskey on the market since Prohibition.

VARIETY/STYLE: Corn

BARREL TYPE: N/A

AGE: 4 months

ORIGIN: Texas

BOTTLE: 750 ml, cork top

ALCOHOL: 46%

PROOF: 92

PRICE: mid-range

RELATED: Berkshire Mountain, Balcones, Hudson, Platte Valley, Georgia Moon

PROPELLERS: !!!! !!!!

Balcones Distilling, 225 South 11th St., Waco, TX 76701, (254) 755-6003, info@balconesdistilling.com, www.balconesdistilling.com

COMMENTS FROM THE BARTENDER:

ANNIE: This tastes like mescal—smoky and woody with hints of citrus and grain.

JEFF: Never saw the smoke coming, but it's the main note in the taste along with oak. A vanilla nose masks the taste.

JOHN: Very sweet nose. It's totally misleading—it actually has a ton of burn and smoke.

BRANDON: Sweet and smoky, perfect with sushi.

BERKSHIRE NEW ENGLAND CORN WHISKEY

SUMMARY: Established in 2007, Berkshire Distillers is located in Great Barrington, Massachusetts. Founder Chris Weld and his family purchased a neglected apple field in the countryside of Berkshire County. After three years of cultivating the trees, the apples began to grow. With an abundance of fruit and some of the best granite-based springwater available, Chris knew he was on to something. Today, Berkshire spirits are available in 19 states. The corn whiskey is made with corn grown just up the road at a local farm. It's then distilled in a pot still and aged over oak, and cherry wood, giving it very unique flavors. As my business partner Jeremy LeBlanc would say, "Its wicked good."

FUN FACT: Chris started selling his spirits door to door out of his truck.

VARIETY/STYLE: Corn

BARREL TYPE: N/A

AGE: N/A

ORIGIN: Massachusetts

BOTTLE: 750 ml, cork top

ALCOHOL: 43%

PROOF: 86

PRICE: mid-range

RELATED: Big Bottom, Hudson, Balcones, Stein, Ole Smokey

PROPELLERS: !!!!

Berkshire Mountain Distillers, 356 South Main Street, Sheffield, MA 01257, (413) 229-0219, chris@berkshiredistillers.com, www.berkshiremountaindistillers.com

COMMENTS FROM THE BARTENDER:

ANNIE: Semisweet and I'm getting a lot of oak. It's not my favorite, but it's doable, I suppose.

JEFF: Interesting flavors of smoky wood and sweet corn. Also like fig or black cherry.

JOHN: Very nice and sweet, like Annie. A bit of smoke in the aftertaste. I like it.

BRANDON: Not sure how to describe this. Reminds me of something homemade by my crazy Uncle Fred. I need some more time to figure it out.

BUFFALO TRACE WHITE DOG

SUMMARY: White Dog is the strongest white whiskey we carry. Coming in at 125 proof, it delivers an authentic moonshine burn. Once the grain has fermented and been run through the still, it's bottled. There is no aging process. White whiskeys are not for everyone, but they're a great way to taste the raw flavors of the spirit. You can get an essence of what was coming from stills in shady hollows, up dirt roads and down in the valleys of the Appalachian Mountains—whiskey that helped build the whiskey industry we have today. Buffalo Trace White Dog captures the flavors of what once was and what probably still is if you look hard enough—but we don't recommend that.

FUN FACT: Buffalo Trace makes two variations: mash #1 is the same as their bourbon recipe, and mash #2 is the same as their rye.

VARIETY/STYLE: White Corn

BARREL TYPE: N/A

AGE: N/A

ORIGIN: Kentucky

BOTTLE: 375 ml, cork top

ALCOHOL: 62.5%

PROOF: 125

PRICE: mid-range

RELATED: Ballast Point, Stein, Silver Lightning, Balcones, Hudson

PROPELLERS:

Buffalo Trace Distillery, 113 Great Buffalo Trace, Frankfort, KY 40601, (800) 654-8471, greatbourbon@buffalotrace.com, www.buffalotrace.com

COMMENTS FROM THE BARTENDER:

ANNIE: Corn and limes! This is truly not pleasant.

JEFF: This corn whiskey tasted very yeasty. Not what I want in my whiskey.

JOHN: I dig white whiskey, and if you do, you'll appreciate the raw flavors of this: warm bread and corn.

BRANDON: This one burns for a moment, but the doughy sweet taste that lingers is very pleasant.

DEVIL'S SHARE CALIFORNIA SMALL BATCH MOONSHINE

SUMMAARY: Ballast Point established its brewery in 1996 and has won countless awards for their beers. We rotate a lot of beers at the Aero Club Bar, but there are two handles that haven't moved in years. Ballast Point Pale Ale and our number one selling IPA, their Sculpin IPA. In 2008, they opened San Diego's first craft distillery. Today, they produce over 40 styles of beers and bottle seven distilled spirits. Master Distiller Yuseff Cherney told us a little about what goes into making their small batch moonshine: "80% corn, 17.5% two-row malted barley and 2.5% malted wheat is the foundation of our white whiskey. The grain is mashed and steeped in our brew house just like our beer, minus the addition of hops, and removed from the husk prior to fermentation. This 'lautering' process produces a more refined whiskey with just the sweet barley malt being fermented into our 'distillers beer.' The 'beer' is then distilled through our custom-built Vendome copper hybrid pot/column still. Only the hearts are kept aged ever so slightly to ensure the whiskey character." San Diego may be known for its sunny disposition, but Ballast Point Devil's Share Moonshine is undeniable evidence of a darker, more mischievous side. This former bootlegger's spirit is surprisingly smooth. There are some less expensive brands out there that you may want to try simply because corn whiskey isn't for everyone, but we believe you'd be hard pressed to find a distillery that puts as much heart and soul into the process of making whiskey.

PROPELLERS:

FUN FACT: Ballast Point was awarded California Distiller of the Year in 2013.

VARIETY/STYLE: Moonshine

BARREL TYPE: N/A

AGE: N/A

ORIGIN: California

BOTTLE: 750 ml, cork top

ALCOHOL: 49.3%

PROOF: 98.6

PRICE: mid-range

RELATED: Prichard's, Ole Smokey, Midnight Moon, Wasmund's, MBR

Ballast Point, 9045 Carroll Way, San Diego, CA 92121, (858) 695-2739, www.ballastpoint.com

COMMENTS FROM THE BARTENDER:

ANNIE: Smells like corn! Tastes like kettle corn with a burn! Super sweet and caramel-flavored. Not a bad moonshine. Great for mixing.

JEFF: Tastes like a mango without all the sugar. Drink on a cold winter day, as it will warm your whole body with each sip.

JOHN: I'm really starting to love white whiskey! This one has a total malt sweetness. Reminds me of a candy I loved as a kid.

BRANDON: This moonshine has a wonderfully sweet nose. It's very drinkable but warming and fruity. Have you ever had a moonshine Manhattan?

HUDSON NEW YORK CORN WHISKEY

SUMMARY: We couldn't agree more with the caption on the side of the bottle of Hudson New York Corn Whiskey that says, "This un-aged sipping whiskey is clear and soft on the tongue with the faint aroma of corn fields at harvest." A lot of whiskeys have wonderful descriptions to sway you into ordering their brand. Hudson's statement, however, is pretty dang close! It's distilled one batch at a time from 100% New York corn. Truly a great corn whiskey, with wonderful flavors and consistency. This is our number-one-selling high-end corn whiskey.

FUN FACT: These guys have one of the most impressive trophy cases you will find: 50+ awards since 2008!

VARIETY/STYLE: Corn

BARREL TYPE: N/A

AGE: N/A

ORIGIN: New York

BOTTLE: 750 ml, cork top

ALCOHOL: 46%

PROOF: 92

PRICE: mid-range

RELATED: Silver Lightning, Buffalo Trace White Dog, Platte Valley, Stein, RoughStock

PROPELLERS: ! ! ! ! !

Tuthilltown Spirits, P.O. Box 320, 14 Grist Mill Lane, Gardiner, NY 12525, (845) 255-1527, www.tuthilltown.com

COMMENTS FROM THE BARTENDER:

ANNIE: God, I just want to bake when I smell this. Sweet corn flavors, a great way to taste and appreciate white whiskey.

JEFF: A little more earthy than roasted corn. Almost like it's paired with cornbread but not as sweet.

JOHN: I love this, but that's no surprise. A perfect balance of flavors. A+.

BRANDON: This is great! The nose is floral bouquet with some notes of yeast and sweet corn on the other end. I could sit back all day and sip on this bad boy.

MBR BLACK DOG KENTUCKY CORN WHISKEY

SUMMARY: MBR Distillery is very proud of the fact that they are a true craft distillery using no outside pre-distilled bulk "grain neutral" spirits or bourbon. They promise that if you see their label on something, it was made at their one-and-only facility in Christian County, Kentucky. If you like smoke, look no further. They "dark-fire," or smoke, the corn in a tobacco barn. Too much smoke for most to enjoy neat or on the rocks, they recommend it in a Bloody Mary on their website, and we couldn't agree more. Top it off with a float of Guinness, and you have one of the best breakfast cocktails you've ever had.

FUN FACT: The distillery gets its name from Mary Beth's maiden name. Paul claims it rolls off the tongue a little better than "PR Tomaszewski."

VARIETY/STYLE: Corn

BARREL TYPE: N/A

AGE: N/A

ORIGIN: Kentucky

BOTTLE: 375 ml, cork top

ALCOHOL: 45%

PROOF: 90

PRICE: mid-range

RELATED: Balcones, Hudson, Stein, RoughStock, Silver Lightning

PROPELLERS: ! ! ! !

MBR Distiller, 137 Barkers Mill Road, Pembroke, KY 42266, (270) 640-7744, info@mbrdistillery.com, www.mbrdistillery.com

COMMENTS FROM THE BARTENDER:

ANNIE: Corn and tequila! Sweet and smoky. I really taste that oak barrel here. Reminds me of inhaling campfires.

JEFF: I prefer my whiskey a bit less smoky. Really easy to drink, though. Besides corn and smoke, no other flavors jump out at me.

JOHN: Ooh, yes, these are growing on me! I love the sweet smoky corn flavors with a mild burn.

BRANDON: It has a powerful smoke with sweet flavors that try to come through but are muddled down by the smoke.

MBR WHITE DOG KENTUCKY CORN WHISKEY

SUMMARY: MBR Distillery was started by Paul and Mary Beth Tomaszewski. This "grain to glass" distillery produces many handmade distilled spirits, including bourbon, blends and flavored shines. The site of the distillery was once an Amish dairy farm. Oh, how the times have changed! Today, you can visit the distillery for up-close and personal tours and probably even catch some free live music, as they often have bands playing right on their front porch. You may be pressed for a glass of milk, but there's plenty of whiskey.

FUN FACT: The Border Collie on many of the labels is named Cassius and was rescued from a local animal shelter.

VARIETY/STYLE: Corn

BARREL TYPE: N/A

AGE: N/A

ORIGIN: Kentucky

BOTTLE: 375 ml, cork top

ALCOHOL: 45%

PROOF: 90

PRICE: mid-range

RELATED: Silver Lightning, Buffalo Trace White Dog, Platte Valley, Stein, RoughStock

PROPELLERS:

MBR Distiller, 137 Barkers Mill Road, Pembroke, KY 42266, (270) 640-7744, info@mbrdistillery.com, www.mbrdistillery.com

COMMENTS FROM THE BARTENDER:

ANNIE: Again, all white whiskey smells like tequila to me. Tastes like smoked corn and sugar with citrus to me.

JEFF: If you inhale deeply, you'll find the notes of peach that are masked by the medium smoke. Not as sweet as other white whiskeys.

JOHN: I think I like corn whiskey now. The more I taste, the more I love. This is good stuff, but I prefer a little more smoke.

BRANDON: Smells like corn and alcohol. The flavors are much softer than expected: cream corn with soft fruit and citrus.

PLATTE VALLEY 100% STRAIGHT CORN WHISKEY

SUMMARY: McCormick Distilling Co. was founded in 1865 as Holladay Distillery by Ben Holladay. It has produced different whiskeys for different owners over the years, and the Platte Valley label is said to be about 25 years old. Platte is made from 100% corn and is aged three years, relatively long compared to most corn whiskeys. This whiskey does benefit from the time in the barrel, with a little more depth than some of its peers. But what really makes it stand out is the old-timey ceramic medicine jar it comes in. As for the whiskey, it gets ordered simply because of the bottle. The whiskey inside gets mixed reviews.

FUN FACT: The distillery survived Prohibition by producing whiskey that was sold as medicine only.

VARIETY/STYLE: Corn

BARREL TYPE: Oak

AGE: 3 years

ORIGIN: Kentucky

BOTTLE: 750 ml, cork top

ALCOHOL: 40%

PROOF: 80

PRICE: mid-range

RELATED: Hudson, Balcones, MBR, Stein, Buffalo Trace

PROPELLERS:

McCormick Distilling Co., 420 Main Street, Weston, MO 64098, (816) 640-2276, www.mccormickdistilling.com

COMMENTS FROM THE BARTENDER:

ANNIE: Super smooth with a little burn that dissipates quickly. Sweet finish and easy to drink. Definitely cereal-flavored.

JEFF: Is it breakfast time? Reminds me of Cap'n Crunch with its sweet corn flavors.

JOHN: This has to be an 80% corn whiskey, and it's a good one. Very smooth. Did I just hear a cow? Where am I?

BRANDON: Sweet corny corn corn! Sweet malty cereal with a smooth finish.

PRICHARD'S LINCOLN COUNTY LIGHTNING

SUMMARY: Lincoln County Lightning gets bottled fresh out of the still and boasts tremendous corn character. While most corn whiskey is made from yellow corn, Prichard's uses white corn for its higher sugar content. It's a good clear whiskey from a very likable company, but it has some pretty tough competition in this catagory and doesn't get much call to action.

FUN FACT: The distillery now sits in the town's oldest schoolhouse. The basketball hoops are still hanging in the gym.

VARIETY/STYLE: Corn

BARREL TYPE: N/A

AGE: N/A

ORIGIN: Tennessee

BOTTLE: 750 ml, cork top

ALCOHOL: 45%

PROOF: 90

PRICE: mid-range

RELATED: Balcones, Georgia Moon, RoughStock, Silver Lightning, Berkshire MT

Prichard's Distillery, 4125 White Creek Pike, Nashville, TN 37189, (615) 724-1600, www.prichardsdistillery.com

PROPELLERS: ❗

COMMENTS FROM THE BARTENDER:

ANNIE: I know I'm hard on the fresh whiskeys and I try to give them a fair share, but the truth is this tastes like burnt corn flavored water.

JEFF: Me and clear whiskeys just don't get along. A strong burn with a corn flavor was all that I picked up.

JOHN: Kind of different! It's a bit rougher than most. I like it; sweet corn with a great burn.

BRANDON: Ah, man. That's a burn I just can't seem to get used to. After the initial blast of fire, you can appreciate some fresh corn flavor. I'm not really sure what to even recommend mixing this with. Maybe some Saint-Germain and citrus.

ROUGHSTOCK MONTANA SWEET CORN WHISKEY

SUMMARY: RoughStock makes their corn whiskey using 100% yellow sweet corn and pure mountain springwater. It's distilled twice in a copper pot still, and just like the Old West, it's bottled up and served without spending any aging time in a barrel. Corn whiskeys are not the most popular bottles on our shelves, only outselling blended grain whiskeys or moonshines by a hair, mainly because most have too much bite, and lack all the wonderful flavors absorbed from barrel aging. If you like corn at all, popped, cob or even out of a can, you've got to at least try a corn whiskey; you may be pleasantly surprised. Grab some while you can—RoughStock recently closed.

FUN FACT: Corn whiskey does not have to be aged like bourbon or rye. It only has a couple of requirements: it must be 80% corn and come off the still at no more than 160 proof.

VARIETY/STYLE: Corn whiskey

BARREL TYPE: N/A

AGE: N/A

ORIGIN: Montana

BOTTLE: 750 ml, cork top

ALCOHOL: 50%

PROOF: 100

PRICE: mid-range

RELATED: Balcones, Hudson, Platte Valley, Georgia Moon, Stein

PROPELLERS: ❗❗❗

COMMENTS FROM THE BARTENDER:

ANNIE: Smells like grain. Sweet, smooth and smoky. Tastes like camp.

JEFF: I was surprised by the smoke in this corn whiskey. It definitely tones down the sweetness.

JOHN: I instantly want Mexican food when I smell this. It's really delicious. Nice, smoky and sweet corn.

BRANDON: It's got to be corn, by the smell. Oh, yeah. Like roasting a cob on a campfire.

SILVER LIGHTNING MOONSHINE

SUMMARY: Stephen Gertman is the president and master distiller of Ascendant Spirits, established in 2011. He makes his Silver Lightning Moonshine by hand and in small batches. It's made from 100% American yellow corn, and they credit the unique California coastal valley marine layer for aiding in the production process. The whiskey comes in an old-time whiskey jug that looks great on the shelf. The clear stuff inside is bottled at 99 proof, but don't let that scare you off; it's pretty smooth and has all the raw flavors that white whiskey lovers could want.

FUN FACT: Silver Lightning Moonshine won Double Gold at the 2013 International Spirits Competition in New York.

VARIETY/STYLE: White Corn

BARREL TYPE: N/A

AGE: N/A

ORIGIN: California

BOTTLE: 750 ml, cork top

ALCOHOL: 49.5%

PROOF: 99

PRICE: mid-range

RELATED: Ballast Point, Stein, Hudson, Balcones, Prichard's

PROPELLERS:

Ascendant Spirits Inc., 37 Industrial Way, Suite 102, Buellton, CA 93427, (805) 691-1000, www.ascendantspirits.com

COMMENTS FROM THE BARTENDER:

ANNIE: The nose repels me and I don't like the taste.

JEFF: Smells and tastes like caramel corn with a peppery afterburn.

JOHN: Huge corn on the nose tells me I'm going to like this. Yep, sweet corn that really gives me a smile I can't even imagine how good this would be after sitting in a barrel for about 8 years.

BRANDON: This is the perfect moonshine!

STEINSHINE CORN WHISKEY

SUMMARY: The Stein micro-distillery in Joseph, Oregon, prides itself on attention to detail. Every part of the process, from grain growth to harvest through fermenting, distilling, filtering and bottling, is done by hand. Steinshine is a great whiskey to try if you want to experience true farm-to-shelf whiskey with some unique flavors.

FUN FACT: Stein Distillery is the first micro-distillery in the eastern Oregon area.

VARIETY/STYLE: Corn

BARREL TYPE: N/A

AGE: N/A

ORIGIN: Oregon

BOTTLE: 750 ml, cork top

ALCOHOL: 40%

PROOF: 80

PRICE: mid-range

RELATED: Thunder Beast, Georgia Moon, Ballast Point, Silver Lightning, MBR White Dog

Stein Distillery, P.O. Box 200, Joseph, OR 97846, (541) 432-2009, whiskey@steindistillery.com, www.steindistillery.com

PROPELLERS:

COMMENTS FROM THE BARTENDER:

ANNIE: All white whiskey reminds me of tequila. And this smells like it, but the taste is a lot sweeter and smoother.

JEFF: Nose of corn, cream corn and earthy notes, a good idea of what a corn whiskey should taste like.

JOHN: White whiskey is really growing on me! This one is very smooth and sweet, and is that horse leather I'm tasting?

BRANDON: I'm always scared to drink clear whiskey that I don't know, but was surprised by a sweet, smooth taste.

★ AERO CLUB ★

ERO CLUB BAR

MALT

Malt whiskeys are rapidly gaining popularity in the States, mainly due to the hard work of many craft distilleries across the country. We are in the midst of a whiskey revolution and Americans are more thirsty for the spirit than ever. We have hordes of wide-eyed patrons pour through our doors looking to try something they've never had, and our remedy for their fever is American malt whiskey.

In the U.K., the government defines a single malt whiskey as a spirit distilled at one distillery using one batch of malted barley, fermented only with yeast, and aged a minimum of three years in oak casks. Those laws don't apply in the States, though it does have to be aged in new charred oak.

Many American distilleries have begun producing single grain, malted barley whiskeys, and the quality just keeps getting better. This is because the distillers take great pride in their farm-to-bottle approach to making whiskey. They source their grain from local farms and are producing small batches with extra attention to detail.

In this section, we try to pick apart some of our favorite American malt whiskeys for you. These are great whiskeys for you to explore, consisting of unique and complex flavors. Don't be discouraged if you're not particularly a fan of Scotch or Irish whiskeys. These American versions will surprise you with an array of enjoyable flavors that only whiskey made in America can provide.

CHATOE ROGUE OREGON SINGLE MALT WHISKEY

SUMMARY: Rogue Distillery is an extension of Rogue Brewery, one of the first microbreweries in the Pacific Northwest. They are known for experimenting with all types of different mash combinations to produce unique flavor profiles. The Chatoe Rogue is made from malted barley that's also used to make Rogue Dirtoir Black Lager. The whiskey is then aged for three months in their ocean-aged barrels. Just like the Dead Guy Whiskey, this is an acquired taste, with some very raw and very young whiskey flavors.

FUN FACT: The general manager of Rogue, Gary Fleshman, was quoted as saying, "Some people like our stuff and some don't, and that's just fine with us."

VARIETY/STYLE: Malt

BARREL TYPE: Oak

AGE: 3 months

ORIGIN: Oregon

BOTTLE: 750 ml, cork top

ALCOHOL: 40%

PROOF: 80

PRICE: mid-range

RELATED: Ballast Point, RoughStock, Prichard's, High West, Corsair

PROPELLERS:

Rogue Spirits, 2320 Southeast OSU Drive, Newport, OR 97365, (541) 867-3660, John@rogue.com, www.rogue.com

COMMENTS FROM THE BARTENDER:

ANNIE: Perfume-y yet sweet on the nose, maybe some banana. It's floral at first but finishes sweet and rich.

JEFF: This rich-tasting whiskey is full of molasses, mixed with a little wood shavings and fruit. A sweet whiskey that left me thinking about breakfast.

JOHN: I would say this is very young. It is very fragrant, like perfume—very floral. I don't think I would drink this again.

BRANDON: I really appreciate a well-crafted American single malt. Medium bodied through and through with a clear and slightly salty finish. Now I feel like going fishing.

CORSAIR RASPUTIN

SUMMARY: The guys at Corsair are mad scientists of sorts, pumping out many crowd-pleasing variations of whiskey with every type of flavor from sweet to spice to smoke, and even some fruit and coffee in there. Their Rasputin hopped whiskey is derived from a Russian imperial stout. The guys modified the stout recipe to create the base for the whiskey, and the flavor profile they've created is a must-try for any craft beer lover. Lots of hops with layers of sweetness.

FUN FACT: Darek Bell, Corsair co-owner, wrote a book showcasing his creative recipes called *Alt Whiskeys: Alternative Whiskey Recipes and Distilling Techniques for the Adventurous Craft Distiller.*

VARIETY/STYLE: Malt

BARREL TYPE: Charred Oak

AGE: N/A

ORIGIN: Tennessee/Kentucky

BOTTLE: 750 ml, cork top

ALCOHOL: 43%

PROOF: 86

PRICE: mid-range

RELATED: Ballast Point, RoughStock, Koval, Journeyman, Stein

PROPELLERS:

Corsair Distillery–Nashville, 1200 Clinton Street #110, Nashville, TN 37203, (615) 200-0320, www.corsairartisan.com
Producer: Corsair Distillery–Bowling Green, 400 Main Street #110, Bowling Green, KY 42101, (270) 904-2021, www.corsairartisan.com

COMMENTS FROM THE BARTENDER:

ANNIE: Super interesting nose, oaky and peppery. Starts citrusy and spicy and finishes with cocoa smoothness.

JEFF: An interesting whiskey. The more you sip on it, the more flavors seem to come out. Pepper, oak, citrus and a smooth, almost chocolate-coffee flavor.

JOHN: Man! Intense flavor! Very complex. Spicy in the front, sweet in the middle, with a nice smooth finish. Also . . . I think I know what brand it is.

BRANDON: Hops! I hate hops! Some strong notes of coffee on the back end, but really, it's like being forced to listen to The Smiths on repeat.

CORSAIR TRIPLE SMOKE

SUMMARY: The Corsair Distillery is owned and operated by Andrew Webber and Darek Bell. The guys are known for experimenting with different blends and with some edgy marketing, as well as a touch of mystery. The whiskey is selling like hotcakes! The triple smoke is created by smoking barley three different ways: cherry wood, beech wood and peat. It is pot distilled and aged in newly charred oak. These ingredients combined with this process create one hell of a whiskey! If you like smoke at all, this is a must-try!

FUN FACT: Triple Smoke was voted Artisan Whiskey of the Year in 2013 by *Whiskey Advocate*.

VARIETY/STYLE: Blended Malt

BARREL TYPE: New Charred Oak

AGE: N/A

ORIGIN: Tennessee/Kentucky

BOTTLE: 750 ml, cork top

ALCOHOL: 40%

PROOF: 80

PRICE: mid-range

RELATED: RoughStock, High West, Rogue, Ballast Point, Angkor

PROPELLERS: ! ! !

Corsair Distillery–Nashville, 1200 Clinton Street #110, Nashville, TN 37203, (615) 200-0320, www.corsairartisan.com
Producer: Corsair Distillery–Bowling Green, 400 Main Street #110, Bowling Green, KY 42101, (270) 904-2021, www.corsairartisan.com

COMMENTS FROM THE BARTENDER:

ANNIE: Super smoky and not in a pleasant way. Almost bitter and leaves a lasting bite. Kind of herbal at the end, too.

JEFF: There's good smoke and then there's bad smoke, and this falls into that category. Smoky and bitter, I'll pass on this one every time.

JOHN: The smoke is a bit much. There is something interesting, though—almost a medicine quality.

BRANDON: Malty, with peat and other smoky flavors. I dedicate this whiskey to my Scotch-loving friends. Tasty!

DEVIL'S SHARE CALIFORNIA SMALL BATCH SINGLE MALT WHISKEY

SUMMARY: Malt whiskey is on the rise with small craft distilleries popping up and each offering up their version of its best, so it may be hard to choose, especially when you have a selection like the Aero Club. We asked Ballast Point's Master Distiller Yuseff Cherney what makes this THE whiskey of choice. "When we set out to create Devil's Share Single Malt Whiskey, we refused to sacrifice quality in favor of expedience; after all, our goal was to craft the smoothest whiskey possible. So we began with pure brewer's malt: 100% two-row malted brewer's barley is the foundation of our Single Malt Whiskey. Select brewer's barley is used to ensure that the same award-winning quality of our beers carries through to our whiskey. This grain is not peated, so there is no smoky quality to the final product. The grain is mashed and steeped in our brew house just like our beer, minus the addition of hops, and removed from the husk prior to fermentation. This 'lautering' process produces a more refined whiskey with just the sweet barley malt being fermented into our 'distillers beer.' The 'beer' is then distilled through our custom-built Vendome copper hybrid pot/column still. Only the hearts are kept and aged in virgin heavily charred American oak barrels for a minimum of three years. Devil's Share Bourbon and Single Malt Whiskey are then proofed down to barrel strength of 122 proof using our onsite reverse-osmosis water. We have found this is the perfect proof for our spirits to interact with the wood and char in our mild San Diego climate." It would seem he's not alone; check out this trophy case: American Distilling Institute 2010: Gold Medal: Whiskey Idiosyncratic, 2011: Silver Medal; Single Malt Whiskey, 2012: Best of Category; Single Malt Whiskey, 2012: Gold Medal; Whiskey, 2013: Best of Class; Whiskey, 2013: Best of Category; Single Malt Whiskey, 2013: Gold Medal; Single Malt Whiskey, Spirits International Prestige (SIP) Awards, 2013: Gold; 2014 Gold Medal for Single Malt Whiskey and Moonshine: World Spirits Awards.

PROPELLERS:

FUN FACT: Extra time and thought were put into the design of the tall, sleek bottle. The dip down the back feels like your hand is on a beautiful woman's back, and the raised letters assure that if the bottle is dug up 100 years from now you will know exactly what it was.

VARIETY/STYLE: Single Malt

BARREL TYPE: American Oak

AGE: 4 years

ORIGIN: California

BOTTLE: 750 ml, cork top

ALCOHOL: 46%

PROOF: 92

PRICE: high-range

RELATED: RoughStock, Corsair, Prichard's, Journeyman, Rogue

Ballast Point, 9045 Carroll Way, San Diego, CA 92121, (858) 695-2739, www.ballastpoint.com

COMMENTS FROM THE BARTENDER:

ANNIE: Vanilla, toast, cinnamon and smoke. Pretty smooth and malty. A little sharp, but it's a nice sharpness.

JEFF: A nice combination of cinnamon, malt, wood and a hint of licorice. Could easily work in a cocktail, but why mix it? It's just great on its own.

JOHN: Very mellow relaxed medium spice. I don't get very much wood. I really like the finish. A must-try neat.

BRANDON: I can really taste the wood and some licorice mixed in with a sweet maltiness. The finish is smooth and pleasant.

GOLDEN SAMISH BAY SINGLE MALT WHISKEY

SUMMARY: The distillery's home is on the quaint hideaway of Samish Island in Bow, Washington. It's an area with very rich agriculture that produces some of the best barley in the country. A true artisan distillery, they use locally sourced products to craft their whiskey. Whiskey guru Jim Murray gave this whiskey an 88.5 rating, which translates to very good to excellent and definitely worth buying. This whisky really lets you experience the barley from this region as well as the craftsmanship that went into the production of the whiskey. A great whiskey to slowly sip and pick apart the flavors. Grab some while you can can—they've recently closed.

FUN FACT: They also offer a Rescuing Single Malt and a selection of handcrafted brandies. They will be releasing more products as soon as they finish doing time in new charred oak barrels.

VARIETY/STYLE: Malt

BARREL TYPE: Oak

AGE: 4 years

ORIGIN: Washington

BOTTLE: 750 ml, cork top

ALCOHOL: 40%

PROOF: 80

PRICE: mid-range

RELATED: Stein, Koval, High West, Ballast Point, Dry Fly

PROPELLERS: !!!!

COMMENTS FROM THE BARTENDER:

ANNIE: Malty and honey on the nose. Flavor is very rich and malty with pleasant caramel, soft vanilla and wood.

JEFF: The first thing you'll notice is a strong burn. As this tapered off, notes of honey, oak and grain showed up in a pleasing combination.

JOHN: The burn is like a quick punch in the gut. After you squint your way through that, it has some pretty interesting flavors of vanilla and honeycomb. Needs help from our old buddy ice!

BRANDON: Okay. It's complex smooth burn that has some pretty cool apple and honey flavors. Kinda like a scotch. Great end of the nighter.

PRICHARD'S SINGLE MALT WHISKEY

SUMMARY: Distilled in one of two large pot stills in Kelso, Tennessee, using water from a nearby steam, Prichard's malt whiskey is produced much like finer Irish-styled whiskeys distilled from malted barley with a very low percentage of rye. It's a unique combination of American and Irish styles with a range of flavors. Try swapping this in for your next Rob Roy.

FUN FACT: Although it didn't make our review list, Prichard's makes a wonderful chocolate-infused bourbon.

VARIETY/STYLE: Malt

BARREL TYPE: New American Oak

AGE: N/A

ORIGIN: Tennessee

BOTTLE: 750 ml, cork top

ALCOHOL: 40%

PROOF: 80

PRICE: mid-range

RELATED: Corsair, Rogue, St. George, Wasmund's, Westward

Prichard's Distillery, 4125 White Creek Pike, Nashville, TN 37189, (615) 724-1600, www.prichardsdistillery.com

PROPELLERS: !!!!

COMMENTS FROM THE BARTENDER:

ANNIE: Very sweet and charred nose. Oak-y, hints of vanilla, oatmeal cookies and even chocolate, which was a bit surprising.

JEFF: I want this to be more. It has a quality just wanting to get out but it's never quite there. It's still unique though.

JOHN: Okay. Sweet grass on the nose. Here it goes—chocolate goodness. Nice lasting finish. Drink up!

BRANDON: Heavy char flavor. Just like an oak tree caught fire and I decided to grow on it. Use this in place of scotch in your Rob Roy.

ROUGHSTOCK MALT WHISKEY

SUMMARY: RoughStock's Malt Whiskey is what put them on the map. Made from 100% Montana-grown and malted barley mash, they use stream water fed from high elevation snowmelt and carefully selected, lightly charred new American oak barrels. The folks at RoughStock proudly produce in small batches, cultivating from grain to glass. This means they are hands on from start to finish. It seems like a lot of our guests either love malt whiskey or make what we call whiskey face, and that's not good. If you are curious about malt whiskey, we highly recommend trying it before you buy a bottle, and RoughStock is a good introduction. They've recently closed, so grab a bottle while you can.

FUN FACT: RoughStock is the first legal distillery in Montana in over 100 years.

VARIETY/STYLE: Malt

ORIGIN: Montana

BOTTLE: 750 ml, cork top

ALCOHOL: 45%

PROOF: 90

PRICE: mid-range

RELATED: Prichard's, Corsair, Golden Samish Bay, Devil's Share, Stein

PROPELLERS: !!!! !!!!

COMMENTS FROM THE BARTENDER:

ANNIE: Spices and oranges! Lots of spice on my tongue minutes after it finishes. I thoroughly enjoyed this one.

JEFF: Scotch is my least favorite of the whiskeys, so I am just not a fan of this, but I appreciate the quality I taste in it.

JOHN: Finally I get a little heat! Slight burn with a vegetable quality. Less sweet, more green tasting.

BRANDON: This whiskey is distinctively malty. There aren't many American single malts around, but this grainy malt could steal any scotch lover's heart.

ROUGHSTOCK SINGLE MALT CASK STRENGTH

SUMMARY: Born from locally grown barley and distilled twice in a copper pot still, this whiskey is aged in charred virgin American white oak. The whiskey is bottled at actual cask strength, not chill filtered and uncut, meaning no water was added to lower the proof before bottling. No open flames, please! This whiskey packs a Scottish punch with a big American fist. Believe it or not, it makes a great Bloody Mary.

FUN FACT: In Scotland, the term "single malt" means the whiskey is distilled and aged at a single distillery. There's no law requiring that rule in the U.S.

VARIETY/STYLE: Single Malt

BARREL TYPE: New American Oak

AGE: N/A

ORIGIN: Montana

BOTTLE: 750 ml, cork top

ALCOHOL: 57.4%

PROOF: 115

PRICE: high-range

RELATED: Prichard's, Corsair, Golden Samish Bay, Devil's Share, Stein

PROPELLERS: !!!

COMMENTS FROM THE BARTENDER:

ANNIE: Herbal-y and almost, tequila-like. Strange, but I can get into it.

JEFF: This starts off with a light fruit nose, mostly pear. Banana, caramel and smoke round out this tasty beverage. A few cubes should help bring out the fruit flavor.

JOHN: Oh, yes! I really like this. Slight burn, sweet candy flavor with a nice aftertaste. I would start the night with this on the rocks.

BRANDON: This is like getting punched in the gut. If you're not a fan of malt, steer clear.

WASMUND'S SINGLE MALT SPIRIT

SUMMARY: Copper Fox Distillery was founded in January of 2000 with some very innovative ideas for making new whiskeys. Founder Rick Wasmund's idea was to use fruit-wood peat and fruit-wood barrels in the traditional whiskey-making process. This single malt whiskey from Wasmund's is on a path of its own. The malted barley is flavored with apple- and cherry-wood smoke and is produced one barrel at a time with a single batch copper pot still, then non-chill filtered to preserve the flavor of the barley grain. And let me tell you, there are a lot of flavors! This is an easy one to figure out: if you love flavors of wood, smoke, cherry or malt, you may have just found your new favorite juice. If you are opposed to any of those flavors, then steer clear. Love it or hate it, respect the craftsmanship. Thanks, Rick!

FUN FACT: Copper Fox claims this is the only single malt in the United States to be malted and distilled under the same roof, and the only one in the world to use apple- and cherry-wood smoke to flavor their barley.

VARIETY/STYLE: Malt Spirit

BARREL TYPE: Used Bourbon

AGE: N/A

ORIGIN: Virginia

BOTTLE: 750 ml, screw cap

ALCOHOL: 62%

PROOF: 124

PRICE: mid-range

RELATED: Ballast Point, Stein, WhipperSnapper, RoughStock, Koval

PROPELLERS:

The Copper Fox Distillery, 9 River Lane, Sperryville, VA 22740, (540) 987-8554, Rick@copperfox.biz, www.copperfox.biz,

COMMENTS FROM THE BARTENDER:

ANNIE: Peaty smell for a clear spirit. Tastes like greens and cinnamon with flowers thrown in for good measure. Definitely use with a mixer.

JEFF: This has a peaty smoke nose that makes me think scotch. The earthy taste is one that I'll pass on.

JOHN: I really want to like this but it's just a little too harsh for me, and if it's too much for me, I could never recommend it to the average human being.

BRANDON: A really moist smell with an oily feel. It must be barrel strength because it's quite warm. I enjoyed the smooth finish and complex flavor after finishing my taster the most.

WESTWARD SMALL BATCH OREGON STRAIGHT MALT WHISKEY

SUMMARY: Westward Straight Malt Whiskey was inspired by Irish tradition but was crafted with a unique American style. It begins with 100% locally sourced Northwest two-row barley. It's fermented with ale yeast, then double-pot distilled. The whiskey also benefits from its no less than two years' aging in the hot Oregon summers and cold, wet winters. If you're a fan of Irish whiskey, you are probably gonna love this stuff. It's a fusion of Irish style and American craft. Just be ready to spend a couple bucks; it's a little higher priced than some of its shelf buddies.

FUN FACT: House Spirits also produces vodka, gin, white dog, aquavit and coffee liqueur.

VARIETY/STYLE: Single Malt

BARREL TYPE: American Oak

AGE: 2 years

ORIGIN: Oregon

BOTTLE: 375 ml, cork top

ALCOHOL: 45%

PROOF: 90

PRICE: high-range

RELATED: RoughStock, Prichard's, Ballast Point, Corsair, Rogue

PROPELLERS:

House Spirits Distillery, 65 South East Washington Street, Portland, OR 97214, (503) 235-3174, www.housespirits.com

COMMENTS FROM THE BARTENDER:

ANNIE: Brown sugar, vanilla and oak. I like it. Give me another, please!

JEFF: Not much to this one. Smells like caramel and cleared out my sinuses.

JOHN: The nose is all fruit. It has a nice burn that is quickly gone with a sweet caramel finish.

BRANDON: Quite peppery. Just a bit of a tingle in my mouth. The finish is much sweeter and tastes like graham crackers.

COCKTAILS

The wonderful world of whiskey grasps the attention of the young and the old. It is a tradition made into a trend that has no intention of disappearing. Whiskey is a complex mix of different grains, flavors and a distillation process that has no bounds. Bartenders and mixologists are honing a variety of skills to develop fine creations known as craft cocktails. The focus is on the art of mixing cocktails using small batch spirits, fresh local ingredients, seasonal spices and syrups. With all the wealth of information provided on the subject, sadly, the knowledge most folks have is limited to the whiskey sour. We thought that we would include some classics with a twist and unique whiskey craft cocktails from mixologists around the country. These unique recipes will enhance and entice your audience, giving them a mixture of different flavors and aromas that will spice up your favorite North American whiskey.

JEREMY'S NORTH AMERICAN COCKTAIL FAVORITES | SAN DIEGO, CA

ONE FOR THE MONEY, TWO FOR THE SHOW

YIELDS 1 COCKTAIL

2¼ oz (68 ml) Bulleit Bourbon

¾ oz (20 ml) Grand Marnier

½ tsp lemon juice

2 dashes Angostura bitters

Ice

Curl of lemon rind, for garnish

Combine the bourbon and the other ingredients (except rind) in a cocktail shaker with ice, shake vigorously and strain into a chilled martini glass. Garnish with a curl of lemon rind.

THE RUN OF THE MILL

YIELDS 1 COCKTAIL

2 oz (60 ml) Buffalo Trace Straight Kentucky Bourbon

½ oz (15 ml) French vermouth (I prefer Martini Rosso)

2 dashes orange bitters

Cracked ice

In a TIN PLAY shaker, add all ingredients and stir well, then strain into a cocktail glass full of cracked ice.

HOT AND BUTTERY

YIELDS 1 COCKTAIL

4 oz (120 ml) boiling water
2 oz (60 ml) Basil Hayden's Bourbon
2 dashes walnut bitters
1 tbsp (14 g) butter
Cinnamon stick, for garnish
1 lemon

Bring the water to a boil. Add your whiskey straight into a coffee or tea glass. Add the water, bitters and butter, and then stir with a cinnamon stick until the butter is dissolved.

Then, to make a string of lemon for garnish, use a lemon zester or sharp paring knife to gently go around the top of the lemon to create a spiral. Clean up the excess with the paring knife. Garnish the drink with a string of lemon and a cinnamon stick. Great for colds!

LA MARQUITA

YIELDS 1 COCKTAIL

Ice

1½ oz (45 ml) whiskey (we like to use Gentlemen Jack for this recipe)

½ oz (15 ml) red cranberry juice

1 tsp homemade rhubarb syrup*

2 tsp pomegranate seeds

In a shaker, combine a scoop of ice, whiskey, juice and syrup. Shake vigorously for a count of 15 seconds, strain and pour into a cocktail glass. In your glass, add seeds and stir for about 10 revolutions. Enjoy!

NOTE: The bitterer your pomegranate seeds are the more they will tend to float on your cocktail. By the end of the sip, note how the pomegranate seeds have taken on a smokier flavor.

---

*RHUBARB SYRUP

2–3 small stalks rhubarb, chopped
1 cup (190 g) cane sugar
2 cups (470 ml) water
¼ tsp cinnamon
¼ tsp nutmeg
½ vanilla bean pod

Combine ingredients in a small pot. Bring to a boil, and then reduce heat to a simmer. Simmer 5 to 7 minutes, then let cool completely. Strain ingredients. Syrup will keep well covered in fridge for 2 weeks.

VERMONT MADE

YIELDS 1 COCKTAIL

2 oz (60 ml) WhistlePig Boss Hog Rye Whiskey

¾ oz (20 ml) Martini Rosso sweet vermouth

1 oz (30 ml) Cherry Heering

½ tbsp (7 ml) absinthe

Ice

Orange zest, for garnish

Add all ingredients except orange zest to a shaker. Stir and strain into a chilled cocktail glass. Express orange oils and garnish with zest.

THE KENTUCKY MINT

YIELDS 1 COCKTAIL

6 mint leaves
5 fresh Bing cherries, pitted
1 tbsp (22 g) simple syrup
Crushed ice
3 oz (90 ml) Evan Williams Kentucky Straight Bourbon Whiskey

Place 5 mint leaves, 4 cherries and simple syrup in a silver julep cup and gently muddle. Add your crushed ice followed by your bourbon. Give a shake and garnish it with a sprig of mint and 1 cherry.

THE JACKASS

YIELDS 1 COCKTAIL

2 oz (60 ml) Jack Daniel's Old Number 7 Kentucky Straight Whiskey

1 tbsp (22 g) simple syrup

¼ oz (7 ml) freshly squeezed lime juice

2 dashes Fee Brothers Whiskey Barrel Aged Bitters

4 oz (120 ml) Goslings Ginger Beer

1 sprig fresh mint, for garnish

Slice of lime

Add your bourbon, syrup, lime juice and bitters to a copper mug followed lastly by the ginger beer. Give it shake and garnish with a sprig of mint and lime.

BLACKOUT

YIELDS 1 COCKTAIL

2 oz (60 ml) Dry Fly Cask Strength Wheat Whiskey (120 proof)

½ oz (15 ml) Green Chartreuse

½ oz (15 ml) Kummel

2 dashes Fee Brothers Whiskey Barrel Aged Bitters

1 lemon

Cinnamon stick, for garnish

Pour all ingredients except the lemon and cinnamon stick into a shaker or mixing glass. Stir and strain into a cocktail glass. Then, take a potato peeler and peel the skin of the lemon from top to bottom. Then squeeze the skin over the drink, releasing its oils, which adds a floral aromatic to the drink. Lastly, discard the lemon peel or swath and garnish the drink with a cinnamon stick. This will change the aromatics of the drink throughout your enjoyment of it and will offer up some subtle wine-like tannins.

BULLEIT PASS

YIELDS 1 COCKTAIL

1½ oz (45 ml) Bulleit Bourbon*

⅔ oz (18 ml) Cynar

¾ oz (20 ml) Imbue Petal & Thorn Vermouth (made with Pinot Gris brandy in Oregon)

3 dashes tea pot bitters

Orange swath, for garnish

Pour all ingredients except orange swath in a down glass. Stir and garnish with the orange swath.

* When constructing this cocktail it must be an absolute stir. It's spirit based and the bourbon itself is pretty aromatic, so you don't want dilution from the ice—just enough to cut through some of the oils and esters from the whiskey.

* This drink needs to be a high rye bourbon; Breckenridge Bourbon also works well.

HOPKIN'S LAST STAND

YIELDS 1 COCKTAIL

2 cups (475 ml) mint tea

2 pinches saffron

1 oz (28 g) honey

2 oz (60 ml) Bully Boy American
Straight Whiskey*

½ oz (15 ml) Pierre Ferrand Dry Curaçao

½ oz (15 ml) freshly squeezed lemon juice

¼ oz (7 g) simple syrup

6 dashes Peychaud's Bitters

Some small shavings of orange zest

Dash of paprika

Lemon swath, for garnish

To make the ice cubes, make 2 cups (475 ml) of tea consisting of mint tea leaves and 2 pinches of saffron and 1 ounce (28 g) of honey while still hot. Once the honey dissolves and the saffron infuses with the mint tea, pour into your ice trays and freeze.

Add 4 mint tea and saffron ice cubes with all ingredients except the lemon swath in a shaker. Shake and double strain into a traditional tulip whiskey glass. Finish with one infused ice cube and a lemon swath.

* Cool mash bill of 45% corn, 45% rye and 10% malted barley. We tried with traditional bourbons and rye but they overpowered the subtle flavors of the drink.

THE DRUM

YIELDS 1 COCKTAIL

2 lemon wedges
2 oz (60 ml) George Dickel Rye
¼ oz (7 ml) Cynar
¾ oz (20 g) kumquat syrup

First, use a brûlée torch to char the lemons. You can use a cast-iron skillet at home to char either side of the lemon. Once they are charred, remove them with a pair of tongs and let cool for a moment.

Once cool, muddle 2 charred lemons with all the ingredients in a shaker. Shake and double strain into a coupe. Enjoy.

AERO MANHATTAN

YIELDS 1 COCKTAIL

2½ oz (75 ml) Maker's Mark Bourbon
¼ oz (7 ml) sweet vermouth
2 dashes Angostura Bitters
Ice
Cherry, for garnish

Add all the ingredients except the cherry to a shaker and stir (if you shake you will bruise the bourbon). Strain into a martini glass and garnish with a cherry.

AERO OLD FASHIONED

YIELDS 1 COCKTAIL

1 tbsp (12 g) granulated sugar

2 dashes Angostura Bitters

Lemon and orange twists

Splash of water

2 oz (60 ml) Fighting Cocktail Burbon

Ice

Cherry, for garnish

Add the sugar, bitters, lemon and orange twists and water to a glass and stir until pasty. Then, add the bourbon and ice and stir. Garnish with a cherry.

AERO SAZERAC

YIELDS 1 COCKTAIL

Ricard, for rinse
2½ oz (75 ml) Russel's Reserve 6 Year Rye
¼ oz (7 g) simple syrup
2 dashes Angostura Bitters
Ice
Lemon twist, for garnish

Rinse a martini glass with Ricard. Combine the ingredients except the lemon twist in the glass and stir. Garnish with the lemon twist.

WHISKEY CADILLAC

YIELDS 1 COCKTAIL

Sugar, for rim

2 slices lemon

2½ oz (75 ml) George Dickel Tennessee Whiskey

¼ oz (7 ml) Cointreau

Ice

Lemon twist, for garnish

Wet the rim of a martini glass and press into sugar to make the sugar rim. Muddle the lemon slices in a shaker. Add the whiskey, Cointreau and ice. Shake vigorously, then strain into the martini glass. Garnish with a lemon twist.

AERO WHISKEY SOUR

YIELDS 1 COCKTAIL

2 slices lemon

2 oz (60 ml) Fighting Cock Bourbon

¼ oz (7 g) simple syrup

¼ oz (7 g) egg white

Ice

Dash of Angostura Bitters

Cherry, for garnish

Cinnamon, for garnish

Muddle the lemon in a shaker, then add the bourbon, simple syrup and egg white. Dry shake vigorously, then add the ice and shake vigorously again. Strain over ice in a rocks glass, and garnish with a dash of Angostura Bitters, a cherry and a pinch of cinnamon.

DANNY AND THE TRAMP COCKTAIL

YIELDS 1 COCKTAIL

2 lemon slices
2 oz (60 ml) Four Roses Yellow Label Bourbon
½ oz (15 ml) Amaretto
½ oz (15 ml) 7UP
Ice

Muddle the lemon slices in a shaker and add the bourbon, Amaretto, 7UP and ice. Shake and then strain over ice into a rocks glass.

CAMP HARTLEY BREAKFAST

YIELDS 1 COCKTAIL

1½ oz (45 ml) Bowen's

2 oz (60 ml) Bloody Mary mix

Ice

Salt, for rim

Lemon and lime wedges, for garnish

Olives, for garnish

Pickled cocktail onions, for garnish

1 oz (30 ml) Guinness

In a shaker, add the Bowen's, Bloody Mary mix and ice. Shake and strain over ice into a pint or highball glass with a salted rim. Garnish with a wedge of lemon and lime, olives and pickled cocktail onions. Be sure to leave room for that float of Guinness!

BE GOOD, OR BE GONE

YIELDS 1 COCKTAIL

Lemon slice

Lime slice

1½ oz (45 ml) Seagram's 7

½ oz (15 ml) elderflower liqueur

Ice

Soda water

Muddle the slice of lemon and lime in a shaker. Add the Seagram's 7, elderflower liqueur and ice. Shake, then strain over ice in a rocks glass. Top with soda water.

WINTER WALTZ

YIELDS 1 COCKTAIL

2 oz (60 ml) Bulleit Rye Whiskey

½ oz (15 ml) Amaro Averna

¼ oz (7 ml) St. Elizabeth's Allspice Dram

2 dashes DeGroff's Pimento Bitters

Star anise, for garnish

Add all ingredients except garnish into a shaker. Shake and strain into a chilled cocktail glass. Garnish with star anise.

BOO RADLEY

YIELDS 1 COCKTAIL

2 oz (60 ml) Wild Turkey Kentucky Bourbon

¾ oz (20 ml) Cynar

½ oz (15 ml) Cherry Heering

Ice

Lemon peel, for garnish

Stir ingredients (except the peel) into a cocktail shaker and strain into ice-filled snifter. Garnish with lemon peel.

WALKER PERCY

YIELDS 1 COCKTAIL

2 oz (60 ml) Maker's Mark Whiskey

½ oz (15 ml) Angostura Bitters

½ oz (15 ml) grenadine

¼ oz (7 ml) lemon juice

¼ oz (7 g) simple syrup

Ice

Lemon peel, for garnish

Add all ingredients except ice and lemon peel in a shaker. Shake and strain over an ice-filled Old Fashioned glass. Garnish with lemon peel.

WHISKEY WARD | MANHATTAN, NY

BERNHEIM MAPLE SYRUP OLD FASHIONED

YIELDS 1 COCKTAIL

1 orange slice

½ oz (15 ml) homemade bourbon cherry*

Ice

1 tbsp (22 g) maple syrup**

2 oz (60 ml) Bernheim Wheat Whiskey

2 dashes Angostura Bitters

Splash of soda

Muddle orange slice and homemade bourbon cherry in a glass. Add ice to a shaker along with your maple syrup, whiskey and bitters, shake vigorously and then transfer back into the glass. Top with splash of soda.

* Fill a mason jar with maraschino cherries and add your bourbon; let sit at room temperature for 2 weeks.

** We make the maple syrup by using Vermont dark maple syrup cut with half water.

LES SWEET TEA

YIELDS 1 COCKTAIL

Ice

2 oz (60 ml) Buffalo Trace Bourbon

¾ oz (22 g) honey syrup*

8 oz (235 ml) brewed iced tea

Lemon slice, for garnish

Fill a 16-ounce (475 ml) mason jar with ice, the bourbon, the honey syrup and the brewed iced tea. Use a barspoon to mix the ingredients. Garnish with a lemon slice.

* We make this syrup by cutting the honey with half hot water.

THE PORTER HOUSE | NEW YORK, NY

DAWN OF THE UNION 1776

YIELDS 1 COCKTAIL

2 oz (60 ml) Basil Hayden's 8 Year Bourbon Whiskey

½ oz (15 ml) Bols Genever

Juice of 2 freshly squeezed lemon wedges

½ oz (15 g) heavy-bodied rum syrup

Ice

2 dashes peach bitters

Sprinkle of cinnamon

Pour the bourbon, Bols Genever, lemon and syrup over ice. Peach bitters are added and the liquid is gently stirred for several moments. Strain into a coupe glass and finish with a pinch of cinnamon. The combination of the herbal Genever, the medium rye-spiced Basil Hayden with citrus fruits and sweet peach offer a taste of a bygone age.

THE ELIXIR | SAN FRANCISCO, CA

THE MONK'S CHERRY

YIELDS 1 COCKTAIL

5 Bing cherries, 1 for garnish

1" (2.5 cm) lavender flower

1 oz (30 ml) Bulleit Bourbon, Sazerac 6 Year Rye or Rittenhouse 100 Rye

¾ oz (20 ml) Green Chartreuse

½ oz (15 ml) Carpano Antica

Ice

1 full lavender flower, for garnish

In a mixing glass, add 4 Bing cherries and 1 inch (2.5 cm) lavender flower. Muddle well and add the liquid ingredients. Fill with ice and shake well for 10 seconds. Double strain into a chilled cocktail glass (preferably a coupe). Garnish with a lavender cherry (See below).

LAVENDER CHERRY GARNISH

Break the long steam off a lavender flower about ½ inch (1.3 cm) from the bottom of the flower. Clean up the stem so it will slide nicely into the cherry. Take a Bing cherry and cut a small slit from the bottom one-third of the way up and off center so as to miss the pit. Pull the stem off and slide the lavender flower into the stem hole, being careful not to puncture the outer skin of the cherry with the end of the stem. Slide the garnish onto the side of the glass.

THE TENDER KNOB

YIELDS 1 COCKTAIL

2 slices Granny Smith or Fuji apple

1½ oz (45 ml) Knob Creek Bourbon

2 oz (60 ml) draft cider

¾ oz (20 ml) agave nectar

10 grates cinnamon

Ice

In a mixing glass, muddle 1 slice of apple and cover with the other ingredients (save the other slice of apple for garnish). Fill with ice and shake well for 10 seconds. Strain over fresh ice in a tall glass (allowing some of the apple chunks through) and garnish with an apple slice.

BENTLEY OLD FASHIONED

YIELDS 1 COCKTAIL

2 oz (60 ml) Breaking and Entering Bourbon

2 dashes chocolate bitters

½ oz (15 g) orgeat syrup

Ice

70% dark chocolate, for garnish

In a bucket glass, add the bourbon, bitters and syrup. Then, add a large cube or ball of ice, stir well and garnish with shaved dark chocolate over the top.

HOLLINGER MANHATTAN PROJECT

YIELDS 1 COCKTAIL

2 oz (60 ml) Rittenhouse 100 Rye Whiskey

½ oz (15 ml) Carpano Antica Formula (sweet bitters)

¼ oz (7 ml) Luxardo Maraschino Liqueur

Ice

Absinthe, for rinse

Luxardo maraschino cherry

In a mixing glass, add the Rittenhouse, Carpano and Maraschino Liqueur. Top with ice and stir for 15 seconds. Rinse a chilled glass with absinthe and dispose of extra. Julep strain the cocktail and garnish with a Luxardo maraschino cherry.

THE KENTUCKY PILGRIM

YIELDS 1 COCKTAIL

1½ oz (45 ml) Wild Turkey Thanksgiving Infusion (page 178)
1 oz (30 ml) lemon juice
½ oz (15 ml) Luxardo Maraschino Liqueur
½ oz (15 g) demerara syrup
Ice
Lemon twist, for garnish

In a mixing glass, add all ingredients (except garnish) and shake well for 10 seconds. Hawthorne strain into a wine glass and garnish with a long lemon twist.

NOTE: To make this into a hot drink, swap in 3 ounces (90 ml) of hot water for the ice.

WILD TURKEY THANKSGIVING INFUSION

YIELDS 1 COCKTAIL

35 oz (1 L) Wild Turkey 101

2 tbsps (20 g) cardamom seeds

1½ cups (150 g) dried, unsweetened cranberries

3 sticks cinnamon

In a wide-mouthed glass infusion jar, place the Wild Turkey 101 and the cardamom seeds. Close and leave in a cool dark place for 1 day. Strain out cardamom and add the cranberries and cinnamon. Close and leave for another 2 days, agitating once per day. Strain solids and store in the original Wild Turkey bottle with proper labeling.

THE OVERLOOK

YIELDS 1 COCKTAIL

1½ oz (45 ml) Rittenhouse Rye

¾ oz (20 ml) Martini Rosso Sweet Vermouth

¾ oz (20 ml) Campari

Ice

Add all the ingredients (except garnish) into a TIN PLAY shaker and stir for 30 rotations. Strain into a martini glass and garnish with a lemon twist.

NOTE: The Overlook cocktail is named after the hotel in Steven King's *The Shining*, and the redness from the Campari takes on the look of the blood pouring out of the elevators. In this case we will say Red Rye, Red Rye.

JACK AND WENDY

YIELDS 1 COCKTAIL

2 oz (60 ml) Wild Turkey 81

½ oz (15 ml) Martini Rosso Sweet Vermouth

½ oz (15 ml) lemon juice

1 tbsp (20 g) apricot preserves

1 sage leaf

Shake up all the ingredients in a TIN PLAY shaker and served chilled in a martini glass.

NOTE: Named after the characters in *The Shining*, this delicious cocktail is ironically brute and a tad sweet.

THE GOOD, THE BAD & THE UGLY

YIELDS 1 COCKTAIL

1½ oz (45 ml) Old Overholt Rye

½ oz (15 ml) Fernet Branca

½ oz (15 ml) Lillet Blanc

½ oz (15 ml) Cherry Heering

½ oz (15 ml) lemon juice

Splash of simple syrup

Splash of club soda

Lemon wedge, for garnish

Pour all ingredients (except garnish) in a highball glass and stir. Garnish with a lemon wedge.

WHISKEY AND CIGAR PAIRINGS CHART

CIGAR NAME	COUNTRY	PRICE	PAIR WITH	CIGAR NOTES
ATABEY BRUJOS	Costa Rica	$25–30	FIGHTING COCK BOURBON	Medium body with toasted nuts, pepper and hickory spice flavors.
BYRON PETIT POEMAS	Costa Rica	$30–35	BALLAST POINT SINGLE MALT	Very dark, full flavor. Oak and spice with a lasting slow burn.
ILLUSIONE ULTRA	Nicaragua	$10–15	EAGLE RARE 10 YR BOURBON	Creamy, spice, cocoa and cherry.
EP CARRILLO EDICION LIMITADA 2011	Dominican Republic	$18–22	OLD WELLER ANTIQUE 107 BOURBON	Wheat toast, raisin, dried cherries and cranberries.
PADRON 1986 ANNIVERSARY SERIES	Nicaragua	$20–30	CORSAIR RYEMAGGEDON	The rarest cigar made by Padron. Full, spicy flavor stemming from aging the tobaccos for a full 5 years.
LAPALINA LIGERO #9	Dominican Republic	$10–30	JEFFERSON'S CHEF COLLABORATION	Nice spice kick, wood, grass and bitter seetness. Great complexity.
DAVIDOFF MILLENIUM ROBUSTO	Dominican Republic	$20–30	HUDSON N.Y. CORN WHISKEY	A rich and highly complex blend of perfectly balanced flavors and aromas.
LIGA PRIVADA	Nicaragua	$17–25	WOODFORD DOUBLE OAKED BOURBON	Rich, meaty smoke with notes of coffee and chocoate. Full bodied, but silky from start to finish.
MAKER'S MARK 650 TORO	Dominican Republic	$12–20	MAKER'S MARK BOURBON	Imbued with Maker's Mark bourbon to provide a sweet caramel-like flavor and scent in this medium-bodied cigar.
BYRON LONDINENSES	Costa Rica	$35–45	JOHN JACOB RYE WHISKEY	Hints of ouzo, soft wheat, with buttercream and fennel.

CIGAR NAME	COUNTRY	PRICE	PAIR WITH	NOTES
BYRON POEMAS	Costa Rica	$35–45	BUFFALO TRACE SINGLE OAK PROJECT	Aged for a full year after production. Heavy notes of oak, spice and chocolate.
HERRERA ESTELI	Nicaragua	$12–16	FOUR ROSES SINGLE BARREL BOURBON	Crisp, clean notes of spice, cedar and roasted nuts. Semisweet vanilla and cream as you burn it down.
FUENTE FUENTE OPUSX	Dominican Republic	$30–40	RUSSEL'S RESERVE 10 YR BOURBON	A near perfect smoke. Smooth and bold with a lingering sweetness.
ALEC BRADLEY FINE & RARE	Honduras	$28–32	BLANTON'S BOURBON	Toasty, savory and berry sweetness.
VIAJE ORO RESERVE	Nicaragua	$15–20	BREAKOUT RYE	Leather, sweet spice and cocoa powder. Perfect balance of bitter and sweet.
MONTECRISTO MONTE	Dominican Republic	$10–15	WHISTLEPIG	Woody with a healthy dose of black pepper, cinnamon and graham.
ARTURO FUENTE LOST CITY	Dominican Republic	$28–35	JEFFERSON'S 10 YR RYE	Incredibly complex and balanced with notes of coffee, cream, leather and spice.
MY FATHER LE BIJOU 1922	Nicaragua	$14–20	BALLAST POINT SMALL BATCH BOURBON	Fuller body with a depth of sweet cream, wood and spice flavors.
ASHTON VSG	Dominican Republic	$9–12	CYRUS NOBLE	Very earthy with notes of nuts and coffee.
BYRON ARISTOCRATAS	Costa Rica	$40–45	ELIJAH CRAIG 20 YEAR BOURBON	This phenominal cigar has it all. Rich, creamy, spicy, coffee, chocolate, chocolate cherries and wonderful toasted nuts.

THE NORTH AMERICAN WHISKEY DRINKER'S BUCKET LIST

Over the years, many great whiskeys have come and gone from our shelves, but there are a few that really stand out. These are whiskeys that are very limited releases, anniversary productions or even just a whiskey that is so outstanding that production of it could not possibly keep up with the demand for it.

In this book, we reviewed whiskeys for you that we currently have in stock, whiskeys that any decent bar probably has sitting on their shelves. So even though we didn't have access to some of our favorite rare or hard-to-find expressions, we felt they needed to be mentioned. These are tasty elixirs that proudly sat at eye level on our wall of whiskey, but unfortunately didn't stick around very long. So we sat down with our guests and staff to come up with the North American Whiskey Drinker's Bucket List. The whiskeys selected for this are some of our all-time bestsellers, favorites and what we feel are whiskeys you simply must try if you come across them.

We set this page up as a checklist that you can take with you on your travels and check them off as you find them. Here are 20 of our all-time favorites.

Good Luck!

- ☐ PAPPY VAN WINKLE'S 15 YEAR FAMILY RESERVE STRAIGHT BOURBON
- ☐ PAPPY VAN WINKLE'S 23 YEAR FAMILY RESERVE STRAIGHT BOURBON
- ☐ MICHTER'S 10 YEAR SINGLE BARREL BOURBON
- ☐ MICHTER'S 20 YEAR STRAIGHT BOURBON
- ☐ EAGLE RARE 17 YEAR STRAIGHT BOURBON
- ☐ ELIJAH CRAIG 18 YEAR STRAIGHT BOURBON
- ☐ JEFFERSON 18 YEAR STRAIGHT BOURBON (PRESIDENTIAL SELECT)
- ☐ MAKER'S MARK "MINT JULEP" GREEN WAX
- ☐ THOMAS H. HANDY SAZERAC STRAIGHT RYE
- ☐ RITTENHOUSE 25 YEAR VERY RARE RYE WHISKEY
- ☐ BLACK MAPLE HILL 23 YEAR RYE
- ☐ VINTAGE BOURBON 17 YEAR
- ☐ VINTAGE RYE 21 YEAR
- ☐ CANADIAN CLUB 30 YEAR
- ☐ WILLIAM LARUE WELLER KENTUCKY STRAIGHT BOURBON
- ☐ HIGH WEST BOURYE
- ☐ ST. GEORGE SINGLE MALT AMERICAN WHISKEY
- ☐ OLD FORESTER BIRTHDAY BOURBON 2007
- ☐ WOODFORD RESERVE MASTER'S COLLECTION MAPLE WOOD FINISH
- ☐ SAZERAC 18 YEAR OLD STRAIGHT RYE WHISKEY

ACKNOWLEDGMENTS

CHAD BERKEY WOULD LIKE TO THANK

To my amazing fiancée Laura Jackman, your confidence and motivation inspired me to do my best. Thank you for all the hours you spent helping me with this adventure. You truly are the queen of my camp! Very special thanks to my longtime friend and employer Bill Lutzius. It has been a pleasure helping you develop your amazing whiskey bar! To the bartenders of the Aero Club, John Wright, Brandon Josefosky, Jeff Deloy, Annie Hobbs, Barbara Combs and Janeal Banzhoff. Thank you for all your help; I know it must have been difficult for you to have to taste all those whiskeys, ha, ha. Extra thanks to Brandon and Jeff, your passion and hard work were a godsend. Max Daily, who may or may not be from this planet, and Jennifer Hasten-Wright for your wonderful attention to detail. To all the loyal patrons of the Aero Club Bar, without you this book would not have been possible, for it was your likes, dislikes and opinions that inspired the writing for this whiskey guide. To Wade and Sanr at Habano Café, it was a pleasure combining our passion for whiskey with your passion for cigars. To Eli and Wyatt Jackman, my personal assistants, thanks for my lucky #5 pencil and the countless cups of coffee. Stephen and Suzanne, thanks for all the help and support. And last but not least, to all my family who are mostly in southwest Pennsylvania where a lot of whiskey got its start. I love you with all my heart.

JEREMY LEBLANC WOULD LIKE TO THANK

To my wife Danielle and my beautiful kids Ava and Gavin, you are the sole reason that I have the drive to work so hard. I want to say thank you to my supportive family back in Boston and Florida. To my good buddies Matt Kukral and Connor Duncan of San Diego's Cucina Urbana, both of these industry professionals advised and supported Chad and I and we thank you for that. You guys are true friends. To Tamara Lee-Sang, thank you for your firm support to create photos that are truly unique to us and our readers. Your special eye for photography has taken a challenging task of these very similar-looking drinks and made them into a work of art. That photo shoot was burning "hot"—no literally burning hot! Thank you to the Taylor family, Joshua, Natasha and Alison. Your antique shop was the perfect place to photograph our collection of cocktails. Your fine assortment of desirables and ageless unique items made the photo shoot shine. I promise that I will never use your stove again! Special thanks go out to the many mixologists who took time out of their busy schedule to share their signature cocktails. Big thanks to Derek McCluster, Mohammed Momeni and most of all Manny Gonzales of The Saloon in Somerville, MA. These guys sure know how to mix it up. Manny, thank you for all your hospitality; I look forward to sharing some of your distilled gin this summer. Chris Hannah from the Arnaud's French 75 New Orleans, thanks for taking the time to send us your amazing concoctions; I promise I will come visit for the Tales of the Cocktail. To my friends in New York, Sandee Wright and Joe Maritato from The Whiskey Ward—an insane place to kick back and try one of their signature whiskey flights. Thank you Barry from the Porter House in New York City, your cocktail will be enjoyed by many. To Scott Coudriet from Lloyd Whiskey Bar in Philadelphia; this establishment has true character. As Jack from *The Shining* would write, "All work and no play makes Jack a dull boy." Well, at the Lloyd Whiskey Bar you can play all you want and it will never be dull. Many thanks to H. Joseph Ehramn whom I was privileged to be a speaker with at the 2014 Nightclub and Bar convention on "*Emerging Spirits Trending*." H. is the proprietor of the famous Elixir in San Francisco, cocktail and brand ambassador and all-around spirit expert. What a wealth of knowledge: thank you, my friend. To our publisher, editor and designer, Will, Marissa and Meg at Page Street Publishing, for giving us this opportunity to express our passion for this wonderful brown spirit. And last but not least, Bill Lutzius, owner of The Aero Club Bar, you are a true friend to both Chad and I and we can't thank you enough.

ABOUT THE AUTHORS

CHAD BERKEY is Vice President of TIN PLAY Precision Pour Flair Tins, LLC. Along with his business partner Jeremy LeBlanc, Chad invented and patented the innovative TIN PLAY Precision Pour Flair Tin and accompanying four-way muddle, jigger and can/bottle opener. Chad brings to TIN PLAY his vast and varied experience, having worked in all facets of the bar and restaurant industry over his 22-year career. Growing up in small-town Pennsylvania, Chad supported his budding career as a professional motocross racer by working in the service industry. When injury derailed his racing ambitions, he focused his full interests on becoming a professional show bartender. He honed these skills in the Virgin Islands, working in several resorts and nightclubs on the Island of St. Croix. Desiring greater challenge, Chad moved to San Diego in 1998, where he began his successful and illustrious bartending career. Working at San Diego hot spots Moondoggies, On Broadway, Jimmy Loves, ALTITUDE Sky Lounge and Confidential, among others, Chad became recognized as one of San Diego's top and most knowledgeable bartenders. Chad currently manages and bartends at one of the countries most established whiskey bars, The Aero Club Bar. This San Diego landmark has been in business since 1947, and has won numerous awards over the years. It's been *Maxim* magazine's "Top Bars," mentioned in the *New York Times* as one of the "things to do in San Diego," and praised in the *Whiskey Advocate*. For the last 10 years, The Aero Club Bar has been Chad's home away from home.

JEREMY LEBLANC began his bartending career in Boston, Massachusetts, and today is the president of TIN PLAY Precision Pour Flair Tins, LLC. He has more than 17 years of experience as a bartender and began his bartending career at one of Boston's busiest and most prominent clubs, The Rack. Moving to San Diego in 1999, he worked at a high-volume tequila bar in Old Town San Diego, which was certified as one of the only two tequila houses in the United States by the prestigious Academia del Tequila. Jeremy helped ALTITUDE Sky Lounge—Condé Nast Traveler's pick as one of the top 10 rooftop bars in the world—become a huge success on the San Diego nightlife scene. He currently serves as the master mixologist and lead bartender of Parq Restaurant and Nightclub, and is the author of The Best Craft Cocktails & Bartending with Flair.

TIN PLAY PRECISION POUR FLAIR TINS are durable and aesthetically pleasing fine bar tools created by Chad and Jeremy. The Precision Pour Fair Tin upgrades a bartender's standard mixing shaker in a multitude of visually appealing, exciting and revenue-generating ways, all while saving the establishment's pour cost. The stainless steel pin inside the Precision Pour Fair Tin functions both as a measuring tool (liquid poured to its height creates the perfect pour) and as a stopper to allow multiple Precision Pour Fair Tin to be stacked so that even a beginner bartender can perform exciting tip-generating multi-drink pours. Just as the Precision Pour Fair Tin has a variety of ingenuous uses, so too does TIN PLAY's 4-in-1 muddle. This open-ended jagged-tooth device was designed to fit over the pin in the Precision Pour Fair Tin for seamless use of the TIN PLAY products. The cavity of the muddle is also a jigger, complete with measuring lines, and the top of the muddle is a bottle cap/can opener. Every bartender using the TIN PLAY products will have an advantage in the highly competitive hospitality industry. Be sure to see our website at www.tinplay.com for more information on these innovative new bar products.

INDEX